"Amore illustrates with an irresistible blend of wryness and affection [the] engaging pleasures [of] *The Woman Who Stole Vermeer*. Rose is terrific company: clever, forthright and flamboyant."

—*The New York Times Book Review*

"Dugdale's fair-minded biographer pronounces her a 'major figure in the annals of criminal history.'"

—*The Wall Street Journal*

"Anthony M. Amore's engrossing new book is the first deep dive into the peculiar life of Rose Dugdale, the 33-year-old British heiress with a PhD who, at the time of her arrest, was also wanted for gunrunning, a bombing attempt, and armed hijacking."

—*The Washington Post*

"Amore charts in this engrossing account the transformation of Rose Dugdale from a privileged English debutante into a committed radical and fighter for the liberation of Northern Ireland from British rule. Thorough research is matched by prose that keeps the reader turning the pages. True crime and history buffs will revel in the saga of this truly fascinating woman."

—*Publishers Weekly*

"A rollicking biography of a female art thief. Amore, the director of security at the Isabella Stewart Gardner Museum, tells the story of a 'fiery, bold, and brash' Englishwoman who stole for nationalistic reasons. A captivating, detail-rich biography of a 'criminal legend.'"

—*Kirkus Reviews*

"Anthony Amore has written an engrossing character study of Rose Dugdale, a remarkable criminal. I'm very familiar with Anthony and his work, and there are similarities in how he analyzes thefts of art to come up with a specific offender profile and my process for analyzing crimes of violence. Why + How = Who."

—John Douglas, legendary FBI criminal profiler,
#1 *New York Times* bestselling author

"Absorbing. Amore provides effective context for Dugdale's radical actions and offers an examination of the significance of Vermeer's art that bolsters the sophistication of her crimes. Readers will be enthralled by the many worlds Dugdale seemed to inhabit. A captivating book that will entertain fans across genres with its seamless blend of true crime, biography, and art history."
—*Library Journal* (starred)

"Masses of detail, with insights into the history and culture of the time when Bridget Rose Dugdale's ideas and activities were front-page news. The views of senior IRA people concerning her remarkable adventures as reputational matters are lucid and compelling."
—**Charley Hill, retired London Metropolitan Police Detective Chief Inspector**

"Amore does a fine job of presenting the facts of Dugdale's life and dispelling the myths about her exploits. A fascinating account of political fervor and purpose and a woman who had the courage of her convictions."
—*Booklist*

"A meticulous account of the impassioned British heiress who robbed the greatest private art collection in the world—riveting."
—**Matthew Hart, author of the award-winning** *The Irish Game: A True Story of Crime and Art* **and the thriller** *The Russian Pink*

"Amore creates a compelling, illuminating portrait of a woman of deep conviction and daring. He has an uncommon nuance in his analysis, and nobody can surpass him for expertise when it comes to the theft of priceless art. The story he tells is a complex one of morality, transgression, and invention."
—*CrimeReads*

"A fine portrait of one of the twentieth century's oddest criminals: Rose Dugdale, reluctant debutante turned art thief and would-be-terrorist."
—**Luke Jennings, author of the Killing Eve novels**

"As beguiling, complex, and deftly wrought a portrait of Rose Dugdale as the Vermeer she so famously stole. A feat of scholarship and storytelling that will surely go down as the definitive account of the many lives of one of modern history's most compelling—and confounding—women."
—**Kelly Horan, author of** *Devotion and Defiance*

"An astonishing personal story and a fascinating art heist tale, *The Woman Who Stole Vermeer* promises to be a page-turner."
—*Amazon Book Review*

# THE WOMAN WHO STOLE VERMEER

# THE WOMAN WHO STOLE VERMEER

*The True Story of Rose Dugdale and
the Russborough House Art Heist*

## ANTHONY M. AMORE

PEGASUS CRIME
NEW YORK LONDON

THE WOMAN WHO STOLE VERMEER

Pegasus Crime is an imprint of
Pegasus Books, Ltd.
148 West 37th Street, 13th Floor
New York, NY 10018

First Pegasus Books paperback edition September 2021
First Pegasus Books hardcover edition November 2020

Interior design by Sabrina Plomitallo-González, Pegasus Books

ISBN: 978-1-64313-850-3

10  9  8  7  6  5  4  3  2  1

Printed in the United States of America
Distributed by Simon & Schuster
www.pegasusbooks.com

For Alessandra and Gabriela
Two remarkable women in their own right

◎

*The socialist of another country is a fellow patriot,*
*as the capitalist of my own country is a natural enemy.*
—JAMES CONNOLLY, Irish Republican,
in a quote posted on the wall of Rose Dugdale's office

*To gain that which is worth having,*
*it may be necessary to lose everything else.*
—BERNADETTE DEVLIN,
Irish civil rights leader, in *The Price of My Soul*

# CONTENTS

# The Revolutionary Rose Dugdale

When Rose Dugdale became international news in the mid-1970s, she emerged as an emblem of the times. Fiery, bold, and brash, she defied the conventions of her birth and of her gender in everything from action to attire. At the same time, she was generous, articulate, and unquestionably bright. Her criminality, combined with her lineage, her degree from Oxford, and her doctorate in economics, made her a curiosity to journalists not only in Ireland and Britain but in North America as well. She was media gold, having abandoned a life of wealth and leisure to take up arms in operations that would almost certainly, if not intentionally, lead her to prison.

Dugdale was also a radical, not just politically but criminally. No woman before her or since has ever committed anything resembling the art thefts for which she served as mastermind, leader, and perpetrator. For these and other crimes, she carries no regrets or remorse and offers no alibis. The ethical decisions she made during her life were her own, formed after years of intense study in universities and on the ground, from Cuba to Belfast.

Hers was an age of conflict. The antiwar movement, assassinations and riots in the United States, massive student protests in major cities in Europe, civil wars from Guatemala to Ethiopia, a recent revolution in Cuba, a coup in Portugal, and the Troubles in Northern Ireland— these were the fires burning around the world, and she studied all of them.

Hers was also an era of liberation, in its many manifestations. Liberation theology was emerging in Latin America, a symbiosis of Marxist socioeconomics and Christian thought meant to combat greed and,

1

thus, liberate the impoverished from their oppressors. Similarly, the Black Power movement was on the rise, and Kwame Ture (the former Stokely Carmichael) and Charles V. Hamilton had recently published *Black Power: The Politics of Liberation*, examining systemic racism in the United States and proposing a liberation from the preexisting order in the country. The Black Power movement would capture Dugdale's attention throughout her life. There was sexual liberation, with free love and changes in age-old gender roles. Dugdale would test these waters, especially in her open relationship with a married man to whom she provided financial support and engaged in a sort of domestic ménage à trois. There was the women's liberation movement, which had started at around the time of Rose's own ideological awakening in the late 1960s, and from the rejection of societal expectations as a young aristocrat to challenging dress codes at Oxford to taking the lead in militant operations in a way few women of her day dared, Rose reflected that movement in the most radical ways. And, of course, there was the struggle for the liberation of Northern Ireland from British colonial rule—the struggle that would become more important to Rose Dugdale than any other cause, or person, in her life.

Dugdale was unusually earnest in her revolutionary activism. She had no thirst for power, no visions of grandeur for herself; her visions were only for the audacious goals of a free Ireland and the end of capitalism. She found fulfillment in joining the fight and in participating in a grand fashion. While much of what she did and what she tried to accomplish was ill-advised and unquestionably criminal, her motives were no secret and her justifications clear. They were also formed wholly on her own and were not the result of her having fallen under the spell of some charismatic man, despite such claims from lazy onlookers.

Her unbridled zeal for her causes was the topic of countless contemporaneous journalistic opinions, and they typically lay somewhere on a continuum, with "Reluctant Debutante Rebelling against Her Parents" at one end and "Poor Little Rich Girl Radicalized by Her Boyfriend" at the other. In fact, neither of these is completely accurate. Yes, there are elements of rebellion against her parents' wealth, and it is indeed correct that her militancy intensified while she was with boyfriend Walter Heaton, but the truth is that her convictions were the result of her own studies, her own mind, and her own soul. Rose Dugdale was her own person—not her parents', not Heaton's, and not the IRA's.

A major flaw in prior examinations of Dugdale is that, generally speaking, they have focused on the superficial—on frivolous matters such as her looks, her hair color, her choice in attire, her onetime wealth, the age difference between her and her love interests, her pedigree, and her résumé. A closer examination of the woman reveals that none of these were the things about which she chose to speak. Ask her about her youth hunting on the family estate, and she'd tell you about the utility of learning to use a rifle. Ask her about her being presented before the Queen, and she'd tell you about the money wasted that could have gone elsewhere. Ask her about her role in university sit-ins, and she'd smile and talk of student uprisings around the world at the time. And while you were certainly entitled to disagree, she had no time for argument. In short order, Rose Dugdale had decided that she had studied enough about economics at university, learned enough in Cuba, read enough about the behavior of the British Army on Bloody Sunday, and seen enough during her trips to Derry and Belfast to have any interest in winning you over with reason or debate. She was fighting a war, and she had made the deliberate decision that she was willing to take many risks, and, if necessary, many lives, to bring change to the world she saw around her.

Dugdale was not the only woman to fight on the side of the Irish Republican movement. An entire division, the Cumann na mBan (the Irishwomen's Council), consisted of women eager to lend paramilitary efforts in support of the men. While most of their work was behind the scenes, there were women fighting on the front lines. In addition to the famous exploits of IRA members Dolours and Marian Price, whose bombings of famous London landmarks and subsequent hunger strikes will be described in detail in these pages, women participated in a number of operations involving extreme violence. In the very same month the Price sisters bombed London, two girls lured three young British soldiers into a house by inviting them to a party. Once inside, the soldiers were killed. Four days later, two other teenage girls were arrested with a 150-pound bomb in a baby carriage. Before the end of 1973 alone, additional women were arrested for attempted bombings, shootings, possession of weapons, and even a rocket attack on a British Army post.[1]

Even beyond these female militants, Rose Dugdale was a groundbreaker in terms of her genres of criminality. Her involvement in an aerial assault on a police station marked the first attack of its kind. Not since World War II had bombs fallen from the sky in the United Kingdom. Yet as daring as that was, it is not the venture from which her notoriety sprang. Instead, it was her theft of nineteen paintings from the Beit Collection in 1974 that left the greatest impression. That it was thought to be the largest such heist in history was remarkable; that the mastermind was a woman was unprecedented.

Many millions in fine art are estimated stolen every year, but it's almost exclusively the work of men. There have been some women who have been accomplices in art heists, the most recent being Rita Alter, who in 1985 appears to have served as a decoy while her husband, Jerry, took what is now estimated to be a $100 million painting by Willem de Kooning, *Woman-Ochre*, from the University of Arizona Museum of Art. Some others have taken works from their employers or pilfered lesser works. But no woman has ever set their sights on art on par with that stolen by Dugdale nor played such a major role in its taking.

The first Russborough House heist (as of 2020, there have now been, incredibly, four) established Rose Dugdale as the great outlier—history's first and only female mastermind and thief of high-value, highly recognizable masterpieces. It must be emphasized that she wasn't just a hired gun or a lookout—she was the force behind the planning and execution of the crime, the leader of, and key to, the whole sordid and fantastic affair. The men who accompanied her were merely muscle. None of them had the knowledge of Russborough House's holdings to target it and wouldn't have known what to select from the walls even if they had. But Rose knew, and she chose very well. In fact, even if she had left behind the Vermeer during the Russborough House job (an oversight she would never have made), most of the other eighteen works would still qualify her take as among the greatest in art theft history. Yet more incredibly, this was likely not Dugdale's only foray into stealing masterpieces.

This makes Rose a pioneer in yet another sense. Stealing high-value art, unlike most other forms of theft, is nearly always a one-off. Thieves find that once they have successfully pilfered masterpieces, unloading them is even harder than the heist. Only Myles Connor, perhaps the world's greatest art thief, stole Rembrandts on separate occasions (as well as many other masterworks in his storied career). Stéphane Breitwieser was the culprit behind numerous thefts of fine art in Europe. But, at least in the twentieth century and beyond, this club is very exclusive. Rose Dugdale's name belongs right alongside those two men in that notorious league.

Dugdale remains a somewhat enigmatic figure, forsaking a life of creature comforts few can realize for a certain rendezvous with prison. Perhaps there was an element of rebellion against her mother's rigid parenting, but it hardly justified the extreme mutiny from a happy, peaceful middle-class British life. And she held great affection for her father, if not for his station in life. She was no one's mere accomplice, no one's errand girl. She was the architect of her own activism, the composer of her own political credo.

Parallels with Patty Hearst's foray into the world of militantism seem, at first blush, natural. Hearst's childhood was close in style and substance to Dugdale's, with both having attended the finest private schools and living with the sort of wealth that they would later rail against. They fought alongside people whose backgrounds were strikingly different from their own. And both Rose and Patty were repeated subjects of the "poor little rich girl" cliché in the popular media, with nary a story written about either that didn't include the word "heiress." However, that's where the parallels end.

Though Hearst and Dugdale were, incredibly, grabbing front-page headlines within just two weeks of each other in April 1974, there exist strong distinctions between the two women. First, Hearst was just twenty and still in college when she was kidnapped. Dugdale was well into her thirties and had already earned her PhD when her criminal conduct began. Second, as Jeffrey Toobin has described in his book *American Heiress*, after being kidnapped and held in a closet, Hearst was seduced by at least one male member of the so-called Symbionese Liberation Army (SLA), and this was a major factor in her transformation. While there's no disputing Rose's love of, if not infatuation with, the activist Walter Heaton early on in her own personal awakening, Heaton was quick to note that anyone who thought it was his influencing her— rather than the other way around—was guilty of a serious misjudgment. Third, Dugdale took a leadership role in her revolutionary activities, while Hearst was a prop for the SLA. When Rose was released from Limerick Prison, she was left in the trunk of a car to avoid the media. Hearst, meanwhile, was positioned with her machine gun and beret exactly where bank cameras would capture her, making her an effective propaganda tool. Fourth, when facing serious criminal charges in court, Dugdale defended herself, using the courtroom as a political bully pulpit. Hearst, on the other hand, was represented by the famed defense attorney F. Lee Bailey. Fifth and finally, while Hearst would later seek commutation and pardon for her crimes, Rose Dugdale would never seek such accommodations. Instead, she wears her convictions like hard-earned battle scars, proud of each and confident in their righteousness.

There is yet another way that Rose Dugdale's art thefts are somewhat unusual, and that is her motive. Typically, thieves steal masterpieces because they believe—wrongly—that they will be able to monetize the works. Art is usually less secure than, say, money in a bank vault or precious stones. The reason for this is obvious: the whole point of a masterpiece is to display it. Whether in a home, a gallery, or a museum, fine art is meant to be appreciated and, therefore, on view. In turn, displaying art means making it that much more accessible than most other things of very high value. The more accessible something of value appears, the more attractive it is to thieves. The problem for thieves, however, is that once they've stolen a masterpiece, it's nearly impossible to find a buyer. The evil billionaires of Hollywood simply do not exist in the real world and are, for all intents and purposes, unprecedented, especially in the Western Hemisphere.

Highly valuable art is also stolen in order to use it as collateral in illicit trafficking, especially in the drug trade. Having a multimillion-dollar painting in your possession instantly proves to the supplier that you're not only a serious player but that you have something of value to offer—or take—if your cash doesn't make it through.

A third motivation for art thieves is the acquisition of a bargaining chip to use with prosecutors if they are caught committing other crimes down the line. People who steal paintings aren't specialists. They steal anything of value they can get their hands on, along with a host of other sorts of criminality. A highly sought-after work of art can make for an effective "get out of jail free" card. And in some cases, the masterpiece that cannot be fenced is nevertheless held for this reason. Why give it back when you can easily hide it and bargain with it later?

While Dugdale's motive for her biggest heist most closely matches this last scenario, it differs from most major heists—except, incredibly, two other Vermeer thefts in the 1970s—in an important sense: she put her own freedom on the line to obtain a chit with which to aid people who, though she had once met, were largely unknown to her. Rose was working for an ideal—a principle—to which she was committed. She wasn't stealing to help herself in any way. There was no personal financial gain to be had for Dugdale through art theft. There was no plot to hide a portion of her take to negotiate a lighter sentence for herself should she be caught. Her reward was in the effort itself. There could be no doubt: Rose Dugdale was a true believer in her cause.

Unlike most, Rose hasn't written a tell-all autobiography. She has given just a handful of short interviews, usually covering unchallenging questions and only with enough time to provide general overviews instead of in-depth responses. A recent interview attempt by a reporter was met with an angry response. "Clear off, right. I'm not answering questions," she snapped while watching a football match in Dublin, speaking in what was described as a "posh accent."[2]

Perhaps due to her reticence, Rose's story has been mischaracterized in recent years. One widely published art crime scholar has incorrectly described her as an "American socialite" (she was neither); who stole "12 paintings" (she stole more than twenty); "on behalf of the IRA" (the IRA disavowed her crimes); "for the release of IRA prisoners" (it was for the transfer of prisoners, not release); "including her boyfriend" (her boyfriend was not in jail at the time and participated in the biggest of the thefts). He has also incorrectly described her as an "art historian" under whose "leadership" the IRA launched a series of violent art thefts. Such mischaracterizations don't do justice to the legacy of Rose Dugdale. Though she can be coy about whether she was actually an official member of the Provisional IRA, the fact is that she was not. Multiple Provo sources made this quite clear when she was dominating the headlines from the mid-seventies until the very early eighties. Rather, she was an ardent sympathizer who fell in with a rogue unit. Similarly, her role in the history of art theft and activism is one that has been mischaracterized, the true story untold. Regardless of what one makes of her tactics, Rose Dugdale was at the forefront of female activism in a period defined by social and political upheaval.

Despite her recalcitrance and the relative scarcity of her own words about her life, Rose's true story should be told. Whether she was a freedom fighter or a terrorist is for the reader to decide. But as to whether she was a pawn in someone else's game, the answer is clear: she was moving her own chess pieces. She remains unrepentant and proud of her past. Even in her seventies, she proudly established a social media presence, and rather than posting her own face for her profile photo on Facebook and

Twitter, she opted for the most famous painting she stole, *Lady Writing a Letter with Her Maid*, as her public image. This book examines what led her to that Vermeer, and perhaps another, and the remarkable life story that has remained untold for decades.

# ONE

## The Reluctant Debutante

It is perhaps by mischance that on the very day that the Nazi auxiliary cruiser *Thor* sank the SS *Britannia* in the mid-Atlantic, a woman was born who would make it her life's work to undermine the British empire. But so it was that on March 25, 1941, Bridget Rose Dugdale was welcomed into the world by her loving parents, Lieutenant Colonel Eric and Caroline Dugdale.

The news of the SS *Britannia* must have come as a shock to Colonel Dugdale, who was a Lloyd's of London underwriter with a specialty in shipping and aircraft insurance. The sinking of the passenger liner was yet another blow that the Nazis had struck against the British during a long air and sea campaign. He knew shipping, and he knew the military, so he was more attuned than most about what his nation was facing. It's no wonder, then, that though his new baby girl was born during the Blitz, he kept little Rose tucked safely away at the country estate he'd purchased just before the war, sheltered from the terrifying German air raids. She would be a Blitz Baby only by date, not by experience.

There's a tale about Colonel Dugdale, probably apocryphal, that is illustrative of the fighting Dugdale spirit. While playing polo, the colonel was struck in the face with such force that a few of his teeth were knocked from his mouth. Unwilling to let a bit of dental damage interrupt his match, Colonel Dugdale dismounted his horse, retrieved his teeth from the ground, and forced them back into place. It is told that they stayed put for several more years. The colonel was, indeed, a man's man; smart, handsome, lean, and athletic, with a confident, understated manner, he served in the cavalry, survived two wars, and was very

successful at Lloyd's. He also served on the board of the technology firm
Scophony-Baird, Ltd.[1] Though a thoroughly formidable man, it was his
wife, the former Caroline Timmons, who dominated the Dugdale children in the household.

Caroline was tall and imposing, with a strong jaw and an intimidating
countenance set in contrast to her large, pretty eyes, and her family had
made a fortune in the slave trade. Later, they grew even richer in Liverpool in the soap business, and then later and with yet greater success
in the cotton mills of Lancashire. She was given to a "baroque taste in
dress, and an overriding sense of the proprieties," and Colonel Dugdale
was her second husband.[2] Her first, John Mosley, was the brother of
the notorious Sir Oswald Mosley, the founder of the British Union of
Fascists. She left that marriage in time to avoid the ignominy of such a
familial association, but not before having two sons with him that she
would bring into the Dugdale brood. With Eric, she gave birth to Rose's
older sister, also named Caroline, and a younger brother, James.

Caroline Dugdale's authoritarian household was one of exacting, if
sometimes arbitrary, edicts. A friend to the youngsters recalled a home
filled with "daunting rules and regulations," such as a prohibition against
the children taking part in the decking of the family Christmas tree until
they reached the age of ten. The younger offspring would presumably be
required to sit and watch as their older siblings frolicked. The Dugdale
girls were also required to curtsey to guests when they entered a room,
and while they were welcome guests at the homes of their friends and
classmates, even the other parents were "terrified" of encountering their
mother.[3]

Despite the firm hand of her mother, little Rose showed early flashes
of independence. She would tell friends of an incident that occurred
at the family farm in which her parents had pierced her ears without
consulting her first. Young Rose was furious. "She said she considered
herself disfigured," a friend recalled. "And she's refused to wear earrings
ever since. But the worst part was they had it done without giving her a
chance to decide on her own. She was angry and she let them know it."[4]

Still, Mrs. Dugdale was intent on raising a family that adhered to her vision of a proper British upbringing and standing despite the impending cultural changes of post–World War II society, and the setting was certainly right. The Dugdales made their home near Axminster in East Devon, on a six-hundred-acre estate called Yarty Farm. Friends from her youth would recall "a farmhouse smartened up to the extent of being 'ludicrously overdone,' with immaculate grounds, a gravel drive, shiny limousines, [and] a dressage ring in which the children practiced on their ponies."[5] Rose also rode at the pastoral Cotley Hunt and was remembered as a pretty, happy girl, "jolly smartly dressed," if not "a bit Londony" in the eyes of some.[6] Of her childhood in Devon, those who spent time with her recall that "she appeared to be enjoying it,"[7] though it is said that she was forbidden to speak to the local village children.[8] A cousin described Rose as an attractive girl, full of life and laughter, "a great giggler," and a daughter "devoted to her father."[9] Rose's cousin made no mention of such a relationship with her mother.

The countryside in East Devon, as well as the family house in Chelsea (not to mention the mansion in Scotland), were a world away from the downtrodden communities of Northern Ireland with which Rose would fall in love during her adulthood. Belfast featured damp, cramped quarters in a city marked by homes lacking the basic amenities. It had been devastated by blitzes itself, when the Germans bombed the city on Easter 1941, killing a thousand people and destroying more than 50 percent of the city's housing. In sharp contrast, money was never an issue for the Dugdales. When asked by an interviewer about similarities between her upbringing and the bucolic scenery of the popular TV series *Downton Abbey*, Rose was defensive: "Well, I think we should go easy on the heiress stuff. I mean, that's something the media have concentrated on but in some sense I'm certainly not an heiress and I'm not an aristocrat, either. And I'm sorry to disappoint you."[10]

Her protest aside, the only sense in which she was not an heiress or aristocrat was strictly in her self-conscious abandonment of such titles.

The Dugdales wanted for nothing and enjoyed every amenity, every leisure. Indeed, in the same interview, Rose let down her guard and remi-
nisced of an enviable childhood. "I lived in the country," she said. "We
had ponies, and a farm, lots of animals and dogs, and all those lovely
things. And hunting, shooting . . . which was very good training in rifle
practice. And, so, it was an idyllic period of my life."[11] The rifle and
hunting training came via experts in the craft, as she practiced alongside her father and his friends—all officers of the British Army. Rose
described that she "learned to move around the countryside without
making a noise, crawling as if I were a soldier in World War I," and
learned to approach a deer without scaring it off.[12] These were skills that
she deemed most useful in her years as a self-described guerrilla. Later in
life, when asked if she was aware at the time of how privileged a youth
she led compared to the many suffering the hardships of post–World
War II Britain, she answered, "The truth is no, we lived isolated from
that reality."[13]

Rose's early education consisted of attendance at the very exclusive
Miss Ironside's, a private school of about 150 young ladies held in a
large stucco house in South Kensington. She described her experience at
the school as years spent studying "with the daughters of aristocracy."[14]
Instructions at the school were said to center upon sitting up straight,
learning to curtsey, and worrying not about exams, "for Mr. Right was
bound to come along eventually."[15] But Miss Ironside's was far from
the stuffy, rigid institution that one would expect from a mid-century
British school for the wealthy. Students were encouraged to call teachers
by their first names or even nicknames. There were no uniforms, and
the girls were taught using the somewhat Bohemian Dalcroze eurhyth-
mics method, a playful approach to learning through awakening and
refining "innate musicality through rhythmic movement . . . ear-training,
and improvisation."[16] The school was founded in the years between the
wars, and one alum remembered it as a "marvelously idiosyncratic educational establishment, in some ways behind the times but in many ways
ahead of them."[17]

While in session at Miss Ironside's, Rose lived in the children's quarters upstairs at her parents' tony Chelsea terrace house in St. Leonard's Terrace, which was located only a short, chauffeured drive away from the school. One girl who knew her at Miss Ironside's remembered her wit and humor and described a "warm-hearted" and "irreverent" little girl. Another described young Rose as "the high-light" of her time at the private academy. Virginia Ironside fondly recalled her young student. "Everyone adored this generous, clever and dashing millionaire's daughter, who was life and laughter," she said.[18] It was high praise from a woman who taught countless young women gifted with Dugdale-like stock.

Rose was raised with servants in her homes, a luxury to which her adult self would be completely inimical. One of the family's employees at Yarty Farm was her beloved elderly French governess, whom she called simply "Mam'zelle." A friend would later recount meeting the governess and being disappointed in the woman she encountered, but this was perhaps due to the lavish exaltations Rose heaped on her cher-ished tutor.[19] Some have posited that Colonel Dugdale's later dismissal of Mam'zelle and another farmhand Rose held dearly led to a later rift in the treasured father-daughter relationship.

After Miss Ironside's, Rose was sent abroad to travel Europe, doing her "finishing" in France, where she spent another three months studying culture. She also traveled to Germany, where she spent four months learning the language and music and stayed in the home of the former secretary of Nazi propaganda, Joseph Goebbels. To Rose, the accom-modations in the postwar era were less than ideal, and she was quick to dismiss that connection by saying that her mother had many contacts in Europe. "It was not a time of luxury," she would recall, somewhat defen-sively. "Germany was poor and the house I was in was no exception."[20] Along the way, she also made stops in Italy, Greece, and Austria. It was part of her mother's plan for Rose. Mrs. Dugdale moved in intellectual circles, her daughter remembered, and had many contacts, allowing her to coordinate the pre-university excursion. She would utilize them to provide her daughter with a worldly upbringing befitting a member of her class.

Back home, marrying well and maintaining wealth would be the next step in her development, as was her father's expectation. But upon Dugdale's return from her trip abroad in 1958, there appeared a sudden urge for a deviation from this charted course. Rose, it seemed, was not at all interested in what awaited her—the debutante Season, or, what Jessica Mitford (herself an earlier reluctant debutante) called "the specific, upper-class version of a puberty rite."[21]

The debutante Season, naturally, couldn't have been more important to Rose's mother. Caroline Dugdale had high hopes, fretting over all the details. "She wanted her daughter to be one of the leading debutantes of the year, and do all the right things and go to the right places and meet the right young men," said Una-Mary Parker, the society photographer who shot Rose for her Season.[22]

The two-century-old tradition was the highlight of London society and an absolute must for the British elite. It would seem unimaginable that a young woman of affluence would choose not to make her grand entrance into society at Queen Charlotte's Ball. The authoritative biographer of the 1958 Season, the acclaimed writer Fiona MacCarthy, herself a debutante that year and a childhood chum of Rose's, recalled, "By and large it was a family tradition. Most debutantes were presented by their mothers, who themselves had been presented. In the circles in which I grew up, curtseying to the Queen was not a matter for discussion, it was just a thing you did."[23]

Presentation to Queen Elizabeth II at Buckingham Palace was no simple trick. One hundred and seventy-eight years after King George III introduced it as a way to celebrate the birthday of his wife, Charlotte, there remained a very strict method to even the curtsey, and the home instruction that Caroline Dugdale had provided her daughters would not suffice. Instead, debutantes perfected the technique using the method taught to them by a dance instructor named Madame Vacani: the left knee was locked behind the right, with a graceful descent, head erect, hands by the side. That would be followed by three sidesteps and another curtsey to Prince Philip.[24]

Perhaps aware of how valuable a chit participating in the Season would therefore be, Rose used it to bargain with her parents. "I kind of came to a deal with my parents that I would do the season, but we'd just have a small season," she later recalled.[25] In return for participating in this unseemly and excessive "marriage market," as Rose called it, they agreed to her attending St. Anne's College at Oxford in the fall.[26] While allowing one's child to attend Oxford might not seem like much of a parental concession, the furtherance of education was not something that Rose's parents had ever envisioned for their daughter. They expected courtship and marriage to a prominent young man. But they acquiesced, and both Rose and her parents were granted their wishes.

Adding to the importance of the event was the fact that the traditional presentation to the Queen was in its last year. When the lord chamberlain announced that the 1958 class would be the last, a record number of applicants flooded in for this final chance to be presented to the Queen. So the stakes for Rose's participation could not have been higher. One thousand and four hundred young women would curtsey before Elizabeth II that Season.

The presentations had fallen out of favor in recent years, and Buckingham Palace had decided to put an end to them. For one, there was talk of bribery behind the selection of the young women participating. This gave the group the whiff of commoners. Princess Margaret, unimpressed with the class of participants, said, "We had to put a stop to it. Every tart in London was getting in."[27] Dugdale herself would later say that the Season was thought to be "presenting . . . the children of aristocrats, but it became more middle-class, jumped-up middle-class people, who aspired to great wealth, presenting their daughters."[28] Furthermore, this was an era in which deference to the crown had been on the decline. A year earlier, Lord Altrincham described the event as including a "truly classless court" participating in an event that should have been "quietly discontinued in 1945."[29]

Still, such a description of classlessness was quite relative. Not only did the debutante class of 1958 feature an array of young ladies with the finest of upbringings and lineage, it also featured a number of individuals who would go on to great fame and, for some, even greater notoriety.

There was Jennifer Mather, later Jennifer Murray, who, aside from being a successful international businesswoman, would go on to become the first woman to pilot a helicopter around the world, and later, the first woman to repeat the feat solo. Fiona MacCarthy would win several literary awards and write for *The Guardian*. Her eponymous biography of William Morris would be described as "one of the finest biographies ever published" in Britain.[30] Nicolette Harrison was also of the 1958 class. She met the Marquess of Londonderry when she was just sixteen, and soon after her coming out was engaged to him. They had two daughters together, but in 1969, she gave birth to a son whom the marquess believed was not his. Blood tests confirmed his suspicions, and if that wasn't scandal enough, it was learned that the child was actually the son of pop star Georgie Fame. Harrison later married the singer.[31]

Perhaps the alum from the '58 Season who went on to have most in common with Rose Dugdale was Teresa Hayter. The daughter of former British ambassador to the Soviet Union Sir William Hayter, Teresa went on to become a radical and, like Jessica Mitford, embraced Marxism and joined a revolutionary Trotskyist group. She described her conversion as having been completed in the tumult of 1968 at Oxford. "I am convinced that by then it was impossible for any student to ignore Marxist ideas," she later wrote, adding that it was this "Oxford period [that] finally turned me into a revolutionary."[32]

Then, of course, there was Rose Dugdale.

Princess Margaret's contempt aside, Queen Charlotte's Ball, even in that final year of presentation before the Queen, was a magnificent event. Hundreds of girls at a time, dressed in gorgeous white gowns, paraded into Grosvenor House as onlookers gawked at the spectacle. And the entire months-long Season was marked by the elegant parties, dancing, and social interaction of a bygone era. With its end, wrote Mac-Carthy, was the loss of "a mad, sad beauty." She recalls it as "the prime example of elaborate social rituals that lingered through the postwar years. Underlying it were concepts of elegance, good manners, belief in protocol, love and respect for Queen and country, qualities which before long appeared impossibly old-fashioned."[33]

It's hard to imagine concepts any less attractive to the woman Rose Dugdale would become. But even in her teens, she recalls that she viewed the debutante Season as something far from the nostalgic, elegant affair that her mother had spent so much time organizing. To her, it was "pornographic—something which cost about what 60 old-age pensioners receive in six months."[34] The debutante tradition was far too classist, far too discriminating. One critic even went so far as to describe the spectacle as "a mixture of the Nuremberg Rallies and the Dance of the Fairies in the Hall of the Mountain King."[35]

"I did it very reluctantly, refusing to take part in anything more than I had to," Rose said. "As a debutante I was out on the social register and invited to parties and balls which I hated . . . God! . . . when I think of the money that was wasted on the whole business. Each dress I wore was tailor-made by Worth."[36] Rose's dismay over the fuss was not lost on her photographer: "As soon as Rose walked into the drawing room in a white organdie dress, white gloves and a little row of pearls, and a tight perm, looking absolutely miserable and most dreadfully awkward, you realised that this girl should never have been pushed into doing something like the deb season. And I think she was very bolshie about the whole thing. She was very ungainly and unhappy about the whole thing—it was a very sticky session. I think maybe Rose should have stayed down on the farm . . . You know . . . with the horses."[37]

Though she was barely nineteen, Dugdale was keenly and pragmatically aware of what being a debutante meant—finding the suitable husband a girl had been preparing for since Miss Ironside's. "The idea was that you would manage to pair off with someone," she said, recalling that "the single young lads in London at the time tended to be military young fellas, who were in the guards or maybe in the horse guards or so." Given her later activities, it's no surprise that she found the young officers to be "very poor company in my view."[38]

Rose would go on to describe the Season as a time in which she was treated "as if you were being sold as a commodity."[39] Mothers put together lists of the young men from which their daughters should steer clear, including categories like NSIT (Not Safe in Taxis).[40] Unsurprisingly, this was not the sort of affair that appealed to young Rose. She had made the deal to attend and to go through the months-long Season of dances and events and dinners, but pairing off with a future husband was nowhere in her plans. "I hated it, I really hated everything about it," she said, mincing no words. "All I really wanted to do was get to college and to pursue ideas which were very current at the time. I mean, coming out was a torture, and I would rather have spent the time traveling to Greece or seeing some of the world, which at that age you know nothing about at all."[41]

In the circles from which the upper-class debs came, learning about that which you knew nothing wasn't a priority for young women of the period. In fact, Rose and Fiona MacCarthy constituted half of all the women from the 1958 Season to go on to university. MacCarthy, in her book *Last Curtsey*, recalls a "self-consciousness about coming from a very frivolous world where ideas were shunned—girls were ridiculed for any aspirations to intellectual life."[42] Colonel Dugdale certainly subscribed to this mentality. Dugdale remembered that to her father, women were thought of as "mere procreators." Her mother, though, held a progressive view on womanhood for her day, instilling in her daughter a belief that "I did not have to accept inferior treatment because I was a woman." Caroline Dugdale's liberalism didn't extend to her son, however, who Rose claims was sent away because he was a homosexual.[43]

In any event, in 1958, Rose would obediently curtsey one last time for her mother, before the Queen, at Queen Charlotte's Ball. It was the last time she would do anything at her parents' command for the rest of her life.

# TWO

# A Weird Orchid Among Daisies

Signs of Rose Dugdale's rebellious spirit showed themselves almost immediately upon her arrival at Oxford, but her revolt wasn't against "the establishment," Great Britain, or any such noble cause. Instead, it expressed itself in her complete and unreserved departure from the compulsory, rigid, prim-and-proper lifestyle instituted under her mother's roof.

First came a drastic change in her attire. Quickly upon commencing her studies at Oxford, no longer would she wear handmade dresses of the finest fabrics with matching velvet heels beneath perfectly set hair. Rather, Dugdale's sartorial preference consisted almost exclusively of men's shirts and trousers, with shoes to match. A principal at St. Anne's College would later note in a letter of recommendation that Dugdale "had a Season before she came up here and for a time became very bohemian in reaction to this!" On one noteworthy occasion, she and a fellow Oxford student, Jennifer Grove, went so far as to disguise themselves as men, combing their hair and donning bulky glasses to hide their faces. Together, they successfully crashed the strictly all-male Oxford Union to protest the exclusion of women, their disguises so good that they sat and read for some time before finally being discovered.* Grove remembered Dugdale as a woman who "hated the frills and the trappings of femininity."[1]

That's not to say, however, that she had become anything like the

---

* The pair also penned a letter to *The Observer*, writing, "Since women may be invited as guests to drink and dine in the Union, and this is not felt by members to be an encroachment on their privileges, why should it not be possible for women to be invited as guests on to the floor of the debating chamber, where they could participate in debates?" "Old Oxbridge," *The Observer*, November 5, 1961, p. 22.

radical who would one day dominate headlines around the world. To the contrary, she was an unlikely revolutionary and still very much her father's daughter, with her attire perhaps her only departure from earlier norms. Grove recalled her with irony. "Well the funny thing is, she was extremely right wing," she said. "We were asked for example to write an essay on the House of Lords and out of the five of us, Rose was the only person who undertook to defend it as an institution. I can remember her saying that breeding counted for something and I suppose this was because she came from a wealthy background and at that time she was not in revolt against it."[2]

Another student remembered Rose as a defender of the class system, with a fine vintage claret within reach, courtesy of her loving dad. She was remembered by others as "bright, serious, perhaps a bit confused," but remained popular and, most interestingly, proud of her family and heritage.[3] Still, the changes in her manner were glaring. At Oxford, she would discover a refreshing meritocracy, giving her what she saw as "the opportunity to meet other students who did not belong to wealthy classes but were there because of their skills."[4]

Her room at St. Anne's is remembered as being a slovenly disaster. Guests were forced to navigate "a heap of clothes, cigarette ends, books, and papers" strewn about the floor. She became a chain-smoker, a cigarette omnipresent between her fingers, the nails of which were severely gnawed. She is even said to have adopted a strange fascination with pain, going so far as to sometimes pour lighter fluid on her hand and set it alight. Rose would later say of her time at Oxford, "I turned into the most disagreeable kind of intellectual, badly dressed and extremely arrogant."[5] Colonel Dugdale, noting the change in his precious child, told a friend, "Never let your daughter go to Oxford, it teaches girls the most abominable manners."[6]

Rose studied philosophy, politics, and economics at St. Anne's, a selection that did not please her parents but speaks to her desire for academic rigor. The PPE track is the premier program at Oxford, where students are pushed to dissect complex philosophical questions with an emphasis on developing sound ethical judgment in a political and economic context. The PPE would have a profound impact on Dugdale, as she honed skills that she would later apply to nearly every aspect of her life. She wrote two major papers in her final year: one an ambitious undertaking that covered the period from 1919 to 1962 and dealt with Britain's relationship with the rest of Europe, Russia, China, and Japan; the other, a study of global monetary institutions, including the International Monetary Fund and the International Bank, with an emphasis on the British balance of payments problem, development, and monetary intuitions.

Dugdale also wrote her first published piece at Oxford, researching and composing "A Radcliffe Bibliography," published in *The Bankers' Magazine* in March 1962. The work compiled the "great flood of articles, lectures, speeches, pamphlets and even books" that were prompted by the Radcliffe Report, the first authoritative examination of the monetary system of the UK in thirty years. The piece was the result of a painstaking examination of dozens of economic responses to the report in the days when such research had to be done without the benefit of internet search engines at one's fingertips. Instead, Rose (credited as Miss R. Dugdale, St. Anne's College, Oxford) put in what must have been countless hours finding articles with such titles as "Non-banking Financial Intermediaries and the Process of Credit Creation" and papers such as *New Emphasis on "Liquidity."*[7]

Earlier, she had completed a compulsory paper on comparative political institutions that included the U.S. Constitution and American politics. While it is tempting to assume that her research for these papers colored her later activism, there is no indication that this was the case. Rather, this background provided the basis for later employment that was much more influential in her development.

Her record at St. Anne's shows an inclination toward leadership. She played a major role in her class, serving as the president of the Junior Common Room, the autonomous undergraduate student organization that served as a student governing function as well as an entertainment and cultural role at the university. She was also secretary for the new

students' Council of Junior Members, a group that consisted of representatives of the men's and women's colleges. Given the era, the com-
ingling of the sexes was considered a "departure" from ordinary life at
Oxford. It was Rose who wrote the group's first constitution. The CJM
was established in 1961 by Oxford undergraduates who argued that they
had no official means of communicating student opinion on university
matters, such as teaching methods, regulations, libraries, and lodgings, to
seniors. Undergrad proponents referred specifically to "the suppression
by the proctors of the [Oxford student magazine] 'Isis' Lecture Reviews
. . . the arbitrary authority exercised by the proctors, and the state of
the university's lecture system [and] the absence of any representative
student body."[8]

Just as she was at Miss Ironside's, Dugdale was well-liked by her
instructors. "She has a most relaxed and agreeable manner . . . she is a
delightful person," one wrote.[9] Another described her as "exceedingly
conscientious and hard-working."[10] Her ability to command an audience
was emerging, too, as it was noted that "she can control an unruly college meeting of 250 without any apparent effort."[11]

Her influence with her colleagues would come in handy during her
very active schedule outside the lecture hall. In addition to the JCR and
CJM, she belonged to many Oxford societies, including the Oxford
University Conservative Club, Labour Club, and Liberal Club, among
others, and she was an elected member of the Jowett Society, which
was similar in nature to the Socratic Club. As if that wasn't enough,
she served as the college representative for Politics, Disarmament, and
Peace, a newly created society. She also found the time to play tennis and
squash for St. Anne's.

One activity in particular displayed a keen understanding of the fine
arts her mother so enjoyed and to which she was exposed back home and
in her travels. She served as a member of the St. Anne's Art Committee,
where, she said, she "attempted, through buying pictures and helping
to organize exhibitions, to forward the 'cultural interests' of the Junior
Common Room."[12]

Despite all the kind words and extracurricular engagement, Rose's grades at Oxford were ordinary, graduating with an unimpressive third. R. G. Opie, a Fellow of New College, Oxford, and Rose's economics tutor, described a young woman who didn't quite fulfill her promise. "She worked quite well and was quite a character round the town. I think she had more mental potential than she realized,"[13] adding that at this point, "she was no radical, and certainly not a Bolshevik."[14]

But it was not to worry; her parents were relatively disinterested in her academic pursuits, and employment after graduation wasn't her primary concern. Besides, for Rose, it was the exchange of ideas that held the appeal of higher education, not grades. "Oxford was a marvelous university to be at. I mean you were never on a treadmill like you have the impression people today are in terms of getting through your exams and getting your points and getting into college in the first place, all that stuff," she later recalled. "Education was what it should be, which was discussing and thinking and reading and forming relationships with people that were your contemporaries." She described her tutors as "wonderful . . . they didn't politicize me; I was just always very enthusiastic to learn something about the world."[15]

In her graduation portrait, she is an attractive young woman, smiling widely, and nothing at all like the dour debutante described by the photographer for the Season. She puts forth a happy, confident visage. The cap and gown suited her well, and one can see optimism in her blue-gray eyes and smiling face. Perhaps her next academic adventure was on her mind.

Moving back into her mother's home after Oxford was not in her plans. Interestingly, she decided to pursue a graduate degree in the belly of the capitalist beast: the United States. She applied for a program at Mount Holyoke, a small liberal arts women's college in South Hadley, an ultra-liberal enclave in the western part of Massachusetts. The school was founded by a pioneer in American education, Mary Lyon, in 1837, whose most lasting words, "Go where no one else will go, do what no one else will do," sound as if they were whispered directly into Rose Dugdale's ear.[16]

As part of her application to Mount Holyoke, Iris Murdoch, a fellow and tutor at Oxford and eventual Booker Prize–winning novelist, recommended Rose "warmly" for continued studies, describing her as "sensible and in no way neurotic." Though Murdoch was clear that Dugdale was an "intelligent 'all-rounder'" who would benefit from continued education, she stated, "She is not an absolutely brilliant student—I would expect her to get a good second class degree." Murdoch pegged Dugdale for a career as "an able administrator or a good university teacher."[17] Mary Ogilvie, the principal at St. Anne's, was a bit more complimentary in her recommendation. "I am quite sure she would be exceedingly conscientious and hard-working," she wrote. "I strongly commend her to you. She is really the best of any names which I have put forward to you up till now."[18]

Dugdale applied for, and was awarded, an internship at the school's newspaper to complement her studies. Comparing her to another finalist, one of the selecting officials said of her, "Rose is also very nice, much more obviously serious, primarily interested in graduate work but also involved in writing, America, system, etc."[19] The biographical data she provided to the Mount Holyoke New Bureau at the commencement of her internship is perhaps illustrative of her feelings about the family back home at St. Leonard's Terrace. In the section where she is asked to list members of her immediate family, including the ages for each child, she typed simply, "J.F.C. Dugdale Father."

Before she even arrived on the continent, her ambition preceded her. When she wrote to the director of Mount Holyoke's News Bureau in March 1962 asking if she could earn her Master of Arts degree in one year, she received a swift response: "Your letter of March 27 disturbs me greatly. It is most emphatically not possible to get an M.A. in one year when you are working 28-hours a week in the News Bureau; if that had been your expectation, you are obviously laboring under a misapprehension." The director, Elizabeth Green, continued. "I feel I should reiterate very strongly the fact that this is a learning position designed only for those young women who honestly want practical training in public relations as well as graduate work."[20] Desirous to retain her internship, Rose wrote back quickly and apologetically. "I am sorry to have given you the impression that I should perhaps find the office work in the News Bureau but a set of chores. This is far from the case. Apart from regarding the internship as valuable training and experience, I also hope and think I shall enjoy it . . . I am sorry to have implied that my real interests lay elsewhere."[21]

At the time, it seemed that the twenty-one-year-old Rose Dugdale was perhaps destined for a career in the media. A press release was issued to the *London Times* and *Evening Standard* in August 1962, announcing that "A London girl, Miss Rose Dugdale" would study at Mount Holyoke and "will receive training in journalism."[22] In a letter of recommendation to Mount Holyoke, Lady Ogilvie at St. Anne's College noted that "[Rose] has specialized in economics and would like to continue with a career, possibly in journalism or in the B.B.C." She went on to write for the college's newspaper, where she had the opportunity to interview both John F. Kennedy and Martin Luther King Jr. while studying for her thesis.

Dugdale's arrival at Mount Holyoke was something of a news item in Massachusetts. On August 23, 1962, the *Holyoke Transcript-Telegram* announced her appointment as a News Bureau intern, describing her as a "keen sportswoman" who "looks forward to taking full advantage of the facilities at Mount Holyoke and has started off by climbing Mount Holyoke and the Mount Tom range." She was described as being fond of skiing, fishing, hunting, and show horses and "anxiously awaiting the arrival of her blue MG sports car from England as she is an enthusiastic driver."[23]

Such an extravagance hardly fit with the anti-materialist who would emerge just a few short years later, but she worked hard not to flaunt her wealth. Many who attended school with her in Massachusetts knew she was well-to-do, but not the full extent of her family's fortune.[24] She used her fast little car to speed not just around campus but across the entire country, to take summer courses at Stanford, using the semester break as an opportunity to see America. Photographs from that time show her smiling widely in full Western regalia: leather cowboy boots, blue jeans, and a plaid shirt, as she sits causally atop her little convertible, legs crossed, with her blond hair peeking out from beneath her cowboy hat. The speed-loving Dugdale made the solo drive from the West Coast back to Massachusetts in just three days.[25]

Dugdale chose to study philosophy and excelled at Mount Holyoke. One of her philosophy professors, Dr. George Tobey, described her as "an extremely intelligent girl. Very attractive. Extremely spirited. She wrote and thought well. She . . . loved adventure . . . just loved adventure!" Professor Richard Robin, who would later become chair of the philosophy department, said Rose was "very bright . . . she had an extraordinarily good mind and wrote a really excellent master's thesis."[26]

That thesis was an analysis of Ludwig Wittgenstein's *The Tractatus Logico-Philosophicus*. Professor Robin described Wittgenstein's work as dealing with neither the social nor the ethical, but was instead "more a theory of knowledge and some philosophy of language—more the technical aspects of philosophy and not so much the practical." In studying Wittgenstein, he continued, "There was nothing in her work within the philosophy department that has much bearing on the revolutionary activities she became engaged in later on."[27]

One fellow student found Rose to be "a little gruff, but she was very sensitive, although many people found her unapproachable. She put on a front of being tough and yet she was soft." The woman recalled that Dugdale would reminisce about the family farm on which she grew up and the family dog that she loved so much. Others remember her as an elusive figure who spent much of her time in her rare private dorm room listening to classical records and reading.[28]

Lisa Lansing, a fellow graduate student, described her as "small, wiry, engagingly foul-mouthed and very civilized in spite of her unspeakable appearance [with] two shirts which she wore interchangeably without sending them to the laundry in between." Her speedy driving was the stuff of legend. Lansing joined Rose for a seventy-mile-per-hour drive along a dark, curvy road in which she narrowly missed a crash. "She stopped the car, turned off the lights and roared with unnerving, hysterical laughter for two minutes. She was alive with adventure and danger," Lansing later recalled. For a small college town like South Hadley in the 1960s, Lansing recalled, Dugdale "was a brilliant exotic" where she "bloomed like a weird purple orchid among daisies." A typical afternoon with Rose "might include a lecture on 'Hamlet'; a perfectly controlled 80-mile-an-hour drive over back roads in her tiny Austin Sprite; scotch and pate on bread; and usually some of her own history." On the time spent with Dugdale at Mount Holyoke, Lansing concluded in retrospect, "What she was doing in rural South Hadley after earning first-class honors in politics, philosophy and economics at Oxford was something of a mystery."[29] Rose's apparent carefree attitude at Mount Holyoke despite the percolating tensions in the United States of the 1960s was perhaps due to the fact that there, as at Yarty Farm, she was in a bubble. Though seemingly happy at the time, with retrospection comes disdain. "It was the sixties and the U.S. was at war in Vietnam, the civil rights movement was booming . . . but I didn't hear anything because the university was a private ghetto of the privileged classes and I was not aware of the historical moment I was living," she said. "It was an odious experience, of a disproportionate snobbery, where money was everything."

In 1964, Rose was back home in Great Britain and traded in her Austin Sprite for another speedster, a red convertible Lotus Elan. That same year, she made a trip back to Oxford to pay a visit to her brother. While there, she ran into Peter Honorine Ady, a fellow in economics at St. Anne's. Ady had written a recommendation for Dugdale two years earlier, in which she praised her versatility and her knowledge of the international arena.[30] Ady was an eminent researcher in development economics and had worked for the United Nations, advising the Burmese government on its finances. Keenly aware of Dugdale's field of studies at Oxford and her knowledge of the American domestic arena, Ady offered her a job as her research assistant, and the two traveled to New York to work on a project for the UN. Their work also took Rose to Rome and Geneva.

Soon after, Ady was given a two-year secondment to the Economics Directorate of the Ministry of Overseas Development as the senior economic adviser to the Labour government. Ady hired Rose into a junior position in the ministry, where they worked for Baroness Barbara Castle, the "left-wing flame-headed political tornado" and former MP who was easily the best-known woman parliamentarian of her time. Castle was a key adviser to British prime minister Harold Wilson—the only woman in his cabinet, where she served as his minister of overseas development, then transport minister, and finally secretary of state for employment and productivity. Her remarkable career would eerily foreshadow the political fights and tropes of half a century later: in 1969, Castle worked on plans for a statutory enforcement of equal pay for women and was later described as having a "nasty temper and a silly unparliamentary approach."[31] Both Ady and Castle were models for Dugdale not just through their accomplishments but in their strength.

Rose's employment took her even further away from the path pre-scribed for the debutantes of her era, for whom the only acceptable "work" would be the sort of leisurely job that was clearly a hobby and not some professional pursuit. In sharp contrast, these two years working under Ady were crucial to the metamorphosis of Rose Dugdale from academic to activist. Working at the Ministry exposed her to the extreme poverty of the developing world. Her focus was commodities, and that, her friend Peter Ayrton said, taught her "how the price of those com-modities is manipulated, and how this can have disastrous effects on the economy of those third world countries." He explained, "That is they can never predict from one year to another, even from one day to another, how much money they're going to have, so that it's for instance impossible for them to make any planning for building roads or hospitals or anything."[32]

For the first time, then, a new element surfaced in the study of economics that Dugdale had undertaken for more than six years, and that was the question of justice. Her old friend from the 1958 debutante Season and London Society, far-left activist Teresa Hayter, understood well what Rose was starting to believe. Hayter, who would go on to become a vocal critic of the World Bank while curiously praising the North Korean model of development, said of Rose's work, "I think the job gave her the opportunity to judge or understand the function of aid to underdeveloped countries and the fact that it's used to prop up corrupt right-wing governments and to preserve a situation from which North Americans and Europeans profit."[33]

From Dugdale's perspective, Western nations corruptly abused their power to take advantage of poorer countries, engulfing the subjugated in a vortex of poverty that was impossible to escape. It was "the nature of imperialism," she said.[34] This discovery was tantamount to the sound of a starter's pistol in her race toward revolution.

Though she was one of the first women accepted as a member underwriter at Lloyd's, Rose enrolled in Bedford College at the University of London in 1966 to work toward a doctorate in philosophy. The institution was a particularly appropriate setting for her. Founded in the mid-nineteenth century by Elisabeth Jesser Reid, an anti-slavery activist, Bedford was the first institution of higher learning for women in Britain. In just a few decades after its founding, the college grew such that it was recognized as a school of the University of London. It boasts such notable alumni as the famed novelist George Eliot, who was born Mary Ann Evans but used a nom de plume to veer from the female norms of her day; Elizabeth Blackwell, the first woman to earn a medical degree in the United States; and the painter—and daughter of Charles Dickens— Kate Perugini. It was a time of great change for the college: over the previous twenty-four months, it had just added a modern science block and library and, for the first time, male students.

At Bedford, Rose chose an unusual field of study: "Proper Names: Their Role and their Objects." The resultant thesis is deeply philosophical and includes references to her earlier investigation into Wittgenstein as well as a thinker she would later revisit, John Stuart Mill. "Traditionally, the conflict over the question what is the role of proper names in ordinary language has centred around two proposals," she began. "A sense-reference account, where the meaning of a name is given by some favoured description of the bearer, or a designatory account, where the bearer is the meaning of the name." She goes on to tackle the philosophical question "what is the role of 'Pegasus' in the sentence 'Pegasus does not exist.'"[35] Her work shows the ability to argue and reason, but it lacks any utility. An excerpt: "It is a mistake to suppose that Mill's view directly confronts the sense view. The notions of sense, in the sense reference theory, and of connotation, in Mill's theory, are quite distinct. As has been suggested, the nearest overlap between these two terminologies, at least for predicate expressions, seems to lie between Frege's reference and Mill's connotation. In Mill 'white' connotes, or implies the attribute, whiteness, which would seem to be closest to the concept white, which is for Frege the reference of 'white.'"[36] It's a work that doesn't seem to fit her personal narrative, either in terms of her interests as a student or her evolution as a revolutionary.

Despite the banality of the thesis topic, her interest in alternative politics was burgeoning. She held seminars at Bedford on Marx, and it was during this time that she, along with a circle of intimates, embarked on an exploration of volume one of *Das Kapital*. This study cannot be overstated, for it is here in this volume that Marx scrutinizes the topic of British imperialism in Ireland. Within, he is unabashed in his support for an independent Ireland and writes extensively on what he views as the exploitation of the island by the British and the Americans. Marx writes about such issues as the uprooting of the cotton and linen industries and of wool manufacturing by England, as well as the subsequent humiliating conditions of Irish agricultural and manufacturing day workers in Britain. And though Dugdale was never to become a devoted Marxist (she had no time for the "babbling of intellectual Marxists and parties," she said), this topic—the British treatment of the Irish—and her desire to respond to it, would shape the rest of her life.

# THREE

# A *Soixante-Huitard*

In 1967, Rose Dugdale accepted a one-year appointment as a lecturer in economics in the sociology department at Bedford College. Employing the same ability to engage a group of students that she displayed as an undergrad, she was well-liked and respected by those who studied under her, despite the fact that they were but a few years younger than she. "She was an inspired teacher," recalled one pupil. "She was genuinely interested in her students, which was pretty rare."

Perhaps evoking her time at Oxford, where she valued the free exchange of ideas over the pressures of testing and grade-chasing, she organized interdisciplinary seminars outside Bedford's prescribed, more traditional curriculum. One former student opined that such practices threatened the established, permanent faculty at the college. Organizing students around purely intellectual challenges was resented by traditionalists at the school, who saw any deviations from the norm as a philosophical siding with the era's rebels. As a result, Dugdale was not renewed for a second year of teaching. She tried to acquire a lectureship elsewhere, applying to work closer to the center of London at Goldsmiths College, but was turned down. Perhaps she had earned a reputation for unorthodoxy. "My feeling is that she became unpopular in academic sociological circles," said one of Rose's intimates.

The traditionalists were not necessarily wrong about Rose Dugdale. She was, in fact, at this stage immersing herself in the literature and philosophy of the far left that would form the intellectual basis for her future fight. The Black Panther Party in the United States had just been formed, and their armed citizens' patrols dispatched to monitor police in Oakland, California. The still-growing movement, a response to the Dr.

Martin Luther King's advocacy of nonviolent protest, instead sanctioned the use of violence to achieve justice in the face of oppression from the white power structure. It was the age of Black Power, and Rose took to the ideology of the movement. At the onset of 1968, J. Edgar Hoover, the Machiavellian director of the Federal Bureau of Investigation, and at that point a living icon of the old guard, looked to undermine the Black Power movement by painting it as a puppet of the Communist Party. The party had, in November 1967, stated, "There can be no question of the right of the Negro people to use violence to free themselves from oppression and to win full freedom." Hoover, in turn, used this endorsement in his annual report to the U.S. attorney general, stating that Black Power had created "a climate of unrest and [had] come to mean to many Negroes the 'power' to riot, burn, loot and kill."[1]

Though the riots of the long, hot summer of 1967 were over, the cause was not, and the entire world took notice when, during the 1968 Summer Olympics in Mexico City, American track medalists Tommie Smith and John Carlos raised their black-gloved hands in support of Black Power and human rights during the medal ceremony.

In the years that followed, the Black Power movement would also use the courts as an effective means by which to communicate its message by breaking with traditional courtroom procedure and spontaneously proselytizing. One of the movement's most prominent leaders, H. Rap Brown, had been imprisoned on charges of inciting to riot and arson and went on a hunger strike. These, too, would be lessons Rose would remember.

By the epochal year of 1968, Dugdale was already walking briskly in her march toward a full transformation from academic to activist. Her excitement was palpable. Speaking of the era, she told an interviewer in her later years, "I think you mustn't forget it was very exciting times. It was times of student revolution, of the May events in Paris, and Black Power in America and civil rights, and . . . the whole world was already in uproar at that time. There were revolutionary movements in Nicaragua, El Salvador, Honduras, Guatemala . . . the world looked like as if it could change and was likely to be changed. And whoever you were, you could play a part in that."[2]

She wasn't quite a Trotskyist, primarily because she seemed to abhor diving into the "Talmudic" texts on the topic that one necessarily would have to absorb. Instead, she was aligning herself with feminist activists, riding the swell that called for action over study. As Teresa Hayter put it, "I'm sure she must have been affected by the prevailing radicalization among students at the time." Indeed, Rose remembers that it was while teaching that she "realized that . . . I had to get involved in changing the living conditions of the most disadvantaged."[3]

The first six months of '68 were so remarkably eventful that it's almost overwhelming, even in retrospect, to consider what exactly had occurred. From an American perspective, James Earl Ray's assassination of Martin Luther King Jr., on a Memphis evening in April, followed two months later by the murder of Robert F. Kennedy in California at the hands of Sirhan Sirhan, stand out as blood-soaked reminders of the tumult of the time. It remains difficult, fifty years later, to grasp that these two dramatic acts of senseless violence could have occurred less than a year after the Summer of Love.

The assassinations of MLK and RFK certainly garner most of the attention of documentaries and books about that year, but to put those two events in a time capsule along with "sex, drugs, and rock 'n roll" to alone explain the year's impact would be a serious misrepresentation of all that occurred.

The year wasn't yet a month old when the North Vietnamese launched the Tet Offensive at Nha Trang, taking the theretofore jungle battle into the streets of Vietnam's cities, and by 2:45 AM on January 31, 1968, the United States embassy in Saigon would be taken over for more than six hours. Just a day later, photographer Eddie Adams captured one of the most memorable photos from the war when he snapped General Nguyen Ngoc Loan executing a Viet Cong prisoner with a pistol shot to the head. For Western audiences, Rose Dugdale included, the scene epitomized the raw brutality and senselessness of a war an increasing number of people no longer wanted to fight. This, coming just weeks after four men, including renowned pediatrician and author Dr. Benjamin Spock, were indicted in Boston for conspiracy to encourage violations of American draft laws, marked a major milestone in the shifting of American attitudes about the Vietnam War. And when the State Department announced on February 18 the highest American casualty numbers of the war (543 killed, 2,547 wounded), prospects for a U.S. victory in Vietnam seemed grim.

The Tet Offensive was the major catalyst for a dramatic increase in the size and fervor of the Vietnam protests that took place in '68. One major demonstration that would have certainly caught Dugdale's eye took place in April, when Students for a Democratic Society (SDS) occupied Hamilton Hall, the administration building at Columbia University in New York. Students gathered to protest the school's connection to a Pentagon-affiliated think tank. When a Columbia administrator tried to meet with the students, he was taken hostage and held in his office. As Bryan Burrough describes in his book *Days of Rage*, the events gave rise to a number of SDS leaders. One, John Jacobs, known as JJ, was certain that they were on the precipice of a new American Revolution, believing there was "concrete evidence that young people working together could bring the country's white elites to their knees." Jacobs, Burrough wrote, "popularized the parallels between Columbia and the Cuban Revolution, who preached that a select group of hard-core rebels could, as Castro and Guevara had with Cuba, lead America into revolution. 'At first everyone thought JJ was crazy,' remembers his friend Howie Machtinger. 'But then events kind of caught up with him, and suddenly what he was saying seemed almost sensible.'"[4] It was this sense of the possible that swept up students across America.

By March, antiwar presidential candidate Senator Eugene McCarthy, buoyed by the work of thousands of student volunteers, came within a couple of hundred votes of beating the sitting president, Lyndon B. Johnson, in the much-watched New Hampshire primary. McCarthy's success sent shock waves through the political landscape. First, RFK, aware of what McCarthy's finish in New Hampshire meant about the nation's voting trends, sensed an opportunity and jumped into the race, putting to rest public debate over his intentions. The formerly hawkish senator from New York—and fierce enemy of President Johnson—adopted an anti-Vietnam stance with the hope of capturing McCarthy's momentum in the race to unseat Johnson, who had been the presumptive Democratic candidate to face Republican Richard Nixon in the fall. The president, meanwhile, unwilling to be cast as the villain any longer, stunned the nation two weeks after Kennedy's announcement during a nationally televised address. The broadcast, which had ostensibly been aired to allow Johnson to tell the country what steps he would take to limit the war in Vietnam, became famous for LBJ's surprise announcement late in the address: "I shall not seek, and I will not accept, my party's nomination for another term as your president."

The tumult of '68 was not solely an American experience, though U.S. policies and student unrest had repercussions in Europe and elsewhere. In March, various smaller rallies against the war in Vietnam culminated in a massive protest at London's Trafalgar Square. It began as a star-studded affair, with burgeoning revolutionary Vanessa Redgrave (who would years later offer to pay bail for the Price sisters) reading out statements of support for the protest from film directors such as Richard Attenborough and Sidney Lumet. The writer and activist Tariq Ali was there, as was Mick Jagger, who drew from the protest the inspiration to write the Rolling Stones hit "Street Fighting Man" ("Hey, think the time is right for a palace revolution"). Despite the size of the crowd, the rally was described by the BBC as "good humoured." But violence erupted when the demonstrators made their way to the American embassy in Grosvenor Square. When hundreds of police officers attempted to hold them off, demonstrators broke through their ranks onto the lawn of the embassy. Police on horseback were summoned, and the peaceful protest devolved into battle. One protestor recalled, "I remember being terrified at being chased down by what seemed like scores of mounted police with truncheons flailing about while the square was blocked off."[5] Redgrave, however, was allowed into the embassy with three supporters to deliver her protest.

Later in the year, another, larger protest took place, with an estimated twenty-five thousand people turning out to denounce the war. Though some ugliness occurred, one thousand police officers had assembled and were able to stem the tide of demonstrators.[6]

As Dugdale described the time, "The battles [could] be traced around the world, from Berkeley, to Latin America, where students have made universities into red bases in active support of guerrilla struggles . . . to the Middle East, with violent clashes between students and state . . . to revolutionary movement in Pakistan, India, Ceylon, Afghanistan."[7]

To be sure, the youth of the West were filled with the spirit of activism in 1968. "In the developed countries, the student movement has spread throughout Germany, Japan, France with the General Strike of May 1968, to Spain, to Italy, where student and faculty strikes have paralysed academic life, to Canada, where one morning the people of a rich, quiet, 'democratic' country woke up to martial law on the street, and back to America, where numerous universities have called off academic life and directed resources to bringing down those structures which perpetuated the Vietnam War," Dugdale wrote of the period and the change she was monitoring very closely.[8]

Of course, she would be the first to acknowledge that in 1968, nowhere was this more vividly playing out than in Paris. Early in May, police forces took command at the Sorbonne in response to a student uprising calling for reforms to education in the country. The students, in turn, took to the streets in the Latin Quarter to continue their protests, prompting clashes with the police. Soon, the students were setting up barricades and intensifying their protests, despite hundreds of injuries to both protestors and police. What began as a protest by six thousand student demonstrators facing fifteen hundred gendarmes snowballed into the General Strike of which Dugdale wrote, in which ten million French workers joined in the protest, crippling Paris and beyond.

The struggle escalated until, on May 24, students temporarily took control of the Paris Stock Exchange and tried to set it ablaze, after having first raised a Communist flag atop it. President Charles de Gaulle then dissolved the National Assembly and called for elections at the end of the month, which rallied his supporters and ended labor strikes. By the middle of June, student protests were banned, and some concessions were made to the demonstrators. Finally, in July, peace was restored. Nevertheless, the demonstrations had made their impact on Dugdale. As her old friend Teresa Hayter would opine, "I'm sure she must have been affected by the prevailing radicalization among students at the time."[9]

As violent and newsworthy as they became, historians still wonder just what, if anything, came out of the Paris unrest. Contemplating this question in *The New York Times*, Peter Steinfels wrote that it is not easy "to discern what it was all about. Adolescent hormones, the death of communism, the death of capitalism or, as André Malraux suggested at the time, the death of God?" His question is a pertinent one: as Andreas Whittam Smith noted in a retrospective on the month for *Independent* on the fiftieth anniversary of the riots, "The country was calm, both politically and socially, inflation was weak, living standards had been rising and there was little unemployment."[10] British philosopher Sir Roger Scruton, who was a student in Paris at the time, said the events actually drove him toward Conservatism. He would later state, "The thing that most struck me about those students in the street was the sentimentality of their anger. It was all about themselves, it wasn't about anything objective. Here they were, the spoiled middle-class baby boomers who never had any real difficulties to cope with, shouting their heads off in the streets, burning the cars that belonged to ordinary proletarians, whom they pretended to be defending against some imaginary oppressive structures erected by the bourgeoisie. The whole thing was a complete fiction . . . they were acting out a self-scripted drama in which the central character was themselves."[11]

Rose Dugdale saw things entirely differently, believing the student unrest to be a critical stage in bringing about true reforms. "The war in Vietnam will not cease because a brand new [Bertrand] Russell or [Noam] Chomsky publishes wiser insights which finally offer the rational proof we were waiting for—that, after all, slaughter, destruction, torture, wage-slavery, are morally wrong."[12] No, it would take *action*, she believed.

Interestingly, though she was swept up with the student movement, Rose Dugdale was twenty-seven years old at the time—slightly older than the college-age boomers shouting alongside her. But despite her years, she was no less a *soixante-huitard*, a "sixty-eighter," as they came to be known. Polemicist Christopher Hitchens counted himself among this group of young students, witnessing the uprisings up close. And despite Sir Roger's views, Hitchens recounts that the time was "real enough to us. And almost every morning, my little transistor radio would wake me with seismic tidings" of upheaval around the globe. Hitchens's view contrasts with Dugdale's in one major way: whereas it served as a springboard for her, he later viewed it differently: "At the time, I thought 1968 was the beginning of something. Later, I understood that I had instead been part of the end of something: the last gasp of red-flag socialism."

Perhaps, but young people around the world were seeing things on their television screens they hadn't seen before. Séanna Breathnach, a Provisional IRA volunteer, remembers that the images being broadcast into Northern Ireland were making a difference: "We saw the state begin to change. We saw the state attacking marches. We saw the police and their brutal approach to people . . . this was the first time it was shown on television." He continued, "Our community had never seen the Troubles on screen before. They had never seen the police attacking people on TV before."[13]

For leftist students at home and elsewhere around the world, Vietnam presented American imperialism in its most ruthless incarnation. Rose Dugdale was following the protests intently. So was Fidel Castro.

By the summer of 1968, El Comandante was inviting European college students who were protesting the war in Vietnam to visit his country to see what his revolution had brought. The first U.S. tourist group to visit Cuba in years arrived there in July via Europe. Journalist Merwin Sigale of *The Miami News*, who had been invited by Castro to look at the diary of the late Che Guevara, encountered nineteen Americans gathered in the lobby of the former Havana Hilton, rechristened the Havana Libre Hotel. Their first event was at the invitation of the North Vietnamese embassy and the Cuban Cinematography Institute, in which the group was shown three films on Vietnam. The group ranged in age from sixteen to sixty-five, and included not only journalists such as Jane McManus, who published a "radical weekly" in New York City, but also some who were merely curious. Few were willing to provide their full names.[14]

To be sure, there were those whose curiosity brought them to Cuba, but, for the vast majority, it was summer school for revolutionaries. By August, the U.S. Secret Service had learned that American students were traveling to the embargoed nation via Mexico and elsewhere. The Western media began reporting that Castro was providing "revolutionary training" to leftist students in the hills of Pinar del Río.

The media had it right: Campamento Cinco de Mayo, or the Fifth of May Camp, named for Karl Marx's birthday, was located in the province of Pinar del Río and enticed students from Europe and the United States. Danish attendees reported attending political seminars led by Cuban instructors focusing on "the need to upset the social structures of other western countries."[15] A French student dispelled rumors that they were being taught guerrilla tactics to import into the cities. "We are studying the Cuban revolution and working to help the *campesinos* (peasants)," the student said. But some of the students told a journalist from the Associated Press that "those attending agree with Cuba's advocacy of armed struggle to make social revolution. And most apparently intend to try to carry out such a policy when they return home."

In the annals of the Castro Revolution in Cuba, it was interesting timing. El Jefe Maximo had begun rationing gasoline due not only to boycotts but also to a currency shortage and an unwillingness on his part to suffer the embarrassment of continuing to ask the Soviet Union for petroleum advances. "We cannot stand the tensions of having empty tanks and awaiting deliveries," Castro said, as he decided to use fuel from military reserves.[16] In addition to this hardship, the tiny nation had recently suffered one of the worst droughts in its history, which severely impacted its vital sugarcane crop for the year. Sugarcane represented a full 80 percent of Cuba's economy. Still, despite severe austerity measures, the economy was expanding, with a rise in cattle and citrus output. With some reason for optimism, the ninth anniversary of the revolution included the Cultural Congress of Havana, a conference hosting hundreds of left-wing intellectuals from around the world to discuss ways to confront and overcome what they described as "imperialist cultural aggression" from the United States in the underdeveloped world. Luminaries including Jean-Paul Sartre and Simone de Beauvoir of France and British authors Graham Greene and Alan Sillitoe attended.[17] It was from this Cultural Congress that the idea for the Fifth of May Camp was born.[18]

It was precisely the sort of place that Rose Dugdale felt she needed to be. "I went to Cuba as a result of a trip that was organized by Castro," she recalled, "[with] a lot of people that had been involved in the Vietnam protests—America was fighting in Vietnam and it was an appalling war that went on—it was imperialism at its very worst . . . and that was a huge boost to any revolutionary movement."

When she and hundreds of her fellow budding revolutionaries arrived at José Martí Airport in Havana, they were greeted by the festive sights and sounds of guitars, bongos, and joyous dancing girls. There were daiquiri rum cocktails and smiles all around. Then students were issued an ID—and made to surrender their passports—before being carted off to the camp, traveling down a grand new road and past a large sign that welcomed them in English, French, and Spanish. The sign was covered in revolutionary slogans and at least one image of an armed guerrilla.[19] Once at the camp, canvas bunk beds, communal showers, and mess halls awaited them. The students were treated to relentless music and fiery political speeches played over loudspeakers located all over the camp throughout most the day. And the Communists ensured that the students followed their orders and stayed in line.

There were mass rallies where Castro addressed the assembled students, speaking for hours as was his well-known wont and receiving his customary numerous, if not requisite, standing ovations. Much of the rest of the time was spent discussing and arguing politics with other students and learning about agriculture—in other words, planting coffee seedlings in the heat and humidity of the Cuban summer. There were movies at night—in Spanish, of course—and a great deal of team sports.

In a radio interview late in her life, Rose remembered, "In Cuba I actually saw a revolution in the making. It was marvelous. We all went, the people who had been involved in the Vietnam demos . . . to what was a month in a camp, and we planted coffee and rubber in the forest and then took part with political lectures in the afternoons, which were with simultaneous translation. And I think the idea at the time was that people who had been involved in Vietnam demos, people in all the countries in Europe, could come together and try to seek some unification in their view and their practice."

Though her timing was a bit off (the revolution had already taken place by the time she visited, and Che Guevara had been dead for nearly a year), her memories were fond. She was clearly in her element, once again engaging in the dialogues she so enjoyed at St. Anne's. Peter Ayrton also went to Cuba and remembers being "amazed" at Rose's "outgoing nature" and ability to connect with everyone she encountered. Despite the class obstacles resulting from her somewhat narrow life experiences and what Ayrton describes as Rose's "posh accent" (something she would later self-consciously try to abandon), the people she met in Cuba—students and Cubans alike—got on well with her. Her obvious upper-class background "never kind of stopped people being able to immediately relate to Rose as a kind of human."[20]

Ayrton recalls one instance when there was a dance for young people organized in a small village outside the city. When Dugdale saw that the

older villagers, who hadn't been invited, were watching from the outside, she insisted that they be included, convincing the Cuban authorities
to call them in. Though she spoke no Spanish, Ayrton recalled, "She
immediately proceeded to dance with them . . . she kind of related for
the whole evening." Ayrton continued, "She had absolutely no problem
of getting on with people from totally different background and spoke
totally different language and everything."[21] Rose's affability with different classes was a stark contrast to the Oxford student she once was,
who had argued about the necessity of the class system. A kinship with
the less fortunate was emerging, one that would never fade.

Not everyone who made the trip returned home inspired. J. P. Goff-
ings went with his fellow French revolutionaries and found the Cubans,
especially the women, to be "very revolutionary" but with an "obsession
for material things," a departure from the anti-materialism of Guevara.
He also believed that the camps served the concomitant purpose of providing the Cuban Secret Service with an excellent means by which to
collect intelligence. And he found Old Havana to be "dirty, falling in
ruins, almost abandoned." "There was nothing to buy," he recalled. "A
few bags of powdered milk and a dozen small boxes of tomato concen-
trate."

There was what has been described as an "uncomfortable match"
between the Cuban Revolution and the French uprising of May 1968.
French students at the camp were startled by the inflexible military
discipline of Cuba and what some saw as "the cult of Che Guevara."
Moreover, some were upset by the fact that Castro's news service scarcely
reported what they had done in Paris or the massacre of hundreds of
students in Mexico, after that nation was swept up in the spirit of '68.
Finally, when Castro's regime was reluctant to condemn the Soviet inva-
sion of Czechoslovakia, French activists were disillusioned.[22]

Hitchens's memories of the Fifth of May Camp aren't any more
romantic. In his memoir, he speaks of the authoritarian command of
guards who strictly controlled what he could see and where he could go.
He tells of a Communist Party official who spoke of a "new man" being

evolved in the town of San Andres. Despite repeated requests, Hitchens and his comrades were not allowed to visit that supposed Utopian commune. The Cuban socialism he witnessed was "too much like a boarding school in one way and too much like a church in another," the latter a reference to the enforced reverence to the memory of Guevara.

But for Rose, the pilgrimage was elating. It's probable that she encountered the same future members of the Angry Brigade* that Hitchens recalls meeting there. It was a new and exhilarating awakening; a realization that there was a world beyond her narrow upbringing and a host of worthy causes just waiting for her to join their fights. "You had the feeling that the world could change, was about to change, and that maybe young people could play a part in that," she said. "The world was just out there and you needed to get sucked in. The problem was how to get involved, it wasn't so much whether to get involved, but how to get involved. I mean, that was the motivating factor in my life."

It wasn't long before she figured out whose cause she would take up and how she would do it.

---

* The Angry Brigade was a far-left group that held protests and conducted a bombing campaign in the early 1970s in protest against a wide-range of government policies including the Vietnam War, internment in Northern Ireland, and sexism.

# FOUR
## *Graduation*

Though 1968 had come to a close, unrest on campuses had not. By 1969, the impact of student revolt had finally hit England, and Rose Dugdale was eager to take part.

There were protests at two of her alma maters. Students barricaded themselves in seven campus buildings at the usually quiet Mount Holyoke College over what they described as "a lack of concern" with the demands of black students.[1] Meanwhile, even Oxford, where staid, sober behavior was a tradition, was not immune to unrest. Students there protested university regulations prohibiting the distribution of leaflets by leftist students that urged workers to resist Britain's policy of wage restrictions. Five hundred students forced their way through iron gates, scuffled with authorities, and staged a sit-in at the administration building.[2] There is no indication that Rose joined students there in solidarity with their cause.

The prestigious London School of Economics experienced its share of the tumult, and Dugdale made her way there to join the students in their siege. Problems at the LSE had begun when the school appointed Dr. Walter Adams as its director in 1967. Dr. Adams was formerly the head of the University College in Rhodesia and was linked to Rhodesian prime minister Ian Smith, whose racist views on white rule in Africa were an affront to the students. Their protests and sit-ins in response to Dr. Adams's appointment led to the installation of iron gates at the school as a security measure. This only further incensed the students, who took to the gates with pickaxes and sledgehammers and tore down a protective wall. Students also occupied a building at the University of London, calling themselves "the LSE in Exile." Militant students kept the respected institution closed for three weeks. Dugdale, of course, found the entire experience inspiring.

Exhilarated, Rose was sure not to miss the opportunity to take part in the next big student uprising in Great Britain, this time at the University of Manchester in 1970, where, like at Columbia in 1968, students took over administration buildings. "Student revolution was very much happening at the time and that was what led me to go to Manchester. Manchester was one of the universities that were occupied by the students. And so to engage in that occupation led to an awful lot of discussions amongst people. It's hard to explain how exciting those times were. They were times of, definitely, revolution," she happily recalled in an interview.[3]

At Manchester, Rose joined a sit-in of five hundred students, after thousands of others followed the lead set by universities in Edinburgh and Warwick to protest the school's practice of keeping dossiers on them. Nine of Britain's forty-four universities saw protests over claims by some students that secret files filled with information about their political activities were maintained by the schools. "Those files hurt us; they contain details of our political activities," the twenty-one-year-old vice president of Manchester's student union worried. "It can be damaging to a person's career. Why, you can be radical at 18, but later on, you're 30, you could very well turn conservative."[4] The lack of foresight on the young students' part aside, the idea that an institution would maintain secret files was particularly troubling for a generation of Cold War students who were sensitive to anything that smacked of Stasi-style activity.

The demonstrations worked, and the administration agreed to end the practice of keeping political or religious files on students. But it was the gathering at Manchester that gave Dugdale an opportunity to discuss the issues that were becoming critically important to her, including what she saw as a college curriculum that was biased toward capitalism. The idealistic meetings that she had with fellow protestors who had come across the Irish Sea to Manchester led to the recommendation that she make a trip to Belfast. Dugdale would later recall that it must

have been around the time of the vicious ambush of peaceful marchers
at the Burntollet Bridge that she was finally moved to go to Ireland for
the first time.[5] Rose's memory failed her: the Burntollet Bridge incident
occurred in 1969, a full year before the Manchester protests. Nevertheless, there was no shortage of violent attacks against peaceful protests in
Northern Ireland in those days, and it is likely that she was prompted by
some such news to make the trip.

Though she seems to have done nothing in Northern Ireland but
observe what she could of the situation on the ground, the journey east
would be one of the seminal moments of Dugdale's life. She and a group
of students went specifically to see Aggro Corner in Derry, Ireland.
This was the epicenter of the Irish fight against colonial Britain. Every
afternoon and extending into the nights and weekends, Catholic youth
known as the Derry Fusiliers (or "hooligans," as the British Army called
them) hurled stones and other projectiles at British troops, who would
often return volley with rubber bullets. Going to Aggro Corner made
her, for the first time, an eyewitness to British colonialism in action, with
heavily armed soldiers and police facing off against civilians, some of
them children, armed only with rocks and bricks.

Most of the action would take place at William Street, beginning
around 4:00 PM. The area had once been a busy shopping area but was
by then a bombed-out "no-go" area into which the Royal Ulster Constabulary dared not venture. Small fires in abandoned shops, armored
vehicles, soldiers, police, and the occasional sniper replaced shoppers
and pedestrians.

At that moment, this woman in search of a cause found her raison
d'être. She had never been to Northern Ireland before, but once there
she "slowly became aware of what was going on, whereas from an
Englishwoman's point of view, this was a British colony and they were
using the army to maintain their power."[6] But even she could not have
foreseen the events that would soon follow.

The first pivotal incident took place in Northern Ireland in August
1971, while she was safely back home in England. Seeking to take a

hard line against violent clashes between Republicans—mainly, the Provisional IRA—and Ulster Loyalists, the prime minister of Northern Ireland, Brian Faulkner, implemented Operation Demetrius. With the blessing of British prime minister Edward Heath, Faulkner ordered the transparently biased arrest and internment of 450 Irish Republicans, but not a single Loyalist.

British intelligence failed, and the massive predawn raids conducted during the operation were a disaster. Peaceful political activists were among the 342 rounded up (more than one hundred couldn't be located) and held without charges or trial at Long Kesh, in Northern Ireland. Many were elderly, long-retired IRA men, and still others had no connection to the Irish Republican Army at all. Moreover, the arrests intensified the violence. In Belfast, at least twelve were killed in resultant rioting, bombings, and shootings. A Catholic priest was among those slain, caught in the crossfire as he administered last rites to a man wounded in the streets. Throughout Belfast, Derry, and their environs, fires consumed neighborhood blocks. Catholics in the ghetto slums worked to construct barricades to protect others from being carried away to internment. In the British House of Commons, MP Bernadette Devlin urged resistance to the operation, saying no citizen would be safe under the internment law. After her election in 1969, Devlin had wasted no time making clear her opposition to the British government's handling of the Troubles. In her maiden speech before the House, she defiantly declared, "There is no place in society for us, the ordinary 'peasants' of Northern Ireland . . . because we are the have-nots and they are the haves . . . The situation with which we are faced in Northern Ireland is one in which I feel I can no longer say to the people, 'Don't worry, Westminster is looking after you.'"[7]

Devlin would prove to be a major force in the outcry against the internment policy, as she gave quarter to neither the politicians nor the press. In an angry speech before ten thousand people in Whitehall organized by the Anti-Internment League, she attacked the press for its failure to report on the treatment internees were receiving and the conditions in which they were held. "The only friends you have are yourselves and the British working class," she told the protestors.[8] As three MPs (John Hume, Austin Currie, and Paddy O'Hanlon) began a hunger strike to demand an inquiry into the treatment of the internees, Devlin threatened to bring disruption to Britain by calling on Irish building workers to engage in a half-day strike and later a general strike to "mess up the system so that the Tory Government can't run London effectively."[9]

An unmitigated failure, Operation Demetrius would have long-lasting ramifications for the Struggles, and action taken as a direct response would set off a chain of events that ended with Rose Dugdale becoming one of the most famous people in the United Kingdom in the mid-seventies. Yet the British would provide Dugdale with still more reason to revolt not six months later.

On a raw Sunday midafternoon, January 30, 1972, in Derry, a massive march was scheduled by Republicans to protest internment. Between ten and fifteen thousand people assembled for a demonstration that would take them from Bishop's Field to Guildhall in the center of the city. It was the very locale that Rose and other Manchester protestors had visited not long before. But the British Army would have none of such a mass demonstration. Before the marchers could make it to Guildhall, they were stopped by army barriers and redirected. As the marchers moved on, and as had become commonplace, some of them broke from the rest and began chucking stones at the soldiers at the barriers. The soldiers responded with rubber bullets, tear gas, and a water cannon to stop the assaults and break up the large crowd.

But the nonlethal exchange soon turned deadly. When protestors tossed stones at paratroopers they noticed stationed in an abandoned building, the soldiers returned fire. This time, the bullets were not made of rubber. Two unarmed protestors were shot and wounded, left bleeding in the streets. A short while later, paratroopers were sent through the barriers to arrest the protesters, and the violence escalated. Soldiers chased civilians through the streets on foot and in armored vehicles, mowing down two more marchers. Paratroopers brutally beat civilians, thrashing them with the butt ends of their rifles, and others positioned themselves behind a barricade and opened fire, killing six civilians and wounding seven more. Even as a television reporter was being taped live from the scene saying, "The army throughout the day have said that they hope to use minimum force," a British officer could be heard yelling, "Keep firing!"[10]

Before it was over, the British Army had fired more than one hundred rounds of live ammunition at unarmed protestors, leaving thirteen dead marchers lying in the streets of Derry on what would forever be remembered as Bloody Sunday.

From England, Rose Dugdale was seeing reports of the Bloody Sunday massacre. She remembered Bloody Sunday as "pure horror." She said, "It was exactly the behavior of a colonial army and that was exactly what you expected the Brits to be doing. They were literally coming in and smashing around them, smashing people around them, smashing heads. It was utterly horrific."[11] It was this event that she would later say was—more than any other—responsible for her foray into Irish politics. "It was the point at which it became obvious that the reasons the British gave for sending troops into Ireland, as a peacekeeping force, was a lie," she said.[12]

Bernadette Devlin was present on Bloody Sunday, and the firebrand brought the level of outrage and injustice felt on the streets of Derry to the floor of the House of Commons. When she rose to speak about the murder of thirteen innocent people, she was denied the right to speak by Selwyn Lloyd, the Speaker of the House of Commons. The British Home Secretary, Reginald Maudling, was allowed to speak, however, and claimed that the British paratroopers had fired on the civilians only in self-defense. Incensed, Devlin crossed the House floor and slapped Maudling in the face.[13]

Rose was now convinced beyond any doubt that the attitude in England about the massacre on that auspicious Sunday in Derry was that "nobody cared" that unarmed civilians had been killed by the British Army. For her, it was a call to action: "There was no question that you needed to do everything you could to support that cause to free the Irish people from the stranglehold which was the British imperialist relations." Dugdale continued, "I remember thinking that, you know, if you are involved in this you need to accept the possibility that at the end of the day you may have to kill people, and I tried to wrestle with that thought and dealt with it so much that I was accepting the recognition that there can come a time when you may or may not want to kill people, but at the end of the day it's the only way to deal with them."[14]

From that moment on, she moved from intellectual activist to militant operative, answering only to herself and her own code. "It was happening right on your doorstep, just across the water, in Belfast," she said. "The overall questions was how to get sucked in."[15] Just as she believed that new arguments from public intellectuals weren't going to bring about an end to the war in Vietnam, neither would peaceful protest and demonstrations free the people of Northern Ireland from the grip of its colonial master. Robin Blackburn, later the editor of New Left Books, saw this when he remarked that Dugdale was "a good militant" but not so good with Marxism.[16] Rose Dugdale was ready for battle. And she was on the precipice of finding her first true comrade-in-arms in her crusade.

## FIVE
## *The Cause*

For the people of Britain, the first week of March 1973 was a time of chaos and inconvenience. Workers throughout the country, numbering more than seven hundred thousand, took part in massive strikes in protest of the government's plan to freeze wages in order to curb a rate of inflation that was approaching 12 percent, three times that of the United States. There was a slowdown by the gas workers that left Britain's homes and shops cold. Hospital workers went on strike, teachers stayed home in select areas, and thousands of civil servants walked off the job, including four women who protested by walking in public wearing only their underwear to demonstrate that their salaries—a mere $40 per week—left them little with which to buy clothes.

The greatest disruption to everyday life was caused by the striking transit workers, especially in the densely populated cities. Only one train was running in London, and it carried just six passengers, as commuters decided not to chance its availability. As a result, major metropolitan centers from London to Liverpool, Glasgow to Birmingham, were jam-packed with cars moving at a crawl or not moving at all. In London, drivers left their homes at 6:00 AM to get to work on time. Still, the streets remained at capacity near noon, with traffic backed up for ten miles. The Automobile Association described it as "Hell on wheels" and told the press, "The capital is like a wheel with spokes of congestion building up around a hub of confusion."[1]

Meanwhile, government officials had good reason to be concerned about the situation in the metropolitan areas beyond the work outages and congestion on the roads. March 8, 1973, was the scheduled date for the contentious Northern Ireland border poll. The plebiscite would determine whether the people of Northern Ireland wished to join the Republic of Ireland or remain part of the United Kingdom via a simple, two-question ballot that asked, "Do you want Northern Ireland to remain part of the United Kingdom?" or "Do you want Northern Ireland to be joined with the Republic of Ireland outside the United Kingdom?"

The goal of the border poll, in the view of its supporters, was to "take the border out of politics," by settling sectarian differences via the vote. But this was a rigged referendum in the view of the Catholic people, their representatives, and those in favor of Irish unity, all of whom believed that the whole of Ireland—not just Northern Ireland—should constitute the electorate. After all, Northern Ireland consisted of just six of the nine counties that made up Ulster, and those six guaranteed a Protestant, pro-Loyalist majority.[2] The results of the vote, therefore, were a foregone conclusion.

Irish MP Bernadette Devlin described the entire thing as a "farce" that was merely being held so that Prime Minister Edward Heath could keep a promise "for once in his miserable life." Her colleague Gerry Fitt warned that even those Catholics going to vote to maintain ties with the United Kingdom might "meet their deaths" at the hands of Protestant gangs mistakenly believing they were voting for a united Ireland.[3]

Fitt's warning was no cynical demagoguery. Violence was in the air, as the vote came at a markedly polarized time in Northern Ireland, even by the measure of that embattled region. Casualties of the Troubles were an everyday affair, with an estimated one in every two hundred people in Ulster having either been wounded or killed in the previous three and a half years. And while bombings had begun to decrease by 1973, forty Protestants and twice as many Catholics were felled by assassins' bullets in 1972, with little prospect for peace in sight.[4]

On March 4, 1973, terrorists bombed St. Lawrence Hall in Belfast, which had been designated as a polling place for the vote. And on March 7, Anton Brown, a British guardsman, was killed by an Irish

Republican Army sniper. The twenty-two-year-old was the tenth soldier to die in about as many weeks. Government officials in Northern
Ireland, keenly aware of the threat of a further escalation of violence
on election day, erected barbed-wire barricades and machine-gun
nests. Leave for all police officers was canceled, and nine thousand
militiamen were put on standby alert. In all, thirty-three thousand
armed men would be patrolling the streets of Northern Ireland
during the plebiscite.[5] Soldiers stacked sandbags and barbed wire to
protect Florian Hall, where ballots would be counted following the
vote.[6]

Meanwhile, at 10 Downing Street, Prime Minister Edward Heath
was scheduled to meet with the incoming taoiseach, Prime Minister–
Elect of the Irish Republic Liam Cosgrave. Cosgrave had been elected
on February 28, 1973, unseating his predecessor, Jack Lynch, whose
party had been in control for the previous sixteen years. Prior to his
election as Irish prime minister, Cosgrave, a Catholic, had, just three
months earlier, come within hours of being removed as the leader
of his party when he supported the Offenses Against the State Act,
a measure introduced to combat the threat of the IRA. He ended
his earlier resistance to the bill after car bombs tore through Dublin,
killing one person and injuring more than two hundred. In declaring
his support for the anti-IRA measure, Cosgrave said, "We have put
the nation before party. We will ensure the government will have all
necessary powers available. This house will protect the people from
this type of thing."[7]

Now having won election as prime minister, he entered his meeting
with Prime Minister Heath with the confidence of the Irish establishment. In an editorial the day before the scheduled conference, the *Irish
Times* wrote, "Mr. Cosgrave is an experienced politician and spent
three years as Minister for External Affairs, as the post then was. He
is not going to Mr. Heath in any spirit of deference. He is the Prime
Minister of a sovereign State, an equal with Britain in the councils of
the European Community. He is going to hear Mr. Heath's exposition

of the White Paper, and he will tell Mr. Heath if he doesn't like what he hears . . . It is as simple as that."[8]

Despite the expected exposition, the "White Paper" to which the *Times* referred was a controversial and, at the time, mysterious British proposal for the future of Northern Ireland that had not yet been released to the public and was thought to still be in draft form on the eve of the meeting. To the annoyance of many, it would not be released until sometime after the plebiscite of March 8. Nevertheless, the meeting between the prime ministers was a high-stakes affair. Expected to last five hours, the *Irish Times*'s political correspondent Michael McInerney opined, "It is realised that failure at this first meeting . . . would be disastrous and so both sides are preparing to do everything possible to secure success. Such success is imperative if there is to be any hope at all for peace and progress in Northern Ireland."[9]

The fact was that peace in Northern Ireland never seemed so far away. In the mid-sixties, Catholic attempts at nonviolent civil rights demonstrations, in the style of Martin Luther King Jr., had been met with (often extreme) violence by radical Protestants. All the while, the Royal Ulster Constabulary, Northern Ireland's police force, had watched on, usually with arms folded. In 1969, sporadic violence throughout the year had escalated into six days of riots in August, in which eight people were killed, hundreds of Catholics burned out of their homes, and the British Army deployed to the region.

It was against this backdrop that a split within the Republican movement emerged, and from it was formed the Provisional Irish Republican Army. The PIRA originated as a paramilitary group defending Nationalists in Northern Ireland, but it evolved into an offensive operation working to force renegotiations with the British over the six counties.

It was to counter the efforts of the PIRA—or "Provos," as they were called—that the British had instituted Operation Demetrius, the measure that allowed for arrest and indefinite internment without charges, ostensibly to prevent violence. It did nothing to stem violence, and, instead, stoked yet more unrest. Then, the violence hit its peak on

"Bloody Sunday." The events of that fateful day "hardened people's hearts," recalled Eamonn McCann, a journalist and civil rights activist who was one of the organizers of the march.[10]

Though all this bloodshed and bedlam that was happening across the Irish Sea, British authorities notified all units, as a matter of routine, when word came in from an informant on March 6, 1973, that Republicans from the Andersonstown battalion were on their way. While tips about incoming militants were not necessarily unique, Scotland Yard was taking no chances given the impending referendum and visit by Cosgrave. The next day, the tipster confirmed the names of two of the Andersonstown Provisionals who were already in London, and from there things escalated quickly. By that evening, all police were on the lookout for the two. The commissioner of the Metropolitan Police, Sir Robert Mark, was in close touch with Home Secretary Robert Carr, as well as 10 Downing Street. The threat level was so high that a meeting was convened that included officers from the serious crimes unit of the Special Branch and officials from the Home Office and the Ministry of Defence.

The Special Branch, at the time the subject of a slick, eponymous television drama, deployed all available units to monitor the major ports. One unit put men and women on two British European Airways flights preparing for departure. Then, at 11:00 AM on Thursday morning, police found the IRA battalion at London's Heathrow Airport. Not two but ten militants were discovered and arrested as they attempted to take flights to Dublin or Belfast. The group was taken to Ealing Police Station, where they were questioned under the strictest security, with everyone seeking to enter the station questioned, including the police officers.[11]

Earlier that morning, at 8:30 AM, George Burrows and Stanley Conley of the Special Patrol Group, their antennae raised, took note of an older, battered green Ford Corsair with a recently issued license plate number for a newer vehicle, NYP 477J, that didn't quite match its bearer. The car was parked on Broadway, a narrow street that ran along New Scotland Yard in Westminster, an obvious target for terrorists.[12]

The two alert constables were no strangers to pressure-filled situations. Just two weeks earlier, Burrows and Conley had responded to the Indian High Commissioner's Office, where Pakistani youths flashing knives, acid, and fake guns had taken hostages. Burrows and Conley, both skilled marksmen, had shot and killed the kidnappers before they caused any more harm.[13]

The constables carefully approached the green Corsair and gave it a once-over. Upon searching the suspicious car, they located fourteen sticks of commercial gelignite—a high explosive most commonly used for rock blasting—both in and under the back seat of the vehicle. Added to the gelignite sticks were thirty small bags of a powdered explosive, all of it wired to an alarm clock set for 3:00 PM. There could be no doubt: a major IRA operation was underway, planned to coincide with the referendum and the visit by Irish Prime Minister–Elect Cosgrave.

The police moved quickly. Within fifteen minutes, the area was cleared and cordoned off, and the bomb was delicately removed from the car. Two explosives experts, Peter Gurney and Major Geoffrey Biddle, spent the next half hour successfully defusing it. The scene was rendered safe by police, who knew at that moment that it was likely the only safe place in the entire city.[14]

The Yard kicked into high gear. First, all officers on duty were notified of the danger of an untold number of car bombs throughout the city. They intensified their search, combing through high-impact locations and landmarks for suspect vehicles. Next, the public affairs branch notified BBC Radio and the city's major newspapers of what they had found, but, hoping to avoid further chaos on the already congested streets due to the rail strike, an evacuation of the city was not ordered.

At 1:56 PM, with no additional car bombs yet detected despite the best work of the police, a call came in to the *Times* of London from a man with an Irish brogue. The Irishman provided the secretary staffing the news desk with the locations of three more car bombs: Dean Stanley Street, New Scotland Yard, and the Old Bailey—the Central Criminal Court of England and Wales. The *Times* immediately contacted Eric Wright, the head of the Metropolitan Police Press Bureau, who in turn also notified the City of London Police.

The Dean Stanley Street car was found within just a few minutes, parked by the offices of the British Forces Broadcasting Service, which was the target. In the trunk of the blue Via automobile, police located another gelignite bomb—smaller than the previous bomb, but deadly nonetheless. Officers quickly cleared the area of people and deftly defused the bomb.

As police frantically searched the vicinity of New Scotland Yard for the car identified by the caller, a sick realization struck the people responsible for communicating his warning: the caller had meant Great Scotland Yard, at the other end of Whitehall, not New Scotland Yard. Police scrambled, and by around half past two, the second car was found: a Hillman Hunter, another midsize sedan. Heroic efforts were made to clear the immediate area, and an explosives officer from the British Army bravely climbed into the car and engaged in a desperate race against the clock to defuse the ticking bomb, but without success. He jumped from the car three minutes before the explosive detonated at 2:43 PM, seventeen minutes before the 3:00 PM time set on the other bombs. The blast lifted people from the ground, and windows as far as a quarter-mile away were blown out of their sashes. Thirty-eight people suffered injuries, mainly from flying pieces of glass and other debris, but no one was killed. However, the worst was still to come.

Emergency personnel responding to this nightmarish challenge to find and defuse bombs, seemingly from a James Bond novel, were doing so in the face of streets jammed with traffic. Emergency service vehicles, including bomb disposal units, fire engines, and ambulances, were stalled by gridlock. Worse yet, the police were working with severely limited resources: the Metropolitan Police were understaffed by five thousand officers, and the City of London Police were working at 80 percent strength. Police officials had no choice but to put out a request to all police officers not directly involved with an emergency response to man the city's traffic lights to help free up congestion.[15] And there was no time to waste—there was still one more bomb.

Meanwhile, a reporter from the *Times*, Martin Huckerby, having heard the news of the car bomb locations when they were called in to his paper, made his way over to the Old Bailey, arriving at 2:07 PM. He was shocked to learn that though he managed to get there quickly, the police were still not on the scene. Huckerby quickly identified the suspect vehicle on his own, across the street from the courthouse, parked by a noteworthy old tavern named the George. He found the policemen assigned to the Old Bailey and notified them of his discovery. Then, wisely, he found a suitable doorway and took cover.[16]

Watching the scene unfold from a safe distance must have been surreal for Huckerby. A century and a half earlier, another young reporter, Charles Dickens, had observed the goings-on at the Old Bailey from across the street at the George. From that location, he witnessed and reported on nineteenth-century London's major trials—and public executions—for the *London Daily Chronicle*. Dickens later used his experiences at the Old Bailey in both *A Tale of Two Cities* and *Oliver Twist*.

As the minutes ticked by, and no additional emergency response personnel arrived, Huckerby grew anxious. "The police who approached did not arrive until 2:35," he reported, a full twenty-eight minutes after the reporter identified the green Ford Cortina estate car himself. Worse yet, "The police did not stop people walking past the car, which was parked in a line of vehicles, until 2:45 p.m."[17] This despite the fact that it was, quite literally, a ticking time bomb. It was just an hour before the scheduled meeting between the prime ministers, and two minutes after the Whitehall bomb had exploded, when the police finally began to block access to the area and evacuate people.[18]

Just then, amid the chaos, a quick-thinking police officer noticed a school bus filled with children stuck in traffic by the Old Bailey. He told all forty-four students and their teachers, en route to a school trip, to get off the bus and run in the other direction. Meanwhile, officers evacuated the courts, but that effort moved slowly. A judge, wearing the traditional wig and perhaps numb to bomb scares, announced in an unconcerned and most British manner, "We seem to have a bomb alarm."[19]

As the courthouse was being emptied, Detective Sergeant Nick Birch was hurriedly escorting nervous jurors out of the Old Bailey at 2:49 PM when, suddenly, the car bomb exploded. The percussion sent Birch twenty feet into the air and across the street. It did the same to his car, which was damaged beyond repair. Patrons of the George, who had withdrawn to the rear lounge and escaped injury, emerged to find the famous public house reduced to shambles.[20] Meanwhile, the children fleeing their school bus were knocked to the ground and showered with broken glass—a fate far less hazardous than what had awaited them on the bus, closer to the bomb. One of the students would tell a reporter, "It was terrible. We had come to London to see St. Paul's and a museum. One of our teachers was hurt."[21]

Black smoke could be seen rising from the spot from miles away. Some cars were tossed on top of each other, while others were blown onto their sides. Glass was piled ankle-deep from innumerable shattered windows. Barristers walked about with bloodstained wigs, and court clerks with blood running down their cut faces were everywhere. People in nearby buildings were thrown from their chairs and across rooms. Dozens more injured people lay bleeding on the sidewalks. Striking hospital workers hastily huddled and voted to go back to work for the day to deal with the injured. The scene was filled with the wounded, ambulances and other emergency vehicles, and countless policemen and firefighters milling about streets strewn with damaged vehicles, broken windows, papers blown from offices, and small fires. At least one of the victims had exposed bones from multiple injuries. In all, more than two hundred people were wounded—many of them seriously—and the press reported that one man died from a related heart attack (though it would later be determined that his death was unrelated to the blast). More than one witness described the scene as "just like the Blitz," the bombing campaign conducted by Nazi Germany that terrorized Britain during the Second World War. Indeed, the bombings were the first Britain had suffered since the war's end.[22]

Irish Prime Minister–Elect Cosgrave condemned the bombings and expressed his "concern and regret."[23] British Prime Minister Heath visited the injured schoolchildren in the hospital. Oddly, he gave the people of his country no reason to remain calm when he said on television, "In a capital of this size, there is always the chance that people with determination to damage, to kill people and to wreck buildings will succeed."[24]

Seán Ó Brádaigh, the information officer for the political wing of the Provisional IRA, Sinn Féin, told the media, "I don't know who is responsible and I have no comment to make. Quite frankly I know nothing except what I heard on the radio." And the "official" IRA released a statement denying involvement in the bombings. "It has never been part of our policy or intention to take action which would alienate the British working-class people or cause injury or death to workers in Britain or Ireland," it read. "The IRA had no part in today's explosions in Britain."[25]

Scotland Yard was already acutely aware that the bombings had been the work of the IRA, regardless of what they or Sinn Féin might say. In fact, they'd known before a single explosion had occurred. Intelligence about the ten individuals officers had intercepted that morning at Heathrow was already being analyzed, and the two main suspects presented an anomaly in the annals of fighting the Republicans: they were women. As the Special Branch officers were conducting their search, they had been aided by photos of both of them. They were the Price sisters: Marian, age nineteen, and Dolours, the ringleader, twenty-two.

Their last name was familiar to Scotland Yard. The girls' father, Albert, had been on the British Army's list of most wanted since Operation

Demetrius had been implemented a year and a half earlier. His exploits were well-known to intelligence services in the United Kingdom. In 1939, when the IRA embarked on a war against the British, Albert Price had joined a number of his Republican brethren on a mission to do battle against their oppressor.[26]

Four years later, Albert and twenty fellow IRA members were being held in Derry Gaol when they pulled off a daring escape, tunneling all the way out of the prison and into the yard of a neighboring home, emerging through the owner's garden. A waiting furniture truck parked on the road drove them to the safety of Donegal.[27] But Albert was hardly done with Republicanism. Decades later, when the paramilitary Provisionals split from the existing IRA, he not only sided with the Provos, he assumed a senior rank and was a suspected member of the secret Army Council.[28]

Albert Price's children did not veer from their familial path. His eldest daughter, Claire, was engaged to another Provisional who was interned at the time the police were searching for Marian and Dolours.[29] Dolours, a waifish, brown-haired beauty, would recall a childhood spent with her sisters listening to tales of the IRA at their father's knee. He was fond of telling his children war stories, such as the time when a friend had been hanged for a bombing with which he was not involved. "As children growing up, that's the kind of bedtime story we would hear. We wouldn't hear Little Red Riding Hood, we would hear, 'They hanged my mate Jimmy,'" remembered Dolours.[30]

As active as Albert was in the IRA, the Price sisters did not grow up in a home simply dominated by a patriarch with dutiful women tucked away in the kitchen. Dolours recalled that "on my father's side, I had a very religious aunt who would've said, 'For God and Ireland.' On my mother's side, Ireland came before God." Two generations of women in their family had preceded them in jail for their Republicanism. As children, the Prices would watch them prepare care packages of sweets and cakes for IRA prisoners on special occasions. It instilled in the young girls a sense that prison was a place where "you got all sorts of wonderful stuff." However, no one's effort on behalf of the cause could match that of their dear aunt Bridie.[31]

Bridie Dolan, their mother's sister, was a beautiful young woman of twenty-five when, in 1938, she went on an IRA errand to retrieve a deposit of munitions in the Catholic Lowers Falls of Belfast. When her escort didn't show up for the dangerous mission, Bridie went on without him. The arms dump exploded, and she was badly disfigured, losing her hands and eyes in the blast. For the rest of her life, Bridie lived with her family. Her grief-stricken mother put the house into mourning. Dolours described the home like "having a wake, but with a living body." She and her sister would swap assignments bringing cigarettes up to their aunt's room, placing them in her mouth, and lighting them for her. The girls hardly enjoyed the task, but they understood it was their duty to this real-life sacrificial lamb to the cause.[32]

Bridie's massive injuries and subsequent life spent in darkness didn't deter her nieces from allegiance to the IRA. Rather, their aunt's patriotism instilled a passion for Republicanism and a sense of duty in Dolours and Marian. "The fact that she was in the state she was in and the condition she was in obliged me in some way to continue the struggle because it validated her sacrifice," Dolours said. "And to have ignored the struggle would have been to make her sacrifice futile, useless."[33]

It was with this generational inspiration that Dolours embarked on the career of a militant. As a student at Queen's University in Belfast, she had tried the route of the peaceful civil rights protestor, joined by her then fifteen-year-old sister, Marian. They were among the marchers viciously ambushed in Derry in 1969 by Protestant extremists at the Burntollet Bridge, as police passively watched it all take place. In the sad saga of the Troubles, the event was what historian Paul Bew called "the spark that lit the prairie fire."[34]

For Dolours Price, that spark was yet another piece of kindling that would erupt into a roaring inferno. Fed up with nonviolence, and not willing to settle for a role in the women's paramilitary branch, Cumann na Mban (the Irishwomen's Council), Dolours, an ardent feminist, swore an oath to the IRA and immediately informed the men in charge, "I don't want to be rolling bandages. No, that's not what I want to do. I want to fight."[35]

Soon, Dolours was transporting explosives by car from Dundalk to battalion areas as often as twice a day, the incendiaries secreted in her door panels. Soldiers patrolling the roads saw her so often they came to know her by her alias, "Rosie." They'd chat with the pretty young Irishwoman, who was not above flirting with the rugged British Army men in order to make it to her destination. Her mission was of primary importance, her predilections a far second. Soon she was helping the cause by participating in armed bank robberies, including one in which she was disguised as a nun. Price attributed her temerity to "the recklessness of youth," and her Republican zeal was lost on none of her superiors. In less than a year, she was promoted to the IRA's intelligence unit and was a member of the über-secret group the Unknowns, which, she said, was run by Pat McClure, but ultimately reported back to Gerry Adams, who had already emerged as one of the leading figures in the Republican movement, in Belfast. As a member of this band of dedicated and ultra-loyal militants, Dolours was involved in the abduction and transport of those marked for death by the IRA for informing. Most notably, she was involved in the disappearance of Jean McConville, a thirty-eight-year-old widow of a Catholic British Army soldier. McConville, the mother of ten, was believed by the IRA to have been providing information to the security forces. Her murder, by a gunshot to the back of the head, was front-page news and would, decades later, make headlines when Price's own admissions implicated Irish politician Gerry Adams in the affair.[36] Adams strongly denies involvement in the McConville murder and steadfastly maintains that he has never been a member of the IRA. The latter claim is believed by few, if any.

It was in this age of Republican activism and violence that Dolours was discussing doing battle against imperialism on their opponents' home turf, just as Albert Price had done decades earlier. That's when the talk turned to targeting specific symbols of the British Empire. In a secret meeting with her fellow paramilitaries, she claimed Gerry Adams announced a "very serious operation" for which he was seeking volunteers. According to Price, Adams described the operation as a possible "hanging job." He gave those unwilling to put their lives on the line the opportunity to leave the meeting. To the disappointment of Price, many did. "I was very shocked and surprised that people were so unwilling to actually undertake such an important mission, which I was only too happy and too willing to undertake," she said. Price assumed the role of officer commanding (OC) for the operation, which was to be the bombing of the Old Bailey and the three other sites on March 8, the date of the referendum on Northern Ireland. "We could set off ten car bombs in Belfast and they would have little effect on the English public opinion," she reasoned. Just one car bomb in England, though, "would change English public opinion to such an extent that they would perhaps begin to call to have their troops taken out."[37]

That a woman would not only volunteer for, but be appointed the person in charge of, such a monumental event was not only a testament to the faith the IRA had in the twenty-two-year-old Dolours Price, it was a dramatic sea change in the way women were utilized in fighting Britain. It was Price who traveled to London to select targets, and she was instrumental in the plan to take four car bombs into the city. Years later, she would recall that the men in the plot weren't nearly as reliable. "The boys had been instructed not to acknowledge each other, to be oblivious of each other. Nothing untoward was to happen," she said. Unequipped with Dolours's sense of duty and obedience, "They of course disobeyed all of that, went to pubs, got drunk, got carried into boarding houses." She encountered her confederate Gerry Kelly outside the art museum in Trafalgar Square and she described him as "leapfrogging over the bollards and shouting . . . in a broad Belfast accent." Despite his lack of discretion, though, she said, "It didn't really matter. We were set to go."[38]

And go they did. The bombings in Britain sent shock waves through the country and made headlines around the world. In the House of

Lords, opposition leader Lord Shackleton heard the IRA's message loud and clear: "We have not yet suffered in London as they have in Belfast, throughout Northern Ireland and in Dublin and I can only pray that we shall not have to face this."[39]

The police interrogated Marian first. Despite being barely nineteen years old, the younger Price was as hard as nails and no less fervently committed to the IRA. She had accompanied her sister to all the key protests in Northern Ireland and, like Dolours, was fearless and said to sometimes be called "the Widowmaker" by British officers.[40] She refused to answer the police's questions. At 3:00 PM, she looked at her watch and smiled, knowing that by then, bombs were exploding in the city.[41]

The interrogation turned to Dolours. Like her younger sister, she provided no information, responding to each question with "I have nothing to say." The Prices were put into cells and stripped of their clothes. When the police handed Dolours a filthy blanket with which to cover herself, she refused it. She was later walked completely naked through the police station in front of a group of police officers. After four days, her mother arrived for a visit. Hardened by decades of fighting the British, Mrs. Price whispered into her daughter's ear, "No tears, not in front of these people." For his part, her father was quick to remind her, "I blew them up before you did. The only thing was I didn't get caught."[42]

The sisters and their fellow bombers would stand trial for six weeks, during which time the legend of the Price sisters would only grow, with stories of their daring feats rapidly spreading throughout Belfast. Onlookers at the court were bewildered by the two young, beautiful women who had caused so much destruction. "When I look at those girls, I kept asking myself what on earth got them into something that should land them in that dock," one oblivious senior officer said, adding, "I couldn't find any answers."[43]

Despite an impending conviction that was all but a foregone conclusion, the Prices did not see themselves spending a long time in prison.

They confided to friends that as political prisoners, amnesty was a possibility. Marian told the judge that she considered herself a prisoner of war. The women even talked of escape; small wonder, considering their father's famous success at the breakout.[44]

The trial was marked by some disruptive behavior by the Republican defendants. When one of the ten, Roisin McNearney, was acquitted after cooperating with authorities, the men in the group hummed the Death March while their fellow defendant, Hugh Feeney, tossed metaphorical blood money at the eighteen-year-old typist-cum-bomber.

The next day, before the other nine were allowed to speak prior to sentencing, Judge Sebag Shaw warned, "I will not have this court turned into a political arena." But his words fell on deaf ears, and the defendants constantly interrupted the judge as he prepared to impose his sentences. Frustrated and seemingly shaken, Judge Shaw said, "Passing sentence on people as young as you are is repugnant to me." Marian shouted out, "Don't worry, we absolve you."[45] The Price sisters were sentenced to two life terms.

All of the convicted immediately declared a hunger strike. They refused to eat until they were treated as political prisoners and transferred back to a prison in Northern Ireland.

# SIX

# *Wally*

To her parents' growing dismay, Rose Dugdale's transition to the direct-action phase of her militancy was underway. It began as a combination of meeting with radicals, assisting revolutionary groups, and writing her first (and only) published call for substantive change.

In 1972, academic Trevor Pateman edited a collection of essays titled *Counter Course*. Compiled as a study in university course criticism, Pateman described it as a "handbook for the use by students . . . who find that their education consists in being processed for a particular niche in the class structure of society."[1] It's hard to imagine a more appropriate platform for Dugdale, as she herself fit squarely into that definition as both a daughter and a student. She contributed an essay arguing for a complete overhaul in the way that economics was taught in universities. It was a topic she understood well as a teacher of economics in the sociology department of Bedford College, where she lectured in seminars on Marxist economics and classes where she said she would "try to show the consequences of certain economic policies."[2]

In "Economic Theory in Class Society," Dugdale explained her view that the major flaw in the contemporary economic model was that it describes the world as naturally tending toward rest, whereas she saw a world naturally tending toward conflict. She argued that one needed only to look at the fact that "students have openly declared war on American capitalism and its tentacles of power across the continents" to see a vivid example. Indeed, she wrote, "students are now fighting out their economics in the streets."[3] Again, she took on John Stuart Mill, arguing against his view that "the ills of society can one and all be overcome by democratic decision in the light of reasoned argument." No, Dugdale explained, echoing her thoughts about the futility of waiting for public intellectuals to dream up new ideas to solve the Vietnam question, direct action was necessary, and students of her day were increasingly aware of this. "Students have begun to see the hypocrisy of 'Yes, indeed society must change—we will bring about change through educational enlightenment and the victory of mature philosophical reason,'" she wrote. Perhaps, she went on, it was more sinister: "Economic policy is not derived from economic theory. Rather, the dictates of economic need and political-economic policies, determine acceptability of the theory—acceptability *by* the ruling classes, *for* the ruling class."[4]

To counter this problem, Dugdale proposed that students demand far less a reliance on instruction in mathematics in the teaching of economics, as this traditional method reinforced "an attitude of passive reception of economics by students. It is not up to the student to question his mentors, still less the theory, until he has grasped all the tools." Once all those tools were mastered, the lessons were done. Instead, she urged a more pragmatic, boots-on-the-ground, agenda-driven economic theory that was "applied to the needs of the working class, to service the workers' revolutionary struggles." She argued that the utility in teaching economics should involve bringing the working class "into the universities to understand the natures of its enemy, capitalism." Indeed, students should be urged not only to oppose capitalism but to fight it from outside its structure, for "to oppose it, from within, is as incorrect as to support it."[5]

Though little-noticed, her essay had roots in long political and philosophical discussions she had had with students while participating in sit-ins at the University of Manchester, about how she saw their curriculum as prejudiced on behalf of capitalism. Interestingly, it was at this very time and with the same group of students that she was invited to visit Belfast.

Both the epoch and the essay provide a vital insight into the character of Rose Dugdale. While analyses by various writers in the years to come would describe her—predictably—as a "poor little rich girl," to assume she was simply a spoiled young woman swept up in the frenzy of student protest and inspired by a boyfriend's working-class heroism would be to severely underestimate the woman. The truth is that Dugdale's beliefs were deeply rooted in a great amount of independent work, study, and thought. Her radicalism came from her own making.

Rose would later recount that the question she most pondered at this point in her life was not *if* but *how* to get involved. The message of her essay was clear: it was not simply a time to put theory into motion; it was a time to skip the theory altogether and go headfirst into action. The enemy was identified; the victims evident. So, she sought to lend a hand, busily making herself known to various groups and causes. When Black Power demonstrators were jailed, she offered to post bail, just as she did for Anna Mendelssohn,[*6] who was arrested and later convicted of conspiracy to cause explosions as part of the Angry Brigade. Rose had previously met with a few of the members of that group, a small band of far-left anarchists in Britain who had by this time successfully waged terror via bombings aimed at Western capitalist structures at home. Eventually, Teresa Hayter introduced Rose to the International Marxist Group, but Rose couldn't be swayed to sign on as a Trotskyist. Instead, she remained true to her own writings—she was described by Hayter as "impatient with the slowness of political work on the Left as it was carried on in Britain at the time."[7]

She wasn't alone in her efforts. Though outgoing, warm, intelligent, and an obvious force of nature, Rose Dugdale didn't have a significant romantic relationship until she was past thirty. She had consciously, even forcefully, planned and directed her young adult life away from the expected goals of finding a suitable man of equal station, marrying, and enjoying a life of privilege. Now, as she began her fourth decade of life, the study of revolution was her central pursuit. As she had decided, she would abandon academics for a crusade, and it was

---

* Described by *The Guardian* as "a poet like no other," Mendelssohn was also an actor, musician, and painter who, in her 2009 obituary, was said to be "beholden to no cultural dictates."

through such engagement that she found the man with which she would form a torrid and strange romance filled with activism, arrests, and domestic upset.

Rose Dugdale met Walter Heaton, a six-foot-three-inch tall, thin self-described revolutionary socialist with longish dark hair and an equally long, dark moustache, while she was hard at work on a protest of great importance to her and her feminist sisters. When married women walked the picket line, they were not being paid strike money because, the trade union argued, their husbands were supporting them.[8] The North London claimants union was involved in the efforts on behalf of the female strikers, and it was around this time that Heaton and Dugdale encountered each other and quickly became not just constant companions but comrades-in-arms.[9] Heaton, the branch chairman of a recently closed factory, took many despondent workers to the claimants union for Rose's help.[10] From her own purse, she established the Tottenham branch of the claimants union, just walking distance from the big Gestetner factory and in an area that can be fairly described as a slum. From their claimants union, which they later renamed the Civil Rights Centre, she and Heaton adhered to the motto "If you don't hit it, it won't fall."[11]

Which of them held greater sway over the other is a matter for debate, but this much is clear: the relationship was symbiotic, and the two went at their causes, and each other, with reckless passion. Heaton said that Rose was smitten with him essentially because of his commitment to working-class issues. She appears to have also been taken by his aggressive, if not abusive, behavior. She would fondly recall that during an argument, Walter, a strong, strapping ex-guardsman, tackled her and shouted her down. It was then that she strangely decided, "This is the man for me."

Heaton was a far more complicated figure than the man portrayed by the media of his day. His military service, often simply referenced with just a passing nod, greatly disturbed him and had a clear influence on the man he would become afterward. Too young when he tried to enlist during World War II, he joined the Coldstream Guards in 1948, and by the age of seventeen, he was aboard a ship headed to Malaya. In an interview later in life, Heaton described traumatic experiences during the deployment. Military intervention there was a convoluted mishmash of anti-communism and corporate cronyism. British foreign policy expert Mark Curtis describes Britain's entry into Malaya that year as the start of a "counter-insurgency" campaign against what was then one of its colonies. According to declassified files, the British employed "very brutal measures" while battling the communist insurgents, including the use of chemical agents. Curtis points to the colony's rich mineral holdings as the primary concern of Britain.[12] British atrocities during the war there were such that in 2015 the British Supreme Court declared that Commonwealth forces had committed mass murder.

Originally told he'd be fighting terrorists, Heaton quickly realized he'd been sent to Malaya because of the country's rich natural resources, with items such as rubber produced in the colony. He came to believe he was fighting for corporate interests, including the Dunlop Rubber Company, which had outsize influence over the government. Heaton patrolled "the worst jungle in the world," filled with snakes and traps, and spent two years sleeping under a canvas tent, while by day helping to force local Malayans into a prison camp called Kampong Coldstream. The twisted British strategy was that anyone not in the camp was not a local civilian and, therefore, an insurgent.[13] Heaton recalled terrible conditions at Kampong Coldstream, where he watched "kids crying as soldiers burned their food and their things." He readily described it as a concentration camp and, later in life, questioned why there had not been greater inquiry into the conduct of the Commonwealth authorities there. There is "no run-out date on justice," he told the press. "Murder is murder."[14] So, whereas Rose had studied the sins of the West in the classroom, Walter had seen them up close and on the ground from a young age in what he called "Britain's My Lai."[15] For him, there could be no more vivid an example of British colonialism at its worst.

Back home, Heaton compiled a dozen convictions for petty offenses, ranging from stealing electricity to robbery, which landed him in lockup and a stint in prison.[16] While incarcerated, the Englishman spent his time reading and developed a romantic attachment to the Irish Republican cause.[17] Both a drinker and a charmer, he had a gift for rhetoric and leadership, having organized his co-workers in a "work-in," which was his attempt to prevent the closure of the Standard Bottle Company. He failed, but it only added to his proletariat credentials.

Heaton's activism also had a strong intellectual foundation. Despite his hardscrabble ways, he was extremely well-read in the revolutionary literature of Marx and Engels. Like Rose, he was a student of Marx's criticism of Britain's colonization of Ireland, and Wally's ability to eloquently pontificate on these topics was an aphrodisiac to her.

Having moved from her posh apartment in Chelsea to the run-down working-class district of Tottenham, Rose was proving her mettle and making her mark in two ways: parting with her riches and fighting for the poor. She took notice of the practice of "squatting" sanctioned by the Provisional Irish Republican Army in Northern Ireland, in which needy families, without permission, occupied newly built housing and refused to leave. The Provos didn't wait for local authorities to allocate the space—they took matters into their own hands and did it themselves, doling out the residences as they saw fit. Inspired, Rose implemented the Provos' approach, employing the rallying cry "Derry today, Tottenham tomorrow."[18]

Popular with feminists and radical students, claimants unions were increasingly popular local organizations that were founded to help British citizens get all the welfare benefits to which they were entitled, and then some. It was just the cause for Rose: an opportunity to work at the grassroots level on behalf of those she described as "the poor and deprived." She took to the people she represented with ease, just as she had with the villagers in Cuba, with whom she connected despite a language barrier. The needy found her to be a soft touch, paying legal costs or bail for neighbors, buying coal for pensioners in the winter, and rescuing tenants who were in trouble with their rent. From this work, she became known to many as the Angel of Tottenham.[19] She even did her best to adopt the local accent, speaking Cockney to the appropriate audiences.[20] Friends worried that some were taking advantage, but if they were, Rose was unconcerned. This was her métier, taking on the British government on behalf of the working class.[21]

The fighting Dugdale spirit emerged in Tottenham. She would depart her office, which she and Wally repainted with the Irish tricolor covering its entire exterior, and show up at local council meetings to shout down the councilors for her clients, making demands, not requests. It was direct action in its purest form.

With the enormous number of activist groups that had emerged, the concept of direct action became all the rage in the sixties and into the seventies. In an editorial titled "Direct Action in London," which addressed a series of violent incidents in the city, *The Guardian* said, "The rash of incendiary devices and letter bombs in London and Aldershot follows an almost classic recipe for creating anxiety. At this moment we not only do not know who is responsible; we do not even know which cause is intended to be served." The editorial went on to state that the most probable answer as to who was behind it was "irregulars in the Irish Republican cause, rather than the Provisional IRA itself." Oddly, the piece states that the Provisionals had not extended their campaign to Britain. The writers' memories must have been short—the bombings at the Old Bailey and elsewhere had taken place just five months earlier.[22]

The traditional, more subtle methods of trying to effect change, such as lobbying those in power, were thought insufficient for the exigent issues of the day. Instead, people—especially young people and students—were taking to the streets in large numbers. For some, direct action meant the nonviolent protest style of Gandhi and MLK. For others, it meant violence and confrontations with police. But it wasn't just about the methods used, argued British peace activist and academic April Carter, who wrote that direct action depended also on the political context and mood surrounding each particular event. Further, its forms were and remain varied. "It may be designed to demonstrate in action the answer to a particular problem—homeless families squatting in empty council houses . . . or it may be a method used to repudiate the entire political system and promote insurrection."[23]

Certainly, Rose would come to run that entire gamut. When a claimant needed representation at the welfare office, Rose would kick open the door and slam her fist on the table while addressing intimidated civil servants. Tagged with a reputation for overturning tables and making a scene, she became so feared that she was banned from at least one office. The approach wasn't always successful. Lynn Cusack, the director of the homeless families' unit in the area, said Rose "hadn't the discipline to maintain working-class support. If she'd organised better she could have had the support of most of the families in temporary accommodation." Instead, she added, "She preferred flashpoint confrontation to political organisation."[24]

Rose Dugdale, who had been raised to curtsey before every guest who entered the room was now earning a reputation for her inability to control her zeal. Cusack recalled that others would come to her office, "sweet as a nut," and get handouts for the squatters, "But not Rose. She'd fly in, and wallop, give me a f— blanket, you f— magistrate's daughter." Rose's friends from the time said that at the mere mention of her name, the authorities froze.[25] Cusack said that Rose told her coldly that, when the revolution comes, "you'll be the first to be ground into the dust."[26]

Nor was she able to rein in her passionate affection for Wally Heaton. The pair carried on an unusually open adulterous affair, right in the presence of Heaton's beleaguered wife, Audrey, with whom he had two daughters, at the time aged fourteen and four. For a while, Dugdale even essentially moved into the Heaton family home, and the two were rather brazen in their behavior. Audrey recalled that Wally and Rose would sit and flirt, ignoring her presence and carrying on like a couple in front of her, leaving Audrey to feel like an outcast in her own house.

"One night," Audrey recalled, "I was sort of uptight about it and I threw a cup of coffee over Wally. I was really mad; they were sitting toasting each other with their cups of coffee, speaking in Gaelic. I couldn't understand it. And they used to leave me right out of the conversation. I used to tell them to get out, but they completely ignored me. There was nothing I could do about it."[27]

On another occasion, Audrey found the two naked in bed in a postcoital embrace. Her disregard for Audrey is surprisingly out of character for Rose, who has been described as a woman much more responsive and trusting of the influence and affection of other women.[28] "I became rather hysterical," Audrey said. "It was a shock. He'd had affairs all his married life but I'd never come that close to it." When Audrey smashed up the room upon the upsetting discovery, she said Rose "just lay there, and, you know, as if it were quite natural. I told her to get out. She got out of bed and she left." Still Rose stopped to leave a note for her lover on the front door that read, "Dear Wally, it was beautiful, I'll see you soon, Comrade, Rose."[29]

Dugdale had spent years employing the strictest of manners. Now she was in Audrey's home, sleeping with her husband, sitting in her living room with her legs up on the chair, her hair and nails dirty, and an omnipresent cigarette dangling from her lips, using vulgar language filled with expletives, delivered in the incongruously posh accent of London's middle class.[30]

Though she was (and would remain) quite defensive about her background, always attempting to downplay her pedigree, Dugdale was still reaping the benefits of wealth. She regularly attended operas and horse races, obvious evidence of her true class. Her father had made her a name at Lloyd's, which established her as an investor and underwriter in the firm as well as a member in the family business. This endowed her with nearly £80,000 (roughly equivalent to ten times that today). Her dedication to her activism was suspect to some, given her wealth and education. She had by then completed her academic work and was officially Dr. Dugdale, an expected achievement for someone of her breeding, but hardly the résumé of a working-class revolutionary. Perhaps to compensate for this, Rose was noted for her tattered clothes and inattention to appearances, except for her parlance. One friend noted that Dugdale had taken to speaking "in old left wing jargon like something out of an old pamphlet from the Fabians."[31]

One incident that is said to have put Dugdale on the radar of authorities took place in 1971, when Dugdale squatted two evicted families into homes in Islington. She then barricaded the street and declared it a "no-go" zone to local authorities.[32] Dugdale lost that standoff but was far from done. Later, three more families squatted in Islington and, when eviction proceedings began, Rose's Tottenham claimants union marched on the housing department, forcing a police response. The squatters, determined to stay put, went on a hunger strike, and, once again, barricades went up and the area declared a "no-go area."[33]

Rose and Wally didn't restrict all of their time and efforts to the poor of the Tottenham district. They also voraciously read Irish history and about the fight for Republicanism, absorbing the writings of James Fintan Lalor, James Connolly, Arthur Griffith, Michael Davitt, and Patrick Pearse.[34] From this intellectual foundation came an ever-increasing fervor to fight on behalf of the people of Northern Ireland and against British occupation. They frequented rallies decrying the internment policy in Northern Ireland alongside activist Pat Arrowsmith, and, though Rose once took issue with the idea of fighting capitalism through leaflets, the couple could often be found circulating pamphlets on behalf of the Anti-Internment League in London.

In the summer of 1972, Rose and Wally participated in a massive protest that led to their first arrest together, this time in support of five longshoremen who had been jailed at Pentonville Prison for refusing a court order to stop illegal picketing. Hundreds of thousands of union workers in Britain staged a strike in support of the five, and demonstrations at the prison brought out activists from myriad causes. The couple was already on the radar of the police when Chief Superintendent Donald Forrest noticed them in Rose's car, which he immediately recognized.

Forrest kept a close eye on the rabble-rousing pair and observed them walking in the area. He reported, "I watched these people periodically, and as the crowd built up and trouble erupted, I saw Heaton and Dugdale moving about among the agitators." Forrest continued, "[Heaton] was shouting slogans, such as 'Rush the Police'; 'Don't Let Them Move You'; 'Release The Five'; and 'Burn the Buses.'" Later, as the protest grew to approximately six hundred demonstrators, a police constable, Peter Butcher, noted that a few groups of "political extremists [were] interspersed amongst them."

Wally began to address the crowd, railing on about the situation in Northern Ireland. But this wasn't the audience for a lecture bent on winning support for the IRA. The protestors grew angry as Heaton fearlessly shouted, "British murderers, British soldiers are murdering brave lads in Derry and Belfast fighting this corrupt government for your cause. We must unite!"

Heaton's claims were met with, "If he doesn't fuck off he'll get his head knocked off," by an incensed British dockworker. Another shouted, "Clear off, leave the British soldiers alone, they're doing all right." Several moved toward Wally, as Rose stood firmly by his side. She saw their action at Pentonville as "a tribute to what existed in Derry."[35] Alarmed at the growing agitation, Constable Butcher tensely cautioned Wally, "You're upsetting these people and might cause trouble." Heaton was unmoved by the warning, derisively dismissing him by saying, "Does the jingle in your pocket match the jangle in your head?"

The constable backed off, and Heaton continued, "One of the brave British soldiers fired a rubber bullet at a woman looking out of her window and shot half her jaw away," to which a dockworker replied, "And the IRA shoot our men in the back!" Another shouted at Wally, "My brother's out there, shut your mouth." When a second police officer tried to warn Wally of the imminent threat posed by inciting the large gathering, he was nonplussed: "This is free speech, I can say what I like." At that, wary of a large-scale punch-up, the officer arrested Heaton. Rose, ever protective of her companion, grabbed the officer's arm, shouting over the crowd, "Just a minute! You've got no right to arrest him!" Another officer intervened, twice ordering Dugdale to let go of his colleague. When she refused, she, too, was arrested.

Walter was charged with "using insulting words whereby a breach of the peace was likely to be occasioned," and Rose with "willfully obstructing a constable of the Metropolitan Police force in the execution of his duty." Predictably, they both pleaded not guilty but were nevertheless convicted. Heaton was fined £30 and ordered to pay £20 in court costs. Rose received no penalty.*

What the police didn't know was that Rose's intentions at the Pentonville Prison protests were far more nefarious than merely standing by as Wally bravely delivered a fiery political speech to an irritated crowd. One of the protest leaders was twenty-nine-year-old Colin Ross, a dockworker who helped run the strike headquarters by day and the pickets outside the prison in the evening. His strategy included keeping the striking dockworkers on one side of the road and away from what he called "the strange groups" on the other—this in a crowd that extended for eight hundred yards.

One evening, one of the picketing dockers told Ross that someone on the other side of the street wanted to speak with him. He was led to two Irishmen he described as having the intimidating presence of the Kray twins, two infamous London gangsters. The pair led Ross down a side street and into an alleyway, while he wondered if he would come out of the situation alive. Once in the dark alley, Ross recalls being approached by Rose, who, with a booming voice, said, "Hello, a great turnout." He was taken aback by the woman wearing what he described as a combat coat with trousers. Her appearance gave him the impression that he had been brought to meet yet another oddball from the protests. But Rose was deadly serious. "You have got enough men here," she said. "We can

---

* The accounts of the incident at Pentonville Prison, including the arrests of Rose Dugdale and Walter Heaton, come from police statements by Police Constable Peter Butcher (August 1, 1972) and Chief Superintendent Donald John Forrest (February 28, 1973), both of Scotland Yard, in files retrieved from the a public records request to the Metropolitan Police.

supply the guns and hand grenades to get your men out of there." Surprised but unswayed, Ross thanked her and informed her that the union intended to peacefully secure the release of its five members. "She looked at me as if I were mad and left," he remembered.[36]

Perhaps she did think him mad not to accept her offer. Yes, negotiations might work to eventually free the five longshoremen, but only with concessions and the existing power structure still intact. Guns and hand grenades could get the job done more quickly and with a much clearer message to those in charge of the corrupt government: true power rests in the hands of the people. Violent direct action, in Rose's view, had the potential to bring about rapid change. This was the lesson that Dolours and Marian Price came to believe, and it was emerging in Dugdale as well.

This was an exciting time for Rose Dugdale. She was doing what she loved: fighting every day for the rights of the underprivileged and now supporting Irish Republicanism in an increasingly active fashion. Moreover, she was doing it alongside a man she adored. She even took to referring to Wally as her common-law husband, despite the fact that he was already married and the bed they shared was in his wife's home. Together, they were taking direct action to another level, and arms and munitions are believed to be at this time taking the place of home heating assistance and squatters' rights. Bringing an end to British imperialism in Northern Ireland had become Dugdale's mission, her true calling. She said, "There was a struggle going on right on my doorstep in Ireland and there was never any doubt that I had to be involved. When I got off the boat in Belfast, I saw the British Army on the streets in their uniforms with their high-tech weapons. I saw British troops raid a set of flats and I found it horrifying. I became anxious to get involved in the armed struggle."[37] She even took up karate to help prepare herself to fight. Perhaps because of her time in post-revolutionary Cuba, where bloodshed was considered a necessary component of the struggle, Rose never bought into the nonviolent protest approach that first entranced Dolours Price. Rather, she subscribed to the dictum of Mao that "political power grows out of the barrel of the gun" seemingly right from the start.

Rose and Wally used the guise of their Civil Rights Centre to get themselves directly involved in the efforts of the Provisionals. Heaton described their efforts as trying "to get children from the Lower Falls area, the Bogside, and the Creggan off the streets, alleviating a very explosive situation," in Northern Ireland by bringing both Catholic and Protestant children back to Tottenham. But the fact was that no one ever saw Wally and Rose with any children.[38] There were no witnesses to these youth outings, no evidence that any such effort ever took place. Instead, it is believed that the couple was transporting weapons across the sea to the Provisionals.

They made frequent trips under the guise of bringing Catholic children away from volatile Northern Ireland to mingle with Protestant children in Tottenham for holiday, and for her part, Rose made an effort not to draw any unwanted attention from the police, adopting what was for her the uncomfortable attire of a young woman of the day: skirts and blouses. But the authorities were well aware of the two aspiring guerrillas and kept a watchful eye on their movements as they increasingly suspected the pair of running weapons to Ulster.

The method the police believed Dugdale and Heaton were using to smuggle arms was not unlike that employed by Dolours Price as she delivered munitions through checkpoints in Northern Ireland. They allegedly concealed the illicit goods within the upholstery of rented vehicles, which they would drive to Manchester and then to Stranraer, where they would board a ferry over to Northern Ireland. The cars would then be driven from the ferry by either paid sympathizers or unwitting tourists. Police believed they had accumulated enough evidence to eventually obtain a warrant.[39]

If they were transporting arms, as the police investigation and the incident at Pentonville seem to clearly suggest, their impact was likely small. The IRA had by then established consistent supply lines and had long before given up on relying on deliveries through the English ports for large caches of weaponry.[40] Still, the work was unquestionably an elixir to their militant souls.

The battle-hungry couple's trips to Northern Ireland, especially to Derry and Belfast, continued throughout 1972 and 1973. They even got themselves arrested in Derry when they refused to identify themselves at a checkpoint while attending a civil rights march.[41] They wore the arrest like a badge of honor. Journalist Tom Mangold reported that while there, they met "rather theatrically with alleged IRA gunmen."[42] It's hard to imagine Rose being any more excited than she must have been upon coming face-to-face with real soldiers on the ground in the war against imperialism.

While on one trip to Derry, Rose met Martin McGuinness, who, in time, would play a key role in politics and become an effective peace negotiator. When Dugdale met him, however, McGuinness was commanding the Provisional IRA in the area.[43] He no doubt wanted to size up this British aristocrat–turned–Republican ally for himself. In County Donegal, she met with a senior member of the Provisionals' Army Council, David O'Connell. It was an impressive feat: O'Connell was said to be the most wanted man in Ireland.[44] Informers reported that O'Connell was impressed by her enthusiasm, smarts, and eagerness to go on active service. He was skeptical, however, of utilizing her, not only because she was British but also because she was a woman. O'Connell had been burned just recently by Maria Maguire, the woman who had once been his companion on trips to Britain to procure arms.[45]

Maguire was a middle-class college graduate who had a love affair with O'Connell but became disillusioned over what she believed was the failure of the IRA to seek a political solution to the Troubles instead of the "sterile and murderous campaign" she felt they were waging.[46] Together, the pair were successful in procuring large shipments of arms for the Provisionals, the sorts that made the efforts of Rose and Wally seem trite. On one trip, O'Connell and Maguire ordered more than four and a half tons of armaments from a Czech arms manufacturer controlled by the KGB.[47] Maguire went on to write a book about her time as a militant titled *To Take Arms: My Year with the IRA Provisionals*, published at the time Rose was ferrying back and forth to Northern Ireland.

It is doubtful that Dugdale would ever have been given access to the training camps, much less the hierarchy, of the PIRA at this point in her life without having first proven her mettle in some manner. So police suspicion that she and Wally were transporting guns to Northern Ireland is most likely accurate. What is clear is that in a very short time, she had quickly earned a reputation for her activism and radical integrity.

Still, no matter how dedicated to the cause of Irish Republicanism she was, Rose was met with great suspicion. "In Ireland, everyone is so mercenary in trying to hold on to what they have that they couldn't understand why a woman would give up a fortune to fight a cause that wasn't hers."[48] Some suspected her of being a police plant. She maintained a low-key demeanor and did everything she could to deny her background, including a donation to the Belfast Citizens' Defence Committee.[49] Nevertheless, her activism also fostered some contempt. Recalling Dugdale's foray into the plight of the Irish, novelist and Sinn Féin critic Eilis O'Hanlon said Rose was "lucky . . . not to have been shot on sight when she turned up in the North offering her plummy voice to fight for Irish freedom." O'Hanlon opined, "Maybe it was the fact that she was such an absurd, jolly-hockeysticks figure that gave her a shield of safety, though even the IRA never trusted her completely." But while O'Hanlon, who grew up in Belfast during the Troubles, recalls her as "essentially a ridiculous cartoon and a laughing stock," she cautiously adds that Dugdale was "no less dangerous for it."

# SEVEN

# *Stealing Home*

While at Tottenham, Rose Dugdale was visited by the noted British anarcho-communist activist Albert Meltzer. Meltzer had been made aware of "a sincere young woman who inherited a fortune and proposed to give it to 'the movement' without being sure what it was she believed in." It's possible that Meltzer's intel about Rose's reputation had come from his close friend Stuart Christie, as Christie was rumored to be associated with the Angry Brigade and Anna Mendelssohn (for whom Rose had once offered to post bail). Intrigued, and always eager to win over supporters to his cause, Meltzer approached Dugdale at her claimants union office with the belief that she was a nonviolent anarchist. As such, perhaps she would be interested in assisting the Anarchist Black Cross organization, a nonviolent group that supported revolutionary causes and provided literature and legal aid for political prisoners. Meltzer made his pitch to Rose, explaining that he and Christie had resurrected the group in order to rebuild and assist the Spanish Resistance in its fight to topple longtime dictator Francisco Franco. Upon hearing this, Meltzer said Rose "closed up like a clam." She then told Meltzer that involvement with the resistance in Spain was "too violent" for her, and she politely showed him the door.[1]

If Meltzer's portrayal of his meeting with Dugdale is accurate, it presents an interesting vignette into her public profile at the time. It stands as evidence of her growing reputation as a person of generosity, especially among the New Left. One wonders how many other pitchmen approached the Civil Rights Centre in Tottenham, hat in hand, looking for help from the benevolent Dr. Dugdale. It was, after all, a highly radical era, with no shortage of movements seeking support for their cause from wealthy, like-minded individuals. Further, it appears that Rose was perhaps carefully cultivating the persona of a nonviolent revolutionary to ward off the police authorities who were carefully watching her. By now, the Special Branch had opened a growing file on her, surveilling her home, work, and travel.[2] As to Meltzer's understanding that she hadn't yet committed to a cause, the fact that she had painted the front of her building green, white, and orange, and hung a large tricolor in the office, should have given him a hint as to whom she had decided to devote her sympathies.

Despite Meltzer's misconceptions about Rose as a pacifist, it is clear that she had by then decided that violent action would ultimately be necessary in order to reach her goals. In later years, she has connected this realization back to the events of Bloody Sunday, which had led her to the realization that killing to further the goals of the revolutionary movement was justified.

Rose's rationalization of violence mirrored that of Frantz Fanon's in his popular book of the era, *The Wretched of the Earth*. Fanon, an intellectual, revolutionary, and philosopher from the French West Indies, wrote extensively about the struggle against colonialism. Though he died of leukemia in 1961, he nonetheless held great sway over the Black Power movement and other later revolutionaries respected by Dugdale, especially Che Guevara. Guevara had traveled to Algeria, the decolonization of which was a central theme for Fanon, and later produced an essay titled "Socialism and Man in Cuba" that was heavily influenced by the author.[3] Fanon's words about the necessities of violence against an imperial power provide an interesting perspective on the attitudes of the day and closely resemble Dugdale's beliefs. "The naked truth of decolonization evokes for us the searing bullets and bloodstained knives which emanate from it. For if the last shall be first, this will only come to pass after a murderous and decisive struggle between two protagonists. That affirmed intention to place the last at the head of things, and to make them climb at a pace (too quickly, some say) the well-known steps which characterize an organized society, can only triumph if we use all means to turn the scale, including, of course, that of violence," he wrote.[4] Rose summed it up more concisely: "It's a terrible thing going out with a gun, but it's an infinitely worse thing to be forced into that position. Nobody kills for pleasure."[5]

To Dugdale and Heaton, British imperialism in Ireland was what was forcing their hand. Rose, perhaps conscious of Fanon's writing regarding Africa, said of Ireland, "Realizing the unfairness of the system led me to the conclusion that armed struggle was necessary. I saw the presence of the British Army in Northern Ireland as a colonial occupation . . . It became quite clear that British imperialism was as present in the so-called British Isles as it was in Africa." She continued, "I realized that the only way to support them was to support their movement, which was rising in arms."[6] She and Wally even traveled to Derry to participate in the Bloody Sunday anniversary march.[7]

Rose and Wally were all in, and this level of commitment to their cause consumed their lives. It required fervor, dedication, and boundless energy. It also required a lot of money. Despite the riches into which she was born, and no earlier indications that she was a spendthrift, the pair had blown through all of Dugdale's money by early 1973.

Heaton insisted that his passion for Rose was not based on her wealth. Instead, he maintained that it was rooted in her high-spiritedness, intellect, and what he called "her somewhat naïve rejection of her privileged background."[8] But at least one of Rose's friends saw a different sort of naivety, claiming that Wally physically abused her. Despite her avowed feminism, Dugdale accepted this violence, her friend believed, because she thought such behavior was "real life, this was the way the working-class lived, this was honest."[9] Still, some believe that Wally saw Rose as his personal benefactor. This was a woman with the sort of means to which he had never before had access. She lavished him with money for fashionable and expensive tailored clothes, and he even purchased a beige Mercedes to drive about town—neither the usual effects of the typical self-described revolutionary socialist.

Her largesse did not end there. She gave Wally £10,000 and, in another odd departure from the feminist credo, explained it away by reasoning, "When you are living together, it is embarrassing if you are clearly the person always dispensing the cash." It was as if she was afraid to infringe on Heaton's role as the man in the relationship by letting the locals see the woman paying at the pubs around town (where, incidentally, their behavior led to them being barred from three). Dugdale also gave an extraordinary gift to Audrey Heaton: £25,000. It's unclear whether her motive was guilt, restitution, or both, but it was a remarkable if not bizarre gesture from a mistress to the wife of her lover. Walter's motives proved much clearer, however, when he put that cash into an account with Audrey that required his co-signature. In time, much of it would be spent by him. In Audrey's view, "Wally wanted her money and he wanted me. But Wally, you know, it's funny really, because he thinks he's doing this for the working class, and they should be on top all the time, and yet he's so materialistic." When she would argue with him over his paramour, he would shout back, "Well, what more do you want, you've got money, you've got coloured TV."[10]

There are varied reports on just how much money Rose had gone through, but all indicate that it was a huge sum. There were her earnings from her time as a lecturer, plus she sold her Name at her father's Lloyd's syndicate, which brought her tens of thousands of dollars. Ever the loving father, Colonel Dugdale was extremely generous with his daughter, even as he watched from afar as she made a mad dash to extremist behavior that was completely foreign to him. His motto, memorized from his time in the army, was passed along to Rose: "Money lost—little lost; honour lost—much lost; heart lost—all lost." He told her, "I can only hope that you keep your honour and your heart."[11] Rose would later say, "My parents . . . did not discriminate against me in any way despite being the black sheep of the family." In all, she inherited approximately £155,000 from her family upon her estrangement, an enormous sum of money in the early 1970s.[12]

Nevertheless, it was now with great lucidity that Colonel Dugdale could see that his dear child was gone. Disappointed and confused, he wrote to her:

> During my life I have lived through two wars and I know that the condition of life of everybody in this country has improved beyond all measure and it is still improving. It surprises me that someone of your acute intelligence does not notice this and that you are not the first person to see that it is completely illogical to brand a whole class of people as being either honourable or dishonourable. I believe that our family have made some contribution to the improvement of life in England. The family on both sides comes from the lines of stock, on one side they have sacrificed their lives for their country, three or four at least died during the wars of 1918 and 1945. On the other side our families have provided employment at a fair wage and under decent conditions of service, and I do not think either branch of your family have anything of which to be ashamed. I wrote you a letter some weeks ago and I told you I would never slam the door. Although you have had all the money that I have to give, you will always find a welcome if you return.

It took Rose more than a month to reply to her father, but when she did, she did not spare feelings:

> Dear Daddy,
>
> I hope that you won't shelter under such sanctimony as accusations that I have cut all love between us away. As one of the boys across the water said to me the other day, I will die fighting the oppressor but I will give my life for the poor people. So let's not have any more about the self-sacrifices of our ancestors who died while ordering the men out of the trenches to death for nothing but the well-being of a handful of rich men who own the world:

there will always be a place for you amongst the brave men who are prepared to shoot in the back those commanders. The jolliest time for Lloyds was the last war, was it not? When Guardsman Heaton takes your money it is his for the taking. You can't take your accumulated theft with you of course, though you can be a man who refuses to dishonor himself and family whilst mothers with children are thrown on to the streets which their ancestors built.

Love . . . ROSE[13]

It was as if Rose knew exactly what she wanted to say to her father for some time, and his letter to her provided her an excuse to address him with contempt not simply for the man he was, but for what he represented—an unjust and predatory society that she wished to distance herself from with ferocity. One can almost hear her reading it aloud to Wally with great self-satisfaction before placing it in the post.

His daughter's relationship with "Guardsman Heaton" was certainly cause for consternation for Colonel Dugdale, and Heaton went out of his way to make sure that it was as uncomfortable as possible for the older man. When her parents had the couple to dinner at St. Leonard's Terrace, Wally told them that their daughter was pregnant. She was not. He only wished to shock and upset them. On another occasion, Heaton was yet crueler, sending a hearse to the Dugdale home. The unsuspecting undertaker informed the family that he had come to take the colonel away. Recalls one family friend, "It is impossible to express quite how vile this rebellion was."[14]

There is no indication that Rose ever took issue with the dreadful way that Heaton treated her father. Greatly pained, Colonel Dugdale wrote to Rose, "If I was able to touch you I would have tried to influence you against Wally."[15] Throughout his entire ordeal with his daughter, he never ceased expressing his love and concern for her. Little did he know that Rose had by then squandered all the money that he couldn't bring himself to deny her, and much of it went to his antagonist Heaton.

It was commonly held that Rose—the Angel of Tottenham—was easy prey for anyone looking for a financial helping hand. "She was a real soft touch . . . she was robbed by everyone," recalled a friend.[16] The exorbitant amounts of cash she bestowed on both of the Heatons aside, Dugdale also used her money to maintain the Civil Rights Centre and to perform good works in the community on behalf of the down-trodden, ranging from direct handouts to beggars to footing the bill for emergency expenses for needy families. And, of course, funds were needed to support the IRA. But now, with a depleted bank account, Dugdale, for the first time in her life, had to consider where she could find the money to continue her endeavors. Soon she would turn once more to the only source she ever knew: her family. But this time, she wouldn't exactly ask.

An additional expense that Rose had taken on was yet another member of the Heaton family. In early 1973, she was introduced to Walter's unscrupulous cousin-in-law, Derek "Ginger" Mann, at his residence in Manchester. Mann had a long history of running afoul of the law. In earlier years, he had even helped to set up "The Firm," the notorious gang led by Reginald and Ronald Kray that would later dominate the criminal underworld in the East End of London.[17] Mann, himself from South London, was not particularly political, but he was always up for an easy score. Mann said Rose made him a scout of sorts, giving the short, tough crook a car and paying him in cash to tour the country, "looking for explosive and ammunition stores that the IRA could raid."[18]

Rose was intrigued by the possibilities that having Mann on board brought to their efforts. While she and Wally were still earning their stripes as militant activists, Mann was a well-established criminal. She envisioned using him to establish a syndicate, not unlike his work for the Krays, except this time the ill-gotten gains wouldn't go to line the pockets of thieves. Under Mann's direction, the group would seek out places to rob of arms, ammunitions, and explosives, as well as "anything that would bring money for the IRA cause." At first, Mann found the concept funny, but in time, Rose's vision worried him: "I thought to myself, what I am doing actually, is sitting with these two people and others, and conspiring to commit treason, and . . . I wouldn't do it." Mann was quick to add that it was the prospect of a long jail sentence for treason that concerned him, not patriotism.[19]

There was a stark difference between Rose Dugdale and Ginger Mann. Whereas Rose was a true believer, Mann hadn't a care for any particular cause outside of himself. His ambition went only as far as the easiest quid. When he observed Rose and his cousin cursing British troops as they appeared on television, he realized that they were intensely serious about doing extreme violence: "It suddenly dawned on me like . . . we were all going to go out thieving to get guns and kill soldiers. Now I don't feel special about the soldiers, but they're a bit like me, aren't they . . . Got a job to do and so on . . . Why should they be shot in the back by us?"

Ginger detected a worrisome extremism, especially in Dugdale. "Rose was very, very fanatical," he recalled. Further, Mann found her difficult to trust, because though she was dedicated to doing things that he considered "bent," still, she came from a proper background. "I could never trust Rose Dugdale at all in any way, and I was surprised really at the tie-up with Wally . . . It didn't seem sort of natural," he said.[20] Indeed, Ginger would never be able to meld into the symbiosis that was Dugdale and Heaton, in terms of ideology or zeal. So, it should have come as no surprise that Mann eventually turned informer for the police against Dugdale and Heaton, who were most interested in intelligence he could provide about the pair's suspected gun-running activities. For his services, the police paid him £3,500.[21]

June 6, 1973, marked the 194th running of the Epsom Derby. The annual race is a famed national spectacle and the middle leg of Britain's Triple Crown, inspiring other such derbies, such as the one held annually in Kentucky, around the world. It's the sort of event that attracts hundreds of thousands of Britons to Epsom to see the thoroughbreds on Derby Day, and Colonel Dugdale, a skilled horseman himself, brought his family to the races. Derby Day 1973 brought a record crowd of a million spectators, forcing organizers to close grandstands and public enclosures for the first time in history. As they enjoyed the warm sunshine on a spectacular late-spring afternoon, the Dugdales were treated to an exciting and improbable race. Morston, a 25-to-1 shot, pulled ahead just five furlongs from the post to win by half a length, stunning the crowd and taking home a prize of more than £125,000.[22]

After a bit more merriment, the Dugdales made the 175-mile trek back to Devon to their estate at Yarty Farm. When they arrived home, the star-crossed family was shocked to find that their home had been ransacked. Thieves had forced open a kitchen window and sacked the place of eight valuable paintings, silver, antiques, and other items said to be worth £85,000. Suspicion immediately fell upon Rose, and for good reason. Colonel Dugdale inspected his home and found that his daughter's room was the one space that had not been invaded, and a lovely dish that Rose had given her mother as a Christmas present remained in place though the other precious items alongside it were now missing. When the staff informed Colonel Dugdale and investigators that the dogs at the farm, who loved Rose so much, had not barked at all during the overnight heist, the heartbreaking truth could not be denied: Rose had stolen from the family. The police were summoned, and the colonel had no choice but to relay to them his belief about his own daughter's complicity in the theft.

Less than a week later, Mrs. Dugdale received a call from an unexpected source: Dr. Peter Ady, her daughter's former tutor at Oxford and employer at the United Nations. Dr. Ady told Mrs. Dugdale that Rose, upon returning a borrowed chest of drawers to her, had asked the unsuspecting academic if she could leave some suitcases with her at her flat at St. Giles, Oxford. Ady had agreed, thinking nothing of it. But now, she said, she found that Rose had left these valuables with her and asked Mrs. Dugdale if she'd care to come to Oxford to get her belongings. Relieved yet exasperated, Rose's mother chose to leave them there, saying that the matter had been placed entirely in the hands of the police and that she must let them handle it. The distressed Mrs. Dugdale told Dr. Ady that her daughter was "off her rocker" and in need of psychiatric treatment.

When the police arrived at Oxford, they found the suitcases under Dr. Ady's staircase in the basement, just where Rose had placed them. The authorities believed that Dr. Ady had been duped and did not implicate her in the crime.[23]

The police were not surprised by any of this. Ginger Mann had kept them well informed. Not only was he aware of Rose's plan, but she and Walter Heaton included Mann's own henchmen, Ronald Sanders, Thomas Card, and Michael Cronin, to pull it off. All five were arrested. Sanders, Card, and Cronin, knowing what they had done and seeking to avoid long sentences, pleaded guilty and were shipped off to prison for terms ranging from four to six years. Rose and Walter, however, pleaded not guilty, which meant that their prosecution for the heist would result in a protracted trial at Exeter Crown Court—exactly the sort of high-profile venue for which Rose and Wally longed. Surely the media attention that it would bring would allow them to make loud statements in support of their cause. They would not be disappointed.

In the fall of 1973, the trial of Rose Dugdale caught media attention in the United Kingdom and made its way into some papers in the United States. She was an oddity, this heiress the press referred to as Dr. Bridget Dugdale, placing great emphasis on her Oxford degree and parents' wealth. For her part, Rose did nothing to lessen the spectacle, choosing to represent herself and take every opportunity to make political statements and charges against her father and all that his class and success represented.

Both Dugdale and Heaton were charged with stealing the property and handling the stolen goods, but it was clear from the prosecution's case that the actual heist was led and perpetrated by Rose. Though not an element of the story at the time, an art heist designed and conducted by a woman is remarkable not only for the era but for the crime. Art theft had been exclusively the realm of bad men, and Rose had shattered that profile with her plan. But at the same time, the scheme was amateurish. She had used men supplied to her by Ginger Mann, a person in whom she placed faith despite the fact that his goals did not comport with hers. It's also not surprising that the plan was designed without Wally actually going to Yarty Farm to steal from the home. It's likely that the pair felt that with his long arrest record, another arrest would place him in greater jeopardy than Rose.

Armed with information provided by those who pleaded guilty, as well as the informant Mann, the prosecutor, John Hall, carefully laid out the details of the heist while Rose and Wally watched on, often kissing each other in the dock. Phone calls had been made to Yarty Farm to ensure that her family had indeed gone off to Epsom for Derby Day, as she suspected. History shows that such public holidays make for excellent heist opportunities, as so many—from citizens to authorities—turn their attention away from common precautions. Rose drove Sanders in her car, while Card and Cronin drove to Devon in another. They parked some distance from the home, and Rose led them through fields to the farm. Once there, she showed them a pantry window to force open, and they made their way into the large, empty house. Once inside, Rose directed the operation. She showed Cronin and Sanders where the family's valuables, especially the silver, was to be found, and they eagerly bagged the goods. Then she turned her attention to the art.

Colonel Dugdale's paintings, though quite valuable, were not the sorts of works that were instantly recognizable. This was a private home, not a museum with artists' names proudly displayed on labels and in guides to assist thieves in finding the big names and, thus, the most valuable works. Instead, Rose, who knew art not only from her own education but also from her mother (who had once worked in a gallery), directed Thomas Card as to which eight oil paintings to take, as well as some rare Meissen figurines. The educated Dr. Dugdale discerned which she suspected could garner the most money and selected appropriately, using Card—a career criminal and car dealer—simply as the mule to lift and carry the works.

Perhaps prompted by Wally's significant criminal history and a touch of classism, Prosecutor Hall stated plainly that the heist had been conceived and planned by Heaton, and he made some effort to describe Rose as merely a lovestruck follower of the career lawbreaker whose criminal record she had not known. This claim is highly unlikely. It is far more probable that Rose would have known and indeed honored Heaton's crimes. They had been arrested and appeared in court together before, and surely his previous brushes with the law had been stated before her.

Curiously, Rose's initial ploy was to portray herself as the victim in the heist. She claimed her intentions were simply sentimental and practical. "I went partly for emotional reasons—I had not been to Yarty for 18 months to two years—and partly to go and collect some of my things," she testified.[24] She claimed that Thomas Card had threatened her life and forced her to participate in the raid, telling her, "If you breathe a word about what we have done, your life won't be worth that much."[25]*

Later, Rose claimed, she was able to find and recover the stolen goods from the crooks and hide them at Dr. Ady's with the intention of returning it. This would lead to some embarrassment for Dr. Ady, when she was forced to admit to the court that she had lied in her statements to the police about her knowledge of the stolen goods while trying to protect Dugdale.[26] The judge informed the all-male jury that it would have

---

* During the trial, Thomas Card would claim he lied in his statement and that Dugdale "did not know we were going to steal the antiques" and that Ginger Mann had set up the robbery, but the court would have none of it. Later, an appeals court cut Card's sentence, believing that he had been "dominated" by Dugdale and that she was the mastermind of the Yarty Farm heist. "Woman 'Did Not Know of Plan to Burgle Father,'" *The Times* (UK), October 10, 1973, p. 4; "Sentence on Art Raid Man Cut," *Irish Press*, November 15, 1974, p. 7.

to consider the improbability of this fantastical tale spun by Rose, who by then was no doubt aware that Mann had informed on her, despite the fact that he had asked a neighbor to post bail for Dugdale and Heaton to cover for himself.[27]

Rose was insuppressibly demeaning toward her parents, who sat in the back of the court room with bowed heads as she condemned them and all they represented. "I regard them as gangsters, thieves and oppressors of the poor," she shouted.[28] She claimed that her father hoped she'd be found guilty "because he thinks the best thing for me would be to divert me from my course of life and get some psychological care." She added, "My parents believe that I am mentally sick because I have not taken the course of life they consider right."[29]

Once her feeble defense had been laid out, Rose emulated the behavior she had admired by groups in Ireland and within the Black Power movement. When told by the judge, Mr. Justice Park, that she had no right to interrogate her father, her intent was clear. "This is a political trial," she said. "My father's life represents something alien to my own."[30] She would go on to use the courtroom as her own bully pulpit, speaking her mind directly to the court and, in turn, to the world, without the filter and decorum of a defense counsel. Wearing a purple suede coat over a white blouse and pale green pants, she ignored the judge's statement and questioned her beleaguered father as he stood in the witness box. When the judge offered to Colonel Dugdale that he may sit, she pounced on the courtesy as proof that was some preexisting agreement between the judge and her father. Colonel Dugdale stood to defend his honor, saying, "If you don't mind me saying so, I have been brought up to have decent manners." Rose, perhaps taken aback by her father's response, replied, "I certainly did not mean to insult you." The judge made it clear to the jury that, before the trial, he had never before met Colonel Dugdale. Rose continued, "I love you and if your life were in danger I would wish to stand between you and that danger," but "at the same time I hate everything you stand for. That has to come out or it doesn't make much sense.

"You love me and yet you hate me for what I do and what I stand for and what I gave your money and your mother's away for. You were concerned that I was squandering your wealth," Rose lectured her father. The charge was spurious. Despite the undeserved torment from Heaton and the near estrangement by his daughter, by Rose's own account, her father continued to treat her extraordinarily fairly. It was as if his derision was something she desired but did not have. She said as much with her very next words: "You have been extremely generous. You gave me a great deal of love and you gave me money to see that I could live the way you lived." Colonel Dugdale, perhaps accustomed by now to his daughter's extremism, was calm in his reply. "If you choose to throw your money out, it's none of my affair."[31]

Rose claimed that her animus toward her father began when, she alleged, he dismissed three employees from the family farm, including her beloved Mam'zelle. But Colonel Dugdale denied not only this as a motivation but the claim that he had dismissed the trio at all. Instead, he offered, the rift between his daughter and her family had begun two years earlier. He testified that just as everyone had their own life to lead, Rose was steering hers on a path far from his. Of the money she had squandered, including a large sum just days before the theft, he refused to be judgmental. "If you chose to throw it out of the window, it was not, frankly, my affair," he stated plainly. Her younger brother, James, who also testified, was sympathetic toward his sister, saying that he felt Rose had difficulties with which he was powerless to help her, and that he was sad to see her in the dock accused of serious crimes.

Through it all, Rose was without a real argument against the charges that would save her from guilt. She made a claim that she and Heaton "would not be in the dock at all if it wasn't for the politics which lie behind this," inferring that they were victims of a system that was unjust from top to bottom. But of course, the choice to carry out the theft had been her own. She made no argument about having accepted the largesse her father had bestowed upon her, earned via the system she so abhorred. She didn't exactly make a Robin Hood argument, either.

Instead, she attacked the system, root and branch. But this was a court of law, dedicated solely to establishing guilt or innocence in the criminal matter at hand. And while she saw fit to delve into the wholly irrelevant matter of her family's money and the system that produced it, she made no mention of her true motives behind the theft—funding the IRA. But they should have been obvious. Even the informant, Ginger Mann, knew that the Civil Rights Centre had become a pretense for IRA fundraising. "The only poor being helped," he said, "were poor Wally, poor Rosy, and the poor boys across the border."[32]

In any event, Rose's arguments against her family's wealth and her father's station in life served more to implicate than exonerate her. After an eighteen-day trial and just three and a half hours of deliberation, the jury arrived at a relatively easy guilty verdict for both Rose and Wally. She was then allowed to address the court, and she did so with a gusto in her remarks she seemed to have been waiting years to deliver to the British government.

Speaking in what one court reporter said was perhaps a symbol of her commitment, Rose "embraced the manners and customs of her adopted class totally. Uneducated speech became an affectation."[33] In a working-class accent, she loudly declared to Mr. Justice Park, without any real rationale, "This trial has been an obvious example of British injustice. No jury could have found me guilty if this had not been the case." She continued, "But in returning a verdict of guilty you have turned me from an intellectual recalcitrant into a freedom fighter, and I cannot think of a finer title." In fact, she had already begun her foray into freedom fighting, and she wasn't done scolding the court. "I am certainly not going to ask for mercy because I don't believe it is a quality you and your ilk know anything of. You will sentence me to the longest sentence you can give me without becoming the laughingstock history will make you. You will do this from fears, and fear of the united strength people of no property, brave men and true. You are afraid of this because one day, and I believe very shortly, these men will brush you aside and deprive you of the power and privilege you have abrogated and abused. Nothing on God's earth gave you the right to judge over the life of man of no property . . . gave you the right to dispose of their life and liberty."

She closed her soliloquy with a flourish: "Power to the people: History will absolve us."

Walter Heaton was sentenced to six years in prison for his role in the heist. He would maintain throughout his life that the theft was the work of Ginger Mann.[34] Never one for understatement, at the time of sentencing, Heaton said, "Not since Christ has there been a greater travesty of justice." He added, "You cannot imprison Rose and me because we don't exist. Bet we are everywhere—invincible, incorruptible, and indestructible."[35] As he was literally dragged from the courtroom, Rose shouted at the officers, "Let him go! Let him go!"[36] The manhandled Heaton raised a fist, and a man in the gallery returned it, proclaiming, "We will carry on!"[37]

Four days later, Dugdale was sentenced. The judge read from a medical evaluation he had ordered: "For an individual of her undoubted intellectual gifts and training, a custodial sentence would only further reinforce the bitterness and resentment, while the chance of practising what she preaches might prove a turning point—that is total poverty and hard work, earning her living free from all safeguards of money and status." The report continued, "She has never had this opportunity and it is the only treatment which might reinforce the consequences of the present crisis. Freedom under these conditions might prove a more difficult retribution than containment."[38]

With that recommendation, Mr. Justice Park turned to his sentence. He told Dugdale that he believed that she had been under the influence of Wally and that he had been the mastermind of the crime.[39] However, he added, "You are fully responsible for your actions." Rose braced for the imposition of a significant jail term. But in a legendary display of poor character evaluation, the judge handed Rose a two-year suspended sentence, claiming that she was "unlikely to offend again." "I think the risk that you will ever again commit burglary or any dishonesty is extremely remote," he said from the bench.[40] She would be made to pay £5,000, but she would walk out a free woman. Rose seemed crestfallen. She was sure that she would be marched off to prison. Further, she seemed to have prepared herself for prison and the romantic role of a jailed freedom fighter, a true prisoner of conscience. The leniency from which she benefitted only caused her more anger, as she railed about the class system of sentencing and everything her family represented: "Class injustice if I may say so. A poor man gets sent away for six years on a lesser charge to one for which a rich girl gets two years suspended."[41]

That rich girl, now freed, told the media, "My hate of the system my parents practice and gain by is stronger than ever." She added, "I am going back to the poor."[42] But though her concern for the less fortunate and downtrodden of Tottenham was genuine, she was ready to move on. Rose Dugdale would spend the next six months engaged in a vicious assault on imperialism, in full-throated support of Irish Republicanism, the likes of which are engrained in the lore of the 1970s forever.

# EIGHT

# *Enter Eddie*

Rose Dugdale said that she did not believe that the judge at Exeter Crown Court knew anything about mercy, and though the sentence he imposed on her proved her wrong, she remained greatly dissatisfied. Perhaps the truth is that she didn't really want clemency. She fully expected him to levy the maximum incarceration allowable by law, the unintended consequence being an increase in her credibility with her fellow freedom fighters. Instead, she was granted her freedom, while Walter Heaton was sent away for six years. She was outraged by the disparity in sentencing. Rose ignored the fact that Mr. Justice Park had to consider that this was the latest in a long history of convictions for her dear working-class Wally, while this was her first beyond mere misdemeanor. To her, this was the very sort of discrimination that she railed against. This was classism at its worst, and she was outraged.

That's not to say her theatrics in the courtroom did not win her acclaim, for she did soon begin to earn a reputation among like-minded activists at home and abroad. American journalist Melvin Lansky, an anti-Communist leftist and the longtime editor of the literary periodical *Encounter*, was taken with her performance. Her theft from her family home, he observed, proved that for Rose, "to expropriate the expropriators was no empty phrase from a dog-eared pamphlet. It was proof of the pudding, the means test of militance."[1] Meanwhile, in Australia, the alternative magazine *The Digger* reported her arrest and conviction with sincere admiration: "British revolutionaries now have a millionaire, Oxford educated, attractive heroine. Her name is Bridget Dugdale, and she was this week found guilty of stealing nearly a quarter-million dollars [*sic*] worth of paintings and silver to support British and Irish civil rights movements."[2] It is curious, of course, that her connections and motives vis-à-vis the Troubles in Ireland escaped the concern of the judge in Exeter Crown Court, but not underground journalists in Australia.

Still, though her credentials were now fully burnished, she had also been reduced to a one-woman show. Even as Wally was shipped off to Hull Prison, Rose still referred to him as her common-law husband, in spite of the fact that he was still very much the lawful husband of Audrey Heaton. He professed his love for her ideology. She would lament, "He has fought all his life. He had none of the education I had, but he knows more about the world than I will ever know."[3] Once inseparable, they were now torn apart. One acquaintance remembered, "On demos they just marched along together, holding up their huge Irish flag, just two people doing their thing."[4] Now, it would be six years before they would be fully rejoined. Rose was, at times, inconsolable.

Outraged at what she saw as an unjust sentence, and perhaps motivated by guilt over her privileged freedom while Wally languished in jail over their shared crime, Rose took to loud protests over his prison conditions. Heaton recalled that when she saw the high-security measures to which he was subjected, she would break out in tears in the prison's visiting room.[5] She was photographed by the media outside the Tottenham Civil Rights Centre, posing in front of homemade picket signs with slogans urging the freeing of Walter Heaton and railing against his solitary confinement at Wandsworth jail, to which he had been transferred. One sign, hand-drawn in capital letters, read, "YOUR FEAR IS GREATER THAN OURS."

Rose was desperate to see her lover again. In November 1973, just weeks after they were separated by Wally's incarceration, Rose forced a trial for an earlier charge of refusing a blood alcohol test after an incident behind the wheel of her car. She had been seen outside a pub in Tottenham and soon after was witnessed driving across a footpath, causing a pedestrian to tumble onto the hood of the vehicle.

Rose turned the simple court appearance into a full-fledged trial. The pedestrian, she argued, was Wally, and she had simply been trying to prevent him from reentering a pub where he had earlier been involved in an argument. There was an ulterior motive to her plan: mounting a trial and using this defense allowed her to call Heaton as a witness. They were reunited, if only briefly. Judge T. K. Edie was unimpressed, noting, "If you wanted to make a stand for liberty, you should have chosen better ground . . . There is nothing to suggest you had an undue amount to drink. If you had taken the test it may well have cleared you, but you insisted on this confrontation. Now I have to punish some-body I have no desire to punish."[6] That punishment amounted to a £25 fine and the loss of her driver's license for a year. "It was worth it to see Wally again," she said.[7] But while she had escaped from court with her freedom twice in less than a month, the Special Branch, still convinced that Dugdale was running arms to the IRA, kept her under close watch.

Throughout the following weeks, Rose occupied herself with orga-nizing a Christmas dance in a local Tottenham hall on December 22, selling tickets for 60 pence each.[8] She still spent much of her time involved in the Republican cause, but, separated from her dear Wally, she was going through a deep personal crisis, with a friend noting that she was "very disillusioned."[9] She faithfully visited Walter in prison three times, until Christmas Eve 1973. The woman whom he described as a "soldier of the people, scourge of the unrighteous" and his "lover and friend" left him with the parting words, "I will avenge you."[10] And then, just like that, the visits to Wally ended and her friends saw her no more. Perhaps fearful that she would soon be arrested again, Rose left her native country and moved to Ireland at the dawn of 1974. With the Vietnam War coming to a close and the student upheavals mostly a thing of the past, she would devote herself entirely to the cause of Irish Republicanism as a soldier on the ground in Éire. She checked in with acquaintances in County Tyrone and stayed in neighboring County Donegal. The Angel of Tottenham left England forever.

Everything about young Eddie Gallagher's life was small-town. All of the inhabitants in his tightknit community in Ballybofey, County Donegal, knew the boy, his older brothers Patrick and Charles, and his younger sisters Mary Rose and Margaret. With the exception of Patrick, who moved to Dublin and then to England, the Gallagher children didn't stray very far from the small family farm maintained by their father, Jim. Eddie's tiny, two-teacher schoolhouse, serving just sixty students, was but a mile from the farm, and his teachers, who knew him well, considered him "above average." His classmates all liked him, and this simple life in his parochial town suited him well.

But catastrophe struck the family. Eddie's beloved young mother, Margaret, succumbed to liver disease when he was just twelve years old. The tragic loss marked a change in the bright young boy's life. His grief was such that his schoolwork suffered, and he increasingly kept to himself. One family friend would lament, "The dice were loaded against him . . . if he had been younger when his mother died, maybe he wouldn't have taken it so badly. As it was, he was just on the point of becoming a teenager and he found that the one person in whom he confided and trusted wasn't around anymore."[11]

In his early twenties, as his relationship with his father grew strained and he began to feel stifled by the confines of Ballybofey, Eddie ferried across to Britain in 1969, where his eldest brother, Patrick, was waiting to show him North London. Eddie spent a couple of years in England, bouncing around without any specific purpose, sharing a flat with a friend who was also working for Patrick Gallagher's contracting company in the tunnels of the London Underground. A co-worker remembered him as "a strong lad and a hard worker" who was "shy and seemed to have an inferiority complex."[12] Though early on he had never displayed Republican leanings or discussed politics, oddly enough, away from Ireland for the first time he found himself becoming increasingly enamored of Irish Republicanism.[13]

The spark was officially ignited in 1971, just a few nights before internment was implemented. Harry Thornton, a Catholic worker from Derry, had the misfortune of his car backfiring as he passed the Springfield Road RUC Station in Belfast. The sound startled a British soldier, who fired at the driver and killed him. Scared, Thornton's passenger jumped from the car and ran. Gallagher witnessed the event and heard a soldier shout, "One down, one to go," as the innocent passenger was chased down by British soldiers who took him into the station and beat him.[14]

Gallagher returned home to County Donegal and patched things up with his father. Nevertheless, in Jim Gallagher's opinion, his son's stay in Britain was more detrimental than even the earlier loss of his mother: "England was the ruination of my son." Mr. Gallagher never elaborated on this characterization of his youngest boy's stay in Britain. But the change in Eddie was clear. Perhaps it was the experience of being an Irishman in another land that set a patriotic flame in his heart. It seems certain that while in North London working for his brother, Eddie fell in with Irish freedom fighters. There are whispers that while in there, he met Rose Dugdale for the first time,[15] but according to Gallagher, he first met Rose at a "doss house"* in Edinburgh in 1974, where they had a shared fascination of "dossers" and their ability to sleep on ropes rather than expensive, yet flea-infested, beds.[16]

Once back in Ballybofey, his neighbors found him a convinced Republican. He signed on with the local branch of Provisional Sinn Féin and was a regular participant in all their activities, including giving speeches and carrying placards at local picket lines. He was young with a lack of prospects but a newfound purpose, which made him a perfect recruit for the Provos, who were in the thick of bombing campaigns in Northern Ireland and could use a man with his native knowledge of the countryside along the border territory. It was the era of booby-trap bombings, a regular occurrence in Ulster. In January 1974, booby-trap bombs killed

---

* A doss house is inexpensive housing for the homeless and vagrants, who are referred to as "dossers."

two young army officers in separate incidents in Derry. The attacks were especially common in rural areas and in open fields, utilizing trip wires or remote-control devices. The Provisionals became so adept at luring soldiers to bombs that the British Army resorted to inspecting suspected sites by helicopter.

One such incident is illustrative of the PIRA technique. In County Armagh, a patrol spotted wires leading across the border that were attached to a massive four-hundred-pound land mine buried under the road in the countryside. Upon further investigation, a second twenty-five-pound bomb was also found attached to the wires. As one reporter put it, "Even the booby-traps are booby-trapped."[17]

It was at this time that Rose Dugdale and Eddie Gallagher were reunited. It's unclear how well they knew each other from his stay in North London, but one thing is indisputable: the two were beguiled with each other in short order after Rose's relocation to Northern Ireland. Though she had been separated from the hapless Walter Heaton for less than three months, and her grief over him was intense and real, she had already moved on. Heaton was crushed, and described Rose as "fish-blooded with no real emotions for anyone."[18]

Despite the fact that she was ill upon arriving in Ireland and may have had pneumonia, Rose and Eddie were a quick couple.[19] Eddie was handsome, with dark thick hair and beard, but he was also a somewhat fragile-looking thin man who was inches shorter than the five-foot-six Dugdale. They both possessed the unique sort of passion that burns in those who have, after years of searching, latched on to the perfect cause to match their zeal. They complemented each other perfectly. Rose was older by six years, well-traveled, and extremely well-educated. What Eddie lacked in worldliness and erudition he more than made up for in life experience. Gallagher had all the working-class authenticity of Walter Heaton, and then some, but he had a background that Walter could never match. For while Heaton had read and cared deeply about the Troubles, Eddie was a true Irishman, born and raised in Ulster, and a Republican fighting for his own country. His was not the cause of another man; it was his own. Rose had fallen in love with the undeniable romanticism of Ireland and the cause, and it was embodied in young, wild Eddie Gallagher.

Though new to the cause, Eddie was not enamored of Provisional leadership. "IRA volunteers were given basic training and thrown in at the deep end against well-trained and equipped British soldiers," Gallagher said of the era, in hindsight sounding like a battle-hardened soldier despite being a relative novice at the time. "When we asked for better and heavier weapons, excuses came down from the top."[20]

Gallagher became perplexed at IRA leadership and what he perceived as perhaps a lack of will. He recalled, "After a while, we began to suspect that the leadership was afraid to move the struggle on to a higher level because they were nervous that the Free State Government would close them down. It would be interesting to have a case study done on how some senior IRA leaders were placed where they were." While his words sounded like those of a disgruntled labor union member, his worries were those of a soldier. "At one stage we just refused to tell them what we were about to do," he remembered, "in case we were ambushed when we arrived to do our job."[21]

Gallagher's attitude toward leadership provides a glimpse into his zeal. Here was a twenty-eight-year-old soldier doubting the seasoned leadership of the war fighters, despite the fact that the Provos were continuing a vigorous bombing campaign and the death toll on both sides of the struggle was approaching a thousand.

This was not enough. Gallagher wanted more. Like his new lover, he was looking for a fight, and with Rose Dugdale by his side, he was ready to strike, with or without permission. Together, they would take matters into their own hands and practice the art of violent expression.

# NINE
## The Bombing at Strabane

Irish Helicopters Ltd., an aviation rental service located throughout Ireland, received a call at its Dublin Airport office inside the Westpoint Hangar in late October 1973. A Mr. Leonard, claiming to be an American filmmaker staying in Dublin, said that he needed to charter a helicopter to do some aerial filming thirty miles north of the city. Mr. Leonard explained that he wished to photograph ancient monuments at Stradbally in County Laois, and then head into Wicklow Mountains for another hour of photography. Arrangements were made for the American filmmaker to come to the airport to look at the helicopters available for the mission.

Mr. Leonard, a well-dressed and prosperous-looking man in his mid-twenties, took a taxi from the Royal Dublin Hotel to the Westpoint Hangar to choose between two helicopters. Both were five-seaters, but after some inspection and thought, he selected the Alouette II, the smaller and more maneuverable of the pair, and agreed upon the rate of £80 an hour. At just past noon on October 31, Captain Thompson Boyes took the controls, and he and Mr. Leonard lifted off. They first headed for Stradbally, where they landed on a farm for the filmmaker to retrieve his equipment.

At about 2:30 PM, two armed men wearing nylon masks appeared from behind the tall, still-green trees that bordered the farm and briskly made their way toward the helicopter while aiming their guns at Captain Boyes. This was no Halloween gag. One of them boarded the aircraft and declared, "We are Provos." His companion, standing at the pilot's door, gun still drawn, told Captain Boyes to do as his partner said, warning, "If you foul up this operation, this man has instructions to shoot you." He then departed with Mr. Leonard while his accomplice directed the pilot to fly to Mountjoy Prison in Phibsborough in the heart of Dublin. Once in the air, the masked man told the pilot to follow the Royal Canal and the railway line to the prison and set down in the yard. The captain did as he was told, landing inside the tall stone rear prison wall, where three top members of the IRA were among those watching a football match in the exercise yard in a compound adjoining D wing, a space reserved for political prisoners.

Prison officers thought nothing of the arrival of the aircraft—they were used to seeing Minister of Defence Paddy Donegan arriving via helicopter. But the three IRA men knew better. Prisoners scattered as the helicopter made its dangerous approach in the tight confines of the yard. The trio readied to run toward it. They quickly climbed on board, and one of them was handed a machine gun as soon as he entered the aircraft. Their fellow prisoners cheered as the three were whisked away before prison guards could intervene. One witness described the guards' reaction: "They did not seem to know what to do. Some of them shouted to the warders at the main gate to lock it. Others seemed to stand by in bewilderment. Within a minute or two of landing, the helicopter rose into the air."

The men were flown to a prearranged location outside Dublin, the Baldoyle Racecourse, where they completed their getaway by hijacking a taxi after binding and gagging the driver. They then sped off to Mala-hide, where they abandoned the car. Meanwhile, Captain Boyes, still shaken, took some time to compose himself before flying back to Dublin Airport. There, police questioned the pilot for three hours.

It was a remarkable prison break—the most dramatic in Irish history, according to the police. "It was just like something out of some bloody film," said one officer. "Nothing like this has ever happened before."[1]

Firebrand Loyalist leader Reverend Ian Paisley was outraged at claims by the Irish government that they were dealing with the IRA: "How in the name of goodness, when the IRA can land a helicopter in Mountjoy Prison and take out these valuable prisoners, can they stick to that story?

It shows the Cosgrave Government is no more able to deal with the IRA than the British Government." Provisional Sinn Féin Public Relations Officer Seán O Brádaigh, on the other hand, gleefully remarked that he was "delighted by the escape."

The escapees were Provisional IRA heavyweights. The leader of the trio was Seamus Twomey, fifty-two, chief of staff of the Provos and a longtime leader in the Republican movement. Twomey, known as a particularly violent individual, had assumed the role of chief of staff a year earlier when his predecessor was jailed. The other two were Joe B. O'Hagan, fifty-one, who, with Twomey, was among the founders of the Provisionals, and Kevin Mallon, thirty-six, who had earlier been acquitted in the murder of a police officer and had just entered Mountjoy weeks earlier on a charge of IRA membership.

The three escapees immediately went on the run, with Twomey the most hotly pursued. All garda stations received photographs and were warned that the Provisional chief of staff was known to utilize disguises. Authorities had learned this lesson the hard way: British soldiers had once searched a home for him and were so fooled by his disguise that they apologized for having disturbed him. Capturing Twomey yet again, especially with his large network of sympathizers, would be a hard task.[2]

Meanwhile, Twomey was obviously impressed and inspired by the effectiveness of taking to the skies. In December 1973, he gave an interview to a German magazine in which he promised, "We will have commando action from the air." The declaration sent British security forces scrambling. In Northern Ireland, antiaircraft guns were deployed alongside existing machine guns capable of use against aircraft, and flying clubs throughout Ulster were warned of possible IRA hijackings.[3] Their precautions would soon be put to the test.

The romance between Rose and Eddie certainly blossomed suddenly and furiously, but such things are not rare in the affairs of the heart, especially when both parties are wildly passionate, impulsive people whose primary mover is the heart before the head. Perhaps it was what drew them together, this impetuousness. It certainly dictated their militancy, and together they decided to take direct action to another level that was, even for Rose Dugdale, extreme.

They had joined forces only weeks before, but already they were part of their own fringe active-services unit, or ASU. The leadership of the official IRA would later disavow any connection to them, but some reports claim that the Provisional's Army Council gave them permission to act.[4]

Rose had been in Northern Ireland for less than two weeks when she made her way out to the village of Gortahork in the northwest region of County Donegal on January 9, 1974. Gortahork was just an hour's drive from Eddie's hometown of Ballybofey, so it was a place he knew well, and therefore a good choice for the launch of an operation. The small locale would later become a hotbed for IRA activity when Gerry Adams built a getaway home there.[5]

Dugdale stopped by the McFadden Hotel and tracked down Captain John Hobday, whom she found sitting in the hotel bar. The captain was employed by Irish Helicopters Ltd. and flew to service lighthouses on the coast, including in Northern Ireland. Rose introduced herself as Stephanie Grant, a freelance journalist working on an article about Tory Island, just across the water. It was a good cover: people in Gortahork predominantly spoke Irish, and though Rose was known to sometimes adopt a brogue back in England and speak that foreign tongue, it wasn't going to pass muster in the village. The subject matter made sense, too. Tory Island was the most remote island off Ireland, but it also hosted a small but robust arts community, complete with its own gallery. The famed British artist Derek Hill even established the Tory School of artists there, teaching the local fishermen to paint the gorgeous landscape.

Captain Hobday told Dugdale, a.k.a. Grant, that he could easily make the trip. The island, just nine miles away, was jokingly referred to as "Elvis Island," for on a clear day one could see from Gortahork that it resembled the profile of Presley lying on his back, the jutting rocks on one end evoking his famous hair. Rose was told that she would have to contact the main office in Dublin, to which the pilot reported, to arrange the trip. After making the requisite calls over the course of a few days, the chartered flight was a go.

Just shy of two weeks later, on January 22, Rose checked into the McFadden, still identifying herself as Stephanie Grant, with two men in tow also identifying themselves as journalists along for the flight to Tory Island. While the educated Dugdale could certainly play the part of a journalist, it's surprising that her two companions did not raise eyebrows. The working-class pair, Patrick Anthony Treacy, twenty, and Eamon McNulty, just eighteen, were local toughs from Strabane who had both moved to Donegal at the same time as Rose. Treacy, a mechanic by trade, had the week before narrowly escaped arrest after an armed holdup of a garda car. McNulty, a factory worker, had been his accomplice.[6]

Staff at the McFadden Hotel did make note that none of the trio had brought along any luggage. And the barmaid recognized "Stephanie Grant" from a visit she had made with Eddie just after New Year's Day (suggesting perhaps that Rose had already been in the planning phase of this operation before leaving Tottenham and maybe even before saying goodbye to Wally for the last time). The hotelier, however, was not in the business of investigations, and all else appeared in order. Rose and her team would just have to wait for the helicopter to undergo some minor repairs before making the flight, and by the 24th, they were ready to go. Dugdale, wearing a heavy-duty parka and slacks, paid the bill and purchased an ordnance map before going out back, where she joined Treacy and McNulty, as well as Eddie Gallagher, who met them at the hotel for the trip. Captain Hobday was at the controls of the helicopter, which he had landed behind the hotel for pickup. Rose took the front seat alongside the captain, and her three male companions climbed in the back of the aircraft.

Shortly after departing Gortahork for what should have been a simple journey, Captain Hobday felt a sharp jab in his side. It was the hard steel of a gun held by Eddie Gallagher in the rear of the helicopter. The aircraft was being hijacked. The pilot was handed a note written on an envelope: "Go to Ards Abbey." Just as she had during the heist back at her parents' estate, Rose took the lead, giving instructions and pointing out the destination on the map—a small stone jetty at Ards Friary in Donegal. The monastery was the perfect spot for their operation: a secluded retreat where there would be few witnesses to their scheme.

After landing, the three men jumped off the aircraft and the pilot stayed put, unsure whether Rose was armed. The two younger men ran to an old cowshed from which they retrieved five ten-gallon milk churns, each packed with one hundred pounds of explosives. Two friars, including the guardian of the monastery, Reverend Friar Simeon, were stunned at the unusual sight of a helicopter landing on their property and approached to investigate. Eddie jumped out from behind a wall and held the friars at gunpoint while the heavy churns were transported to the helicopter. Treacy and McNulty loaded four of them, but even after they had dismantled the rear seat, there was insufficient room for the fifth—it would have to be left behind. With his accomplices and their four bombs all on board, Eddie told the priests, "No telephoning now for half an hour," and joined them on the chopper, this time squeezing his slight frame up front with Rose.

With Eddie's gun again trained on him, Captain Hobday took off and followed Dugdale's instructions to fly to Strabane, a Northern Ireland border town just about twenty miles away. The first part of the mission had gone as planned, but as the airspeed accelerated, the aircraft struggled under the weight of the milk churns, and the luggage compartment doors started to open. Two more milk churns were discarded, dumped into Mulroy Bay, an inlet near the north coast of Donegal. As they continued on toward Strabane, Treacy and McNulty worked to attach fuses to the two remaining churns. A nervous Captain Hobday noticed that one of the young men, apparently confused and perhaps himself edgy, lit a fuse on one of the bombs before they neared their target. His mistake caused a flurry of disarray on the aircraft, and Gallagher quickly ordered his young accomplices to put out the fuse, which one of them did by ripping it straight out of the churn. This delay forced the pilot to fly a circuit around Strabane once more while the fuse was replaced. Finally, Rose directed Captain Hobday to approach a large white building: the local police station in Strabane.[7]

Attacks on Strabane were the normal state of affairs for the beleaguered town for years before and decades after, and it had seen more than its fair share of sorrow. In 1971, a twenty-eight-year-old deaf and nonverbal man by the name of Eamonn McDevitt was killed by Royal Marine Commandos as he innocently played with a rubber bullet that had been fired at demonstrators. The incident fostered a deep hatred of the British military in this 90 percent Catholic town. In addition to the shootings and riots, by 1974, the small town of about ten thousand had seen a staggering two hundred bombs in five years, reducing much of it to rubble.[8] According to a report in *The Guardian*, "The 'troubles,' . . . have probably affected Strabane more than most other Northern towns, mainly because of its closeness to the border, providing easy escape routes for the Provisionals after bombing missions." It continued, "Much of the town centre, including the town hall, has been demolished by the bombers and almost every building has been bombed directly or indirectly." Indeed, even Rose's heavily fortified target—the constabulary—already bore scars from a prior IRA rocket attack.[9] Though Strabane had already seen so much unthinkable mayhem, it had never been attacked from the sky—until now.

As the helicopter lowered closer to its intended target, the bombs were dropped out of either side of the aircraft by Treacy and McNulty. One fell harmlessly into the nearby Mourne River. The final churn came closest to its target, landing in a rose garden adjacent to the police barracks. But it failed to explode. When Gallagher shouted that the police were firing at the helicopter, the captain took it down to just about fifty feet. The attack was over. It was a fortunate near miss for the Strabane police barracks, a failed attack that could have had catastrophic results.

Captain Hobday was directed to fly to "the Free State"—the Republic of Ireland—and land beside a major roadway. He did as he was told, flying to Cloughfin in Derry, where he dropped off his four captors by the road and left, unharmed.

It was clear from the nature of Rose's directions that she had formed only a general escape plan. Once on the ground, she and Eddie stopped a car driven by John Patterson, traveling from Strabane to his home in Castlefin, and told him at gunpoint to get out of his car. The four militants climbed in and told Patterson not to telephone for half an hour before speeding off, leaving Patterson behind.[10]

An officer of the First Battalion of the Royal Fusiliers, Major Richard Earle, had witnessed the attack from the ground in Strabane, bewildered by the sight of a helicopter hovering near the barracks and the unexpected vision of milk churns falling harmlessly to the river and ground. In a town that lived under the pall of incessant explosions, where mothers worried about their children becoming another casualty of the Troubles and the police had seen their own fatalities, the failed operation came as a welcome relief. Major Earle said, "I think the effect generally was good for morale because it's always satisfactory to see one's enemy making a fool of himself." The officer continued with understandable dark humor: "There was some useful discussion in barracks on this new military weapon—The AGMIC—the air-to-ground milk-churn, and some unfavorable comparison between this attack and others which we've been subjected to in the past, such as Dunkirk and Tobruk."[11]

His sarcasm provides an unintended peek into life in Northern Ireland at the height of violence. Here was a major being asked about an attempted terrorist attack in which five hundred pounds of explosives had been obtained to inflict widespread death and destruction upon unsuspecting police officers. By any standard, this should have been cause for great concern, not ridicule. But such was the climate of the day.

Indeed, Rose Dugdale described the operation as a "military action"[12] that she found both "operationally very important and exciting."[13] She attributed the failure to deploy the milk-churn bombs on the intended target to their inability to "persuade or force the guy that was driving the helicopter to hover sufficiently in order to land them on the barracks."[14] She acknowledged that there was also technical deficiencies in their plan: "The tops on milk churns are quite loose and you can just bang them down, and obviously if you were going to land that from a height, it was going to break up. So, the hope of being able to explode the bombs in that particular spot was not realized."[15] She also boasted that she had taken part in all aspects of the operation, including the preparation of the bombs. And she didn't see the operation as a total loss. For her, "the goal was to attack the British Army" and "to make the Brits aware that they could be attacked from the sky as they could be attacked on the sea. And it was to force them into recognizing that they needed to take more security precautions."[16] While a bombing operation, especially one of this size, clearly held the potential that people might die, she insisted, "I can't say it was something I thought of at the time." Still, she admitted that the taking of lives was on the table: "It was something that I thought of sometime before . . . that you couldn't really be involved in a revolutionary movement unless you saw that there was an inevitable outcome that you yourself would get killed or somebody else would get killed as a result."[17]

Naturally, authorities immediately suspected that the bombing was an IRA operation. Not only were the Provos engaged in a yearslong bombing campaign, but the modus operandi was eerily similar to the Twomey escape from Mountjoy. Between the escape and Twomey's warning of future air attacks, government officials were rightfully humiliated. Shortly after the Strabane incident, the Irish Minister for Justice, Patrick Cooney, reported to a cabinet meeting that the government was reviewing security and regulatory measures to counter assaults by air. But the fact that the Dugdale operation had happened so soon after Minister Cooney had firmly stated his intention to suppress IRA activity stung the Irish government. Dugdale had not only used a similar method, but she had even used the same helicopter rental service. Moreover, great

concern was expressed over failures on the ground after the two hijackings, as no perpetrators were apprehended after landing. Worse yet, in
the Strabane attack, the incident had occurred in an area with a large
police and military presence, where roadblocks and searches were a daily
routine.[18]

There were additional collateral effects from the bombing attempt.
Though no one was arrested immediately after the hijacking, the Special
Branch strongly suspected that "Stephanie Grant" was Rose Dugdale.
They were not yet certain that Eddie Gallagher had been one of her
accomplices. Whether she was actually a member of the IRA or a free
agent wasn't their main concern—bringing her in for interrogation was.

They turned their attention to Walter Heaton, who was safely secured
in prison and had no role in the Strabane attack. Regardless, he was
shuffled from institution to institution and classified a category "A" top
security prisoner because of his affiliation with Dugdale. What's more,
as a former guardsman and an Englishman, he said his warders considered him "the ultimate traitor" because of his activities against his own
country on behalf of another. Upon first hearing of Rose's attempted
bombing at Strabane, Walter assumed she had done it to bring pressure
on prison authorities to improve his conditions inside.[19] "I felt let down
by Rose because she played right into the hands of the police by those
bombings and made it worse for me inside prison, because they held
me guilty by association with her activities, so that I must have been
some kind of terrorist supporter," he later said.[20] To add to the pain, his
assumption proved wrong: she had completely moved on, and his plight
was neither her concern nor her aim.

Walter had acknowledged that Rose didn't value personal relationships much, and perhaps he was right. Her parents were left to deal with
a daughter they described as "incomprehensibly militant" and who was
all but lost to them.[21] She knew it caused them pain, but she was laser-fo-
cused on her cause and on herself. "It was tragic for them, I'm quite sure
it was. I know it was. But at the same time, it was just something that had
to happen. And, I mean, this was my life and this is what I wanted to do

and there wasn't any stopping me. I had the opportunity to come over to Ireland and to get involved and that was exactly what I wanted. That was a Godsend, and," she said with great understatement, "one thing led to another."[22]

Indeed, there was no way her family could stop her at that point. But the police would try. Rose, keenly aware that she was their main suspect in the bombing fiasco, was now a person on the run. Though a stranger in a strange land, it was the life she had made for herself, and there's no evidence that she did anything but embrace the role of the freedom fighter at large.

## TEN

## The Intersection

Anthony Roach, a young solider with the British Army, had wrapped up his weekend break in Manchester and boarded a bus to head back to duty at an army garrison in Catterick, North Yorkshire. The bus was filled with fifty people, all of them soldiers or their families, who were traveling by coach rather than train because of a labor dispute that forced the cancellation of all British rail services on Sundays in February 1974. It wasn't much of a hardship, though. The trip would take only about two hours, and since it had already grown dark, Roach took the opportunity to slouch in his seat and pass the journey with a nap.

At just past midnight, as the bus rolled along the M62 highway south of Leeds, a fifty-pound bomb, secreted in the luggage compartment toward the rear of vehicle, exploded. The blast tore through steel and flesh alike. Roach remembered that he "just felt the top of my head lift off . . . my ears were buzzing. I'll never know how I got out alive."[1] The longtime bus driver, Rowland Handley, who also served as a director of the coach service, heroically managed to maneuver the vehicle for an additional 150 yards in order to get it to stop against a hard shoulder on the highway. He did this despite being struck in the head by the bus's windshield, which had fallen and crashed upon him. With blood streaming down his face, Handley instinctively made his way to what remained of the back of the bus. "I saw a young child of two or three lying in the road. It was dead. There were bodies all over the place. I was in Cyprus with the RAF, but I never saw anything like this before," he said. The soldier, Roach, echoed that sentiment, unable to recall carnage of this sort in Northern Ireland where he served during so many bombings. When a resident who heard the explosion left his house to see the mayhem, he found "what looked like bundles of rags" and only later realized that he had passed "three or four bodies." Then he saw Handley, the bus driver, who was repeating, "I've finished with driving—I've finished with driving."[2] It was a horrifying scene of death and carnage.

Twelve people were killed in the blast, including a family of four with two children, ages five and two. Fourteen others were seriously injured. The explosion blew wreckage and body parts as far as 250 yards down the highway. In a time of frequent bombings, this one was particularly devastating, killing more people than any other terrorist bombing in England.

The Secretary for Defence, Ian Gilmour, called the attack "a terrible outrage." The British Under-Secretary for the Army, Dudley Smith, visiting his men and their families after the attack, called it "diabolical," and was less measured than Secretary Gilmour: "One does not begin to understand the mentality of people who will do this kind of thing, whatever they are trying to achieve," he said. "It is killing for killing's sake."[3]

Investigators, however, immediately understood exactly the mentality that Secretary Gilmour had pondered. This was clearly the work of the IRA. The only question that remained was whether it had been pulled off by a cell in Britain or a group that traveled over from Northern Ireland, as had been the case with the bombing of the Old Bailey.

Police also knew the motive for the attack. Just a week before, the IRA had shown that they were on the verge of a new campaign to force the British to move Dolours and Marian Price and their colleagues, Gerry Kelly and Hugh Feeney, all of whom had now begun a hunger strike, from English penitentiaries to a prison in Northern Ireland. They kicked off the warning in dramatic fashion: armed men took over buses and trucks at gunpoint in Dublin, leaving them at strategic points around the city with simulated bombs inside to apply pressure on the Irish government to bring the Price sisters home. This came just a few months after life sentences were handed down on the Old Bailey bombers—now referred to as "The Winchester Eight." The IRA statement on the sentences had ended ominously: "The day is long past for Irish people to lie under the lash of British imperialism. In due course, retribution will be exacted."[4]

It was no idle threat. West German diplomat Thomas Niedermayer* was kidnapped by two men who used a ruse to lure him out of his sub-urban Belfast home. The forty-five-year-old diplomat's captors demanded the transfer of the hunger strikers. His whereabouts unknown, militant Loyalist leader Reverend Ian Paisley told the media that the IRA had murdered Niedermayer because the British government failed to meet the prison transfer demands.[5] The standoff over the jailed Old Bailey bombers was at a fever pitch.

Retribution was not only on the minds of the IRA. The Ulster Freedom Fighters (the cover name for the Ulster Defence Association), in response to the coach bombing, announced a campaign of sectarian vio-lence that they said "would continue until the IRA ceased its bombing operation in England." Claiming responsibility for shooting attacks that killed three while wounding eight more in revenge for the bombing, the UFF told the *Belfast Telegraph*, "This is to let the IRA see it does not pay . . . we will not stop until the 12 have been accounted for, and the IRA must come to the realization that there is no point in these useless killings."[6]

Despite the threat of more killing by the UFF, the fact was that nothing the Unionists could do would stop the IRA. Rather, a Loyalist campaign of revenge would only serve to increase the body count. The Republican fight would continue, and now the Provos had icons to inspire them: the Price sisters. They were already making headlines in Britain and Ireland with regularity, and Dolours drew special atten-tion. The young female leader, bright and bold, captured the attention of the public. To the British, she represented a most serious threat: Who would see someone such as her as a potential bomber? To the Irish, she was both the embodiment of patriotism and, at the same

---

* The Niedermayer abduction and murder left a chain of tragedy in its wake. His wife, Ingeborg, overcome with depression, walked into the sea and committed suicide ten years to the day of her husband's funeral. In 1991, his daughter Gabriele also committed suicide, followed by her sister, Renate, in 1994. Finally, Gabriele's husband took his own life five years later.

time, an emblem of all that was lost in the struggle to unify Ireland. In fact, her fame had grown to such a point that rumors were emerging that Dolours would stand—from prison—as a candidate for Parliament representing West Belfast. Though the law prohibited her from voting, it didn't deny a prisoner the right to appear on a ballot. It was an interesting ploy. The rumor alone made headlines on both sides of the Irish Sea and increased awareness for the hunger strike.

Meanwhile, word from the archaic 150-year-old HM Prison Brixton was not encouraging. As the hunger strike continued, all reports indicated that Dolours was seriously ill. *The Guardian* reported that she was in danger of dying. Prison officials had taken to force-feeding the hunger strikers, a brutal process by which liquefied food was literally poured into them through a tube and against their will. Marian described it in great detail: "Four male prison officers tie you into the chair so tightly with sheets you can't struggle. You clench your teeth to keep your mouth closed but they push a metal spring device around your jaw to prise it open. They force a wooden clamp with a hole in the middle into your mouth. Then, they insert a big rubber tube down that. They hold your head back. You can't move. They throw whatever they like into the food mixer; orange juice, soup or cartons of cream if they want to beef up the calories. They take jugs of this gruel from the food mixer and pour it into a funnel attached to the tube. The force-feeding takes fifteen minutes but it feels like forever. You're in control of nothing. You're terrified the food will go down the wrong way and you won't be able to let them know because you can't speak of move. You're frightened you'll choke to death."[7]

Eerily, the very room in which the Price sisters were force-fed was the same space where, fifty-four years earlier, Terence MacSwiney, the Irish playwright and Sinn Féin politician, had died during his internment after a seventy-three-day hunger strike of his own.[8]

The force-feeding was harrowing and continued for 167 days, sometimes twice a day. To make matters worse, Dolours remembered that "if you were sick enough, they would measure how much sick you brought up after the tube had been removed. That had a very, very traumatic effect on both myself and Marian."[9] Still, the Price sisters remained extraordinarily strong. "To be on a hunger strike, you've got to condition your mind, and convince your mind that food is bad," Dolours said. "To have food, to take food, is failure. It is wrong."[10] Though effective for a hunger strike, the mentality would have long-term consequences for both sisters' health.

According to official documents kept by the British government, the Price sisters suffered tremendously. Their medical records showed "a large degree of vomiting, mouth abrasions, tooth damage, and fainting attacks." It was especially damaging to Dolours, who "was particularly prone to vomiting and physical weakness, a problem . . . attributed to her erratic mental state (as evidenced by her bouts of weeping and irritability) and her slender build." The reports depicted "a vivid sense of pain and trauma in the prison."[11]

There were eight specific demands behind these horrid conditions to which Price sisters and Feeney and Kelly subjected themselves. In addition to the immediate return to Ireland to serve their sentences with other Republicans, they demanded political status and the customary practices for such prisoners: the right to wear their own clothes; one food parcel per week; the right to send and receive any amount of letters; the right to be together; the right to refuse to do prison work; and the right to an open visit every week.[12] Visitation had already become another hot-button issue. Relatives were forced to apply for visiting certificates, and that process included a visit with a police officer to determine the suitability of the applicant. This rule applied even to the girls' parents. Once approved, the Price family would make a three-day journey aboard trains and a boat for the two-hour visit.

A measure of support for the Prices came from two British Members of Parliament. Renée Short, a Labour MP, wrote to the Home Secretary, Robert Carr, urging him to examine the process for visitor application and added that force-feeding was "a horrifying business. I understand Miss [Dolours] Price is very sick, has been losing weight, and that her

health is in very grave danger."[13] British government officials dismissed
such concerns, insisting that the Price sisters' health was not in danger.
But MP Bernadette Devlin McAliskey, who was a friend of Dolours's and
knew the condition of all four of the prisoners before their strike, was
"deeply concerned" by their condition after visiting them. She added,
"I believe that the real reason they are not being returned to Northern
Ireland is that Mr. Carr is afraid there might be an amnesty for political prisoners there. The Government is prepared to see people go free
after committing crimes in Ireland, but it does not want to risk releasing
someone who has struck at the heart of the Empire."[14]

MP McAliskey's suspicions were not without merit, because sympathy
for the Price sisters was far from universal. In London, one editorial
after the coach bombing reminded that while force-feeding is "abhor-
rent," the British authorities were "right to refuse to be blackmailed by
the hunger strike of the Price sisters and two of the men." It went on
to express concerns that, if the four were transferred to prisons back
home, "it would be easier to arrange their escape from a Northern Ireland prison and to keep them out. The women's prison in Armagh, for
example, is quite close to the border."[15]

Albert Price, their father, was asked about his daughters' condition.
He reported that Dolours was undeterred. "Dad, it's one way or the
other," Dolours said. "We'll go home to Armagh or we'll go home somewhere. We'll go home."[16] Mr. Price was much less sanguine. "I don't
want them to die, but if they do die—I have lived a good life and I've
always been a Republican." Then he added, with a sense of foreboding,
"I'll become a very violent Republican and can anyone deny me that?"[17]

◎

The events of February 1974 would make it a pivotal month in the life
of Rose Dugdale. Her entire future would be shaped by the events both
within and outside of her control. For the first time in her life, she was
on the run, fully dependent upon people hardly known to her. Alongside

Eddie Gallagher, her dedication to the Republican movement was still ablaze, perhaps more than ever, and the pair would pay careful attention to important events that would dominate the news for weeks to come.

Regardless of the results of the attempted bombing at Strabane, in the view of the police Rose had elevated her status from gunrunner and rabble-rouser to bona fide terrorist seeking to inflict mass casualties. Added to her dangerousness was the great embarrassment she had caused the police and even the Irish prime minister by so quickly foiling their efforts to quash IRA operations—especially by air—in the aftermath of the Mountjoy Prison break. Rose traveled the Irish countryside, going from town to town and staying at safe houses with people friendly to the cause. "We were constantly moving to people who were hugely supportive. I mean, that's been the wonderful thing about Ireland," she would remember wistfully years later, "that the people in the country have such generosity and such welcome for people who are trying to fight to free the country. It was a wonderful experience."[18] When asked later in life by radio host John Murray if these friendly people were giving succor to a terrorist, she readily answered, "Yes," but blamed government control of the media for such a term. "The language of terrorism really only came in when the Brits told the media to behave like that and use 'terrorist' . . . I mean, who is the terrorist today?"[19]

Her experiences meeting the people of Ireland only deepened her resolve. As she traveled, she saw poverty that she blamed on the country's imperial oppressors and talked about "meeting some of the poorest people you could ever meet living in the west of Ireland, where the lack of development deprived people of any kind of livelihood."[20] What she was seeing and experiencing was confirming what in college and in Tottenham had been mere educated speculation: colonialism was subjugating the people of Northern Ireland.

Dugdale recalled a period of great action while on the run. She wasn't interested in merely laying low—she had come to Ireland to be a fighter, and fight she would, seeking new ways to bring the battle to the British. "Every day was really dependent on whether an operation would be successful and how you could expand your activities," Rose said.[21] Still, she had to take care to keep her head down. The M62 coach bombing had meant that police were conducting sweeps of homes, and now, intensive efforts were in place to identify and capture those involved in the helicopter missions at Mountjoy and Strabane.

The Republican movement maintained an impressive network of safe houses and sympathizers able to allow wanted confederates to remain on the move and active during their war. The system extended not just throughout the north but throughout many Western countries, including the United States and Canada (and perhaps it still does). Because she had the benefit of traveling with a native in Eddie Gallagher, and perhaps others in their loosely formed ASU, Rose Dugdale—a former British debutante who had met the Queen—was privy to such assistance. She recalled that she "drove around a lot and had to get through checkpoints where I was fairly recognizable." She took to disguises as well. "I just cut my hair to something red-colored . . . and disguised myself as a fella which I remember being very awkward," especially when visiting random hotels to use the facilities and being unsure about which restroom to use.[22] This was Rose's life on the run, a time she appears to have largely enjoyed.

Members of the Provisional IRA were accustomed to the realities of prison or pursuit. And like Albert and Chrissie Price, their families were aware of the perils that faced their Republican children. So, in late 1973, when police visited the home of factory worker Harry Duggan Sr., in Feakle, County Clare, it wasn't a surprise. Still, the news was not good: they had come to inform him that his namesake, Harry Duggan Jr., a twenty-one-year-old carpenter, had been killed in Northern Ireland while fighting alongside fellow Provisionals.[23] It was not new information to Mr. Duggan. He had been informed of the sad news by Provos who also visited, saying that Harry Jr. had been buried with honors in a local cemetery.

Mr. Duggan went searching for his son's burial site, but no matter where he looked, he could not find where his son had been interred.

Mr. Duggan's search was fruitless for good reason. Harry Jr. was not dead. Rather, he had gone over to England under the assumed identity Michael Wilson, and using that nom de guerre, he was able to carry out additional operations as a member of an Active Service Unit free from the pursuit of police throughout the United Kingdom.[24] It was around this time that Duggan connected with Rose Dugdale and Eddie Gallagher, who were operating in their own fringe ASU.

Though on the run and planning operations, Dugdale was paying very close attention to the news out of Britain about the plight of the Price sisters. The force-feeding and persistent refusal of the British government to agree to transfer them and Feeney and Kelly infuriated both Dugdale and Gallagher. Further radical action on their part by then was inevitable. As the Provo statement after the Winchester Eight sentencing read, "Their heroism will inspire thousands more to drive home the struggle for freedom to a victorious conclusion."[25] But with their aerial bombing plot successful only in terms of embarrassing the government and putting targets on their backs, Rose would have to find a different way to take decisive action.

## ELEVEN
## *The Guitar Player*

On February 24, 1974, Rose Dugdale officially became a fugitive from justice. Police, who had long been working to establish sufficient cause to arrest her, had ample reason to suspect her involvement in the bombing at Strabane and in running munitions across the border. Finally, they obtained a warrant issued out of Manchester under the Explosives and Firearms Act, formally charging her with conspiring to smuggle arms and explosives to Northern Ireland and with possessing guns and explosives. The *Irish Press* reported "a massive hunt" for Dugdale as a result of the warrant. British soldiers in Ulster were given copies of her photograph and physical description.[1] But the search wasn't limited only to Northern Ireland, as police in England, Scotland, and Wales busily searched homes where they believed she could be hiding out. They also warned the public that Dugdale was dangerous, announcing it "imperative" that she be located and appealing to the public for their help.

A spokesman for the police provided a detailed and polite description of Rose, calling her "a vivacious and beautiful woman who rejected the rich life of her parents and society acquaintances." They added that Dugdale was prone to wearing "jumpers and jeans, but she could now be wearing skirts and high heels. She is 5 ft. 6 in. tall, with blue eyes and pale complexion." Police went on to warn that Rose might be disguised: "She normally wears her brown hair long and straight, but she may have purchased a wig or altered the style," and though her normal manner of speaking was with a "cultured voice," she might have adopted an Irish accent.[2]

Meanwhile, the British Army in Northern Ireland released its own wanted poster, and it painted a different portrait of the target. Featuring a large, unflattering photo and description of Dugdale under the large heading "HAVE YOU SEEN THIS WOMAN?," it described not a "vivacious and beautiful woman" but a woman of "mannish appearance" with a "sallow" complexion and wearing "dirty and untidy" attire. It urged that "if recognized she should be detained." The lack of coordination on the messaging gave hint to the fact that while the authorities were now actively working to arrest Rose for her radical criminal activities, they weren't close to apprehending her. They couldn't even be certain on which side of the Irish Sea she was hiding. Moreover, while her exploits were well-known to the police and, increasingly, to the media, what led her from aristocracy to criminality was the fodder for debate. Some saw her as a spoiled scion looking for adventure, while others posited that she was the brainwashed disciple of the radical men in her life. While neither was accurate, one thing was for certain: Rose Dugdale's life was as much a puzzle to the press as were her whereabouts to the police.


Nearly everything about the Dutch master Johannes Vermeer is a mystery. His technique, the figures within his works, his life, and even his death are all puzzles that are today the obsession of art historians, academics, writers, and art lovers throughout the Western world. He will likely forever remain an enigma, unless some centuries-old diary is unearthed, indisputably written in his hand or that of his widow or one of his many children. Even then, the questions that surround him and his works are so vast that it would be nearly impossible to address them all.

Precious little is known about the artist's life. What has been found provides a sparse view of an enigmatic existence in seventeenth-century Holland, much of it from an examination of unearthed and cryptic public records of his day. He was baptized on October 31, 1632, the son of Reynier, an innkeeper who dealt in art, and his wife, Digna. His father's profession meant that his son grew up in a home surrounded by paintings and in an atmosphere of appreciation for fine art. However, nothing is known of his endeavors until 1653, when he was admitted to the Guild of Saint Luke, an association of craftsmen named for the patron saint of artists, for whom he ultimately served two terms as dean. In order to become a member of the society, aspirants must have first completed a long apprenticeship. But details about his time as an understudy are unknown and, therefore, there exists a gaping hole in his biography. The wealth of artists in his orbit in Delft makes identifying his teacher yet more difficult. A possible candidate is Carel Fabritius, a student of Rembrandt's, who arrived in the city three years before Vermeer joined the guild. Vermeer biographer Anthony Bailey draws a comparison between Fabritius's bare plaster wall of his famous painting *The Goldfinch* and those of Vermeer's works, especially *The Milkmaid*. But the timing of Fabritius's own admittance into the guild makes it more likely that he was an adviser to the artist rather than the skilled hand that guided a young Vermeer's understanding of composition and technical artistry.[3]

Life in Delft the year following Vermeer's admission to the guild was marked by the massive explosion of a powder house that leveled much of the town and took countless lives, including that of Fabritius, who was acknowledged at the time to be Delft's best painter. Like the Price sisters, who catapulted from obscurity to fame through a devastating blast, we see Vermeer first mentioned as an artist of some acclaim as a result of the catastrophic explosion. A later poem lamenting Fabritius's death comforts the reader by mentioning that Vermeer "masterfully trod his path."[4]

Just months before Vermeer joined the Guild of Saint Luke, he married Catharina Bolnes. Catharina was the product of a more affluent family than Johannes, but unlike the Vermeers, the Bolnes family was Catholic—a minority population unable to hold civic office and held in low esteem by the Reformed Protestant majority to which her new in-laws belonged. Marrying a Catholic was frowned upon by society as well as his family, and Vermeer was struck from the family record.

Despite her initial disapproval of him, he moved into his mother-in-law's home in the Catholic area known as Papists' Corner, where he remained for the rest of his life.[5] His decision to convert to Catholicism appears to have been heartfelt, and none of the couple's eleven children were baptized outside of the faith. And despite much speculation about eroticism in his paintings, including lurid theories about the sexual role of maids in the household, there's no indication that Vermeer's marriage to Catharina was anything but devoted.

The intrigue surrounding the painter is such that he was famously nicknamed "The Sphinx of Delft" by the nineteenth-century French art historian Théophile Thoré (writing as William Bürger). After a century and a half of obscurity, Vermeer's renaissance came courtesy of Thoré, when the Frenchman toured the museums of the Netherlands in 1842 and happened upon the artist's painting *View of Delft*. Thoré was not immediately besotted with the painting, but, as Bailey writes, by 1860 he "was caught by the Vermeer fire and wanted to know all he could about the mysterious Delft master."[6] His fascination with the work and the artist led him on a quest to find other paintings by the then-obscure artist's hand. He bought those he could afford; those he couldn't, he urged friends to purchase. Thoré went on to compile photographs of all the paintings he attributed to Vermeer, which art historian and curator Elizabeth E. Gardner posits was the first such compilation of his works.[7] The catalog contained seventy paintings.

The actual number of works thought to have been produced by Vermeer has changed dramatically in the years since Thoré's research. Today, his total has been halved, with scholars and historians debating between thirty-four and thirty-seven extant works. However, the conventional wisdom is that there are now thirty-six works generally accepted as authentic Vermeer paintings, with a thirty-seventh, *Saint Praxedis*, the most hotly debated among scholars, especially after a declaration by Christie's auction house that it was indeed an authentic work by the Delft master.

This fine-tuning of his oeuvre is a relatively recent development. In Rose Dugdale's time, there was a wide chasm in the estimates of his extant paintings. The Associated Press estimated that "only about 40 paintings have been attributed to him with any certainty," while Sir Hugh Leggatt, a high-society art dealer, countered, "There are very few Vermeers left in the world—fewer than 30."[8] Regardless, his total body of work, as we know it today, represents an unusually small output of paintings for his time, with artists in his circle producing closer to fifty per year. The scarcity of his paintings only adds to the artist's allure, and to the value, as well.

Vermeer's widely acclaimed technical acumen has also been a subject of great wonderment. His intoxicating domestic scenes evoke silence. His mastery of light, unsurpassed. How did he accomplish such perfection? Mauritshuis director Emilie Gordenker writes, "Vermeer's technique continues to baffle us. We apply theories about the camera obscura on his compositions, harness the latest technical analysis and imaging techniques, but as the artist Stephen Farthing said recently in a documentary film about him: 'We still can't figure out how he did it.'"[9] Similarly, the subjects of many of his works leave experts wondering what exactly Vermeer was telling us. After starting his career painting historical scenes, he turned to domestic life rather abruptly, leaving observers to ponder the narratives. Renowned Vermeer scholar Arthur Wheelock said, "[His] paintings are always puzzles. I think that's what's fascinating. He never tells you exactly what they're about and that leaves us that opportunity to engage ourselves and depending on how we view that day or that month we can sort of respond . . . in different ways."[10] Peter Schjeldahl, an art critic writing for *The New Yorker*, takes it a step further: "With Vermeer, our eyes and minds squabble over what we are beholding. Is it image or paint, realism or reality?" He adds, "There is a discomfort—a prickling itch—in my experience of him. Looking and looking, I feel I have only begun to look."[11]

What is not a mystery but rather nearly universally accepted is Vermeer's greatness. The famed French novelist Marcel Proust, like his countryman Thoré a great admirer of the artist, included Vermeer's *View of Delft* in a key sequence in his book *In Search of Lost Time*. For Schjeldahl, this marks a transition in art appreciation. He writes that "by keying his account . . . to a Vermeer, Proust installed a milestone of art criticism, displacing Raphael as Europe's cynosure of artistic perfection."[12] In a poll conducted in his native land, Vermeer recently surpassed Rembrandt as the nation's most beloved painter.[13] Wheelock attributes his popularity to "the poetic ways his images are portrayed." He goes on, "It is in the way he uses light and color, proportion and scale, to enhance the moods of his figures. He imparts nuances of thought and meaning to his scene which are at once understandable but not totally explicit. Ultimately, however beautiful of sensitive his paintings may be, they continue to appeal because they can never be completely explained."[14]

It is this aesthetic, combined with the dearth of available works, that makes Vermeer's paintings among the most valuable and coveted works of art in the world. With nearly all of them owned by public institutions, they rarely come up for auction. The most recent, *A Young Woman Seated at the Virginal*, was sold over a decade ago for more than $30 million at Sotheby's on July 7, 2004, and is his only painting now in private hands.* Though listed in 1904 as a Vermeer when it hung in the collection of Sir Alfred Beit in Ireland along with the artist's *Lady Writing a Letter to Her Maid*, the attribution of the painting was long the subject of controversy and doubt.[15] A century later, after ten years of intense study and technical analysis of everything from the pigments to the costumes in the painting, researchers found that there was more than enough evidence to prove it a true work by Vermeer.[16] It was the first of his works offered at auction since *A Street in Delft* was sold in Amsterdam in 1921. Back then, *A Street in Delft* went for about $214,000, or nearly $2.8 million in today's dollars. Just as his popularity continues to grow, the value of his paintings skyrockets.

---

* The painting is in the Leiden Collection in New York.

In his own day, Vermeer's paintings sold for less than 100 guilders, or roughly the equivalent of a few thousand dollars today.[17] That, combined with his income as an art dealer and financial help from his mother-in-law, was sufficient to support his outsize household for a brief period of time. But, eventually, the combination of a large family and dire geopolitical events would change his fortunes. By 1675, Vermeer's prospects diminished. A national economic depression in Holland brought on by invasions by the French and, later, the English, left him unable to sell art or pay his mounting debts. In December of that year, perhaps struck by a severe illness and great stress, he collapsed and died suddenly at the age of forty-three.

Left with ten minor children, Catharina was forced to make good to her family's creditors on her own. Though she had hoped to hold on to her husband's paintings, they would necessarily become currency. A month after Vermeer's death, his widow approached the baker Hendrick van Buyten and surrendered two paintings by her husband—*Lady Writing a Letter with Her Maid* and *The Guitar Player*—in order to settle a debt of more than 600 guilders, or about three years' worth of bread for the family.[18] Today, those two paintings combined would fetch well over $100 million. In time, they would be separated, but fate would tie them together once more in a most unusual way.

The life of a museum security guard is marked by silence. Even when the galleries are open, visitors come to look at art in quiet contemplation. For the overnight guard, the quiet is such that the biggest challenge is often staying awake. Guards on evening shifts walk darkened galleries, accompanied only by those whose portraits line the walls. The few sounds are but those of his footsteps and perhaps the creaks of a settling building, especially in an older facility, like the Kenwood House in Hampstead Heath, London.

Kenwood House is an eighteenth-century mansion seated on 112 acres of parkland, given to the people of Britain by the family of Lord

Iveagh, the Guinness brewery magnate and philanthropist who amassed a fortune in fine art. Born in Dublin and educated at Trinity College, Lord Iveagh was the richest man in Ireland when he died in 1927, just two years after acquiring Kenwood House. With the mansion and estate, he also bequeathed over sixty masterpieces by artists such as Thomas Gainsborough, Anthony van Dyck, Frans Hals, and Rembrandt, whose *Self Portrait with Two Circles* is among the most important pieces in the collection. When it was handed over to the people in 1929, Kenwood House became a public art gallery under the administration of the London County Council.

The building itself was redesigned drastically from the original home built on the site in the early 1600s. It changed hands a number of times before becoming the weekend getaway for 1st Earl of Mansfield and his wife and nieces in 1754. The earl commissioned a major remodeling, and, as the house descended through the subsequent Earls of Mansfield, various architects worked to conserve and further beautify it until it was purchased by Edward Cecil Guinness in 1925. During the Second World War, Kenwood House housed military servicemen, and shortly after the war, realizing the need for significant repairs, Lord Iveagh's Bequest Trustees gave control of the entire estate to the London County Council (which would later become the expanded Greater London Council [GLC].)*[19]

Guarding Kenwood House was not without risk. Some of the world's best-known and most valuable works adorn its walls. In 1972, thieves stole two works by the eighteenth-century Venetian artist Francesco Guardi from the institution. Though the paintings, worth about $60,000 each at the time, were recovered just weeks later, the Greater London Council decided to take no further chances, installing what they described as "the most sophisticated burglar alarm system."[20] That system must have given the two night watchmen on duty on February 24, 1974, a sense of some security as

---

* In 1986, Kenwood House was handed over to English Heritage, which controls it today.

they patrolled the vast building, checking the low-lit, ornate rooms for signs of trouble.

Suddenly, at 11:00 PM, the routine silence of the evening was broken. The two guards were shaken by a loud crash coming from one of the rooms. When they reached the source, they found the broken glass of a window adjoining a newly empty expanse of burgundy damask wall covering. Thieves had smashed through a metal barrier, broken open a ground-floor window, and stolen a painting—Vermeer's *The Guitar Player*. Though it took the guards just a minute or so to get to the scene, it was too late. The culprits had already made their getaway, disappearing into the darkness of the evening, but not before cutting the telephone line to the building to delay calls for help. One of the guards ran off the grounds to notify police and found a padlock the thieves had cleverly placed on the exterior of the doors to prevent his departure. Meanwhile, his partner stayed behind and examined the smashed window. As the cold winter air filled the room, he was no doubt bewildered by the fact that the famous Rembrandt self-portrait, depicting the master in his old age and located just steps from the Vermeer, had been left behind.

Detective Chief Inspector Arthur Pike and his men swiftly arrived at Kenwood House from the Hampstead Police Station. They had been alerted to the incident by the new alarm system and began their investigation upon arrival. They determined that a sledgehammer had been used to smash through the steel-barred and shuttered window. The deputy leader of the Greater London Council, Illtyd Harrington, arrived later and was clearly shaken by the scene. "The violence that was used on the window was pretty terrifying," he said. "There was a lot of brute force exercised."[21] Unfortunately, there was no video coverage of the room, and no significant forensic evidence to lead the police on their hunt. Investigators questioned possible witnesses in the area but to no avail. Hampstead Heath was a popular spot for gay men to discreetly meet in the evening. As such, those in the nearby park respected one another's privacy and avoided taking note of what others might be doing. It was an ideal route for a quiet, surreptitious, late-night getaway.[22]

News of the heist made its way across the world with haste, and the authorities were pressed for a comment. A spokesman for Scotland Yard betrayed how few clues investigators had gathered when he said, "We are looking for either a master thief or a madman. It could be the work of someone who does not know what he has done or has no idea of the value of what he has got. But so far we think it is a master thief who has planned the operation over a number of years."[23]

He had good reason to lean heavily toward a deliberate operation. The odds that "someone who does not know what he had done" might arbitrarily smash the correct window to allow them to indiscriminately grab one of the world's most valuable paintings were slim. The Vermeer, situated next to a large window, was the undoubted target. The fact that the Rembrandt was left behind might easily be explained by pragmatism: *The Guitar Player*, at just twenty inches by eighteen inches, was far more portable than the much larger Rembrandt, and no less valuable. Early estimates were as high as $4.5 million, but at least one expert opined that *The Guitar Player* was "really priceless . . . of immense international artistic importance."[24] Either way, it was a long way from the 300 or so guilders Catharina Bolnes had received from her baker for the painting some three hundred years earlier.

*The Guitar Player* is a work of immense genius, with Vermeer's mastery of light at its peak. He defies convention in the work, placing the subject to the far left of the composition, in the same direction as the woman's glance. The viewer is left to wonder if she is alone in her room or accompanied by a friend, a vocalist, or other instrumentalists. Or perhaps there is a mirror out of view that reflects the stunning, delicate light upon her. Art critic Nigel Gosling describes "inexhaustible layers of curious delight" and gushes over Vermeer's skilled articulation of fabric, exclaiming "what magic translation of pigment into silk."[25]

Exactly who served as the model for the rosy-cheeked young woman, with her perfect dangling ringlets of hair, is up for debate. Author John Michael Montias guesses that it could be Vermeer's daughter Maria, who would have been seventeen or eighteen at the time it was painted.[26] Her yellow, fur-collared, satin jacket is perhaps a giveaway that the model might be a family member—it appears in six of the artist's works and is listed in an inventory of his possessions.[27] It could actually have belonged to Catharina, who is known to have owned a few fur-lined jackets.[28] Even the instrument is a matter of fascination, as the guitar, with its strings still vibrating in Vermeer's work, was gaining in popularity at the time, overtaking the lute, which had appeared in so many previous Dutch works.

In all, it was an unusually wise choice: a quick study of criminology shows that art thieves are rarely great students of art. The theft of *The Guitar Player* points to a particularly knowledgeable thief, one who came to Kenwood House knowing that the theft of this specific work would be sufficient to meet their ends, whatever they might be. But with little evidence and no witnesses to the crime, Scotland Yard hadn't much to go on. The Yard announced that ports of entry were being watched closely, and decided it important to broadcast an image of the painting to the public, in case innocent eyes happened upon it. But when the company that held the rights to the image told the BBC and ITV its fee—£10— both determined the cost excessive and decided instead to stick to verbal descriptions on the radio. Given these circumstances, Scotland Yard seemed resolved to lay their bets on what they believed would be inevitable ransom demands. Then, the unbelievable happened.


Nella Jones, a forty-two-year-old single mother of three, lived in a flat in East London with her children. From the age of seven, she had believed herself a seer. She described being overcome with a sense of intense loneliness that would be accompanied by premonitions of deaths and even bombings. She also believed she had the power to heal.

Her involvement in sleuthing began one Sunday evening in 1974, as she was busily tackling a pile of ironing in front of the television. A news report caught her eye—the story of a major art robbery accompanied by an image of Kenwood House. The place was unfamiliar to her. In fact, she had never been anywhere near the posh suburb in which it was located in her life. But when the broadcast mentioned that the art was still missing, she unconsciously announced aloud, "Well, of course they haven't found them, they're looking in the wrong place." Her words were followed by images flashing in her mind that she could not ignore. She ran to grab pencil and paper and sketched what she was seeing. It was a map, and on it she had drawn two crosses. She then drew the back of Kenwood House, despite only having seen an image of its face, and added a large field, trees, and a mesh fence. Overcome by what she had envisioned, she knew she had to act. For the first time in her forty-two years, she called the police.

Scotland Yard directed her call to the police at Hampstead, to whom she described her entire vision: "If you stand behind Kenwood House with your back to the house and look straight ahead, as if that is 12 o'clock, at 11 o'clock there's a kind of lane and if you go down this lane there's a little pond and some railings and over there you'll find something to do with the picture."

Her information was politely taken, and, to her surprise, she received a call from detectives a short while later, who picked her up and took her to the police station for an interview. Nella showed them the map she had drawn, and the detectives decided to take a chance on the clairvoyant. They drove her to the location and, once there, she and the detectives found a new mesh fence, just as she had described. They climbed over it and followed her lead, the February air chilling them to their bones. Finally, skepticism got the better of one of the detectives, who became annoyed and grumbled, "What are we looking for?" Nella replied, "I don't know, but it's metal and it's very important." Soon, she stopped dead in her tracks. At her feet lay the broken metal alarm box that had been on the back of *The Guitar*

*Player*. An earlier search by police and their sniffer dogs hadn't found it, but Nella's instincts had.

As the stunned detectives drove Nella back to the police station, it became clear why they were willing to take a chance on her: they had earlier found the frame to the Vermeer precisely where she had told them when she first called it in.[29] Detective Chief Inspector Pike reported, "The corner of the frame was completely smashed, the wooden supports were broken and the glass was separate and smashed." He was quick to add that specialists from Kenwood House said this did not mean that the painting itself was damaged, as it was still likely on its stretcher. DCI Pike, however, was not about to tell the public that Nella had found the frame. Instead, it was put forth that two park keepers employed at Kenwood found the dark ebony Dutch frame around lunchtime while patrolling the area.[30]

Nella would go on to achieve some notice as a famed clairvoyant after this case and a number of others in her day. Though many remained skeptical of her sixth sense, she had her believers at Scotland Yard, who are quick to point out that she never asked for money for her successes, which is quite rare.[31]

Meanwhile, with the painting's frame recovered, the ransom demands police anticipated for the actual painting began coming in. Soon after word of the theft became public, *The Guardian* received a telephone call from a man with a deep West Indian accent. "I am the one who took the Vermeer," he said. "We have the picture at Highgate. We are from Grenada."

The caller, who identified himself as "Harry," warned that more raids would ensue: "We want a half a million pounds worth of food for the people of Grenada, the poor people. We want it within 14 days. If we don't get the half million pounds worth of food, we shall destroy it. There will be more raids." "Harry" told *The Guardian* he also wanted "free paraffin kerosene given to the old people of Highgate and Archway as well as the money for food." As to why he chose to contact the newspaper instead of the people in charge at Kenwood House, he said, "We don't like dealing with the Greater London Council because they don't treat colored people very well," adding that if the GLC did not provide the payment, he would approach the wife of Harold Wilson, the opposition Labour Party leader and soon-to-be prime minister, to get it.

Before he could hang up, the reporter at *The Guardian* wisely asked for proof that the caller was holding the Vermeer. "We can take a bit off and send to you or we can burn a bit and send that to you," the caller said. Then came the key question for anyone claiming to possess a stolen painting: What is on the back? Surely the person in possession would know the answer to this key bit of information. "It's a bit dusty," came the reply. "That is all I'm going to say."

Then "Harry" hung up.

Police had no choice but to take the threat seriously. GLC deputy leader Harrington was eager to agree. "It is a strong possibility that this call could be genuine," he told the press. "I say this because of the crudity of the method of entry, and because of certain advice I have taken of our people during the day—responsible people in the art world."[32]

A political motive for the heist was highly plausible. Grenada had just received its independence from Britain earlier in the month. In addition, a similar demand that just been publicly made in the United States by the Symbionese Liberation Army, the captors of Patty Hearst, who demanded that her wealthy family distribute food money to needy Californians in return for her release. Yet more similar was the theft of Vermeer's *The Love Letter* in Belgium just two and a half years earlier. That painting, insured for $5 million, was stolen from the Brussels Fine Arts Palace by a thief who demanded that a ransom of $4 million be sent to the Bengali refugees of East Pakistan, who were at the time suffering through a tragic humanitarian crisis. The thief, a Belgian waiter named Mario Roymans, stole the painting by staying behind in the museum after closing, yanking the painting from the wall, and attempting to leave through a window. Unable to get the framed work through the window, the brutish thief cut the canvas from the frame with a potato peeler and tucked the masterpiece into the back of his pants, damaging the work. He caused yet more harm to the painting when he buried it in the forest and later dug it up for fear of rain, finally hiding it in a pillowcase under his mattress. He was ultimately captured two weeks after the heist, when a service station owner and his wife overheard Roymans talking to the media from their public pay phone. When he fled on his motorbike, the couple bravely chased him down, trapping him as he hid under a pile of straw in a cowshed.[33]

In Hampstead, a visibly anxious Harrington, concerned that the Grenadian caller was serious about destroying the Vermeer on his watch, offered an unspecified reward, saying only, "We will not in any circumstances enter into any discussions involving a massive amount of money." He worriedly told the media, "We are dealing with people who are acting out of desperation. We don't believe the Grenada call was a hoax." He pleaded that the painting not be destroyed, arguing that it would bring only "animosity for the people responsible and their cause."[34]

Despite Harrington's belief in the call, something wasn't quite right about the Grenada ransom. One Grenadian commentator said, "Grenadians do not go in for this sort of thing as a general rule," adding that the country was not, in fact, short of food.[35] And the island's prime minister, Eric Gairy, told reporters, "Grenada is not interested in that type of money at all."[36]

But it was politics of a different, and more likely, sort that soon entered into the recovery efforts surrounding the painting. While much attention was focused on the Grenadian caller, a switchboard operator at Capital Radio in London spoke with a caller who said, "We have got the painting and will destroy it unless the sisters are returned to Ireland. Ask the GLC what color the padlock on the door is." The caller, speaking with a brogue, could have been bluffing. However, a few days later, another ransom demand was made, this time to Illtyd Harrington at the Greater London Council, through his secretary. The man on the line spoke with a thick Irish accent, and he stated that *The Guitar Player* was tucked safely under a bed. In a tremendously cavalier aside, he proceeded to inform the secretary of the special pleasure he derived from making love on a bed above such a valuable work of art. Then came his demand: the transfer of Irish Republican Army prisoners out of Britain and into prisons in Ireland. He mentioned only two prisoners by name: the Price sisters. And before the call could be dismissed as just another crank, the Irishman included details about the condition of the painting's frame that had not been made public.[37]

Based on the information about the frame, investigators had good cause to shift their attention to the IRA. The Grenadian had put forth nothing to prove his claims. The Irishman, on the other hand, soon drastically upped the ante by providing a key piece of physical evidence. On March 6, the *Times* received a typewritten demand: "Send the Price sisters back to Ireland to finish their sentence." But the letter wasn't alone. Pinned to it was a small one-inch by one-quarter-inch strip of brown canvas, carefully cut from a painting, and alleged to be from the Vermeer. Here at last was the proof of life investigators and the GLC nervously awaited. A spokesman for Kenwood House expressed concern for the painting but added, "I will say in favor of whoever cut the strip of canvas, that it was done very neatly with a razor blade. Of course, we don't know yet if it came from the Vermeer, but the person had some respect. Probably he knows that its value would be reduced by treating it carelessly."[38] Thankfully, the strip had come from the tacking edge of the stretcher and did not damage the painted face of the work.

Because Kenwood House's own experts could not positively identify the strip as it was, Scotland Yard immediately commenced rigorous chemical and forensic tests to determine the authenticity of the canvas and utilized the powerful optical microscopes and spectrometers of the day. It would be a painstaking, time-consuming process.

The Yard also contacted the National Gallery to use a Vermeer from that museum for comparisons with the strip in question and brought in experts to assist in the authentication process. Early word was that it was likely indeed cut from *The Guitar Player*, and this prompted Harrington to turn away from the Grenada angle and toward the Irish. He impulsively made a statement: "I believe it is in their own best interest to follow our instructions. If these people are Irish it may be easier for them to leave it at the Irish Centre at 52 Camden Square, where they can merge with other visitors going in and out." In exchange, once the painting was returned, he would personally approach the Home Office to discuss the transfer of the Price sisters from Brixton Prison back to Ireland. He warned that failure to return the Vermeer could cause public opinion to "harden against sending the sisters back."[39]

While the analysis of the swatch of canvas continued and news of the demands related to the Price sisters made headlines each day, sources within the Provisional IRA insisted to reporters that they knew nothing of the heist, which suggested that a fringe element of sympathizers may have been the culprits. Then word came from the Price sisters themselves through their father, Albert. "The girls asked me to make a public statement for the return of the painting unharmed to the people of London," he told the press. "They want no gimmicks. When they return to Ireland it will be on their own merits, much as they appreciate people trying to help them."

It was a startling statement, pointing unequivocally to the theft having been committed without the go-ahead of the Provisionals. The sisters were intent on winning their transfer through their hunger strike, based on their belief that they were political prisoners, and not because of an extortion. Albert revealed that Dolours herself had just two years earlier traveled to Kenwood House to take in the Vermeer masterwork.[40] "My daughters told me they want the painting returned unharmed. They are art students, and they appreciate the value of the picture to the people of London," he said.[41] Albert's statement on behalf of his daughters came in the wake of a statement that protests in support of all nine imprisoned Republicans outside of their respective prisons would increase in the coming days.

As Scotland Yard hinted that the result of the testing was just days away, another letter—which included a familiar theme—arrived at the *Times* from the same people who had mailed the canvas.[42] This time, the message was yet more threatening:

> the price sisters have given no sign of gratitude all we have established is that a capitalist society values its treasures more than humanity therefore we will carry our lunacy to its utmost extent the painting will be burnt on st patricks night with much cavorting about in the true lunatic fashion [43]

The threat sent a chill through the Greater London Council. Nella Jones, the clairvoyant, contacted its deputy leader. "Don't worry, Mr. Harrington," she said. "The picture won't be burned. It will be found in a cemetery just as I told you it would."[44]

Just as this ominous news was making its rounds, Scotland Yard released early word on the results of the analysis of the canvas the *Times* had received in the mail. "It is highly probable that the piece of canvas was taken from the painting" by Vermeer, they said.[45] The Price sisters' advocates were the real thing—they had the multimillion-dollar painting and were threatening to burn it. Their deadline was just four days away.

On the eve of St. Patrick's Day, Albert Price again made an appeal for the painting on his daughters' behalf. "I appeal to those who have the painting to return it," he stated. "My daughters do not want it destroyed or damaged, nor do I."[46] It was a heartfelt appeal. Albert knew for sure now that he was speaking to kindred spirits sympathetic to his daughters and the cause of Republicanism writ large.

His statement came just in time to run in the press on St. Patrick's Day, and all through that day, authorities worried. Police told *The Guardian*,

"The picture could already be in ashes in someone's backyard. And no one would know, now or ever."[47] It was an oddly pessimistic view, but one built on years of dealing with the IRA. Scotland Yard knew all too well that the IRA didn't deal in idle threats. Still, as the deadline came and went, there was no further word from the painting's captors. No more threats, no sign of the painting having been destroyed—nothing.

# TWELVE

# The French Visitor

Rose Dugdale stood out on the rocky pier at the port of Baltimore, across the harbor from East Donegal. She faced the cool, breezy, early-spring air and looked out contemplatively at the sea. She was a long way from Yarty Farm in East Devon, a lifetime away from the safe postwar cloister in which her father had kept her as a child. The six years since she'd visited post-revolution Cuba had been eventful by design. As a result, she knew what fate awaited her, at least in the short term; after all, the die had been cast by her own hand.

It had been an amazingly eventful four months since she said goodbye to Tottenham. She had committed herself to direct action and to the cause of Irish Republicanism, escalating from activist and financier to arms trafficker and aerial bomber. She was also now actively trying to get the Price sisters and their compatriots transferred from cells in Britain back home to Northern Ireland as political prisoners, which, to her, they undoubtedly were. She knew she was being hotly pursued, and police now also suspected that she might be the woman involved in a hijacking of one of their vehicles at gunpoint in March. Her crimes were serious, and she knew her day of reckoning was inevitable, especially given her recent exploits.

Ten days earlier, she had rented herself and Eddie a small remote cottage in pastoral Reenogreena, Glandore, in West Cork, as far from the mayhem of Northern Ireland as possible. She told the landlord, a farmer named Con Hayes, that Eddie was her husband, and she, as a wanted woman, provided an alias for herself: "Mrs. Merrimee." She agreed to a price of £10 per week, and Hayes would occasionally allow her to borrow his small, battered, black Morris Minor automobile to make the long trek into town for groceries and such whenever her husband took their car. She had borrowed the car again that day, for her visit to the rocky shore. Eight days had passed since she had successfully pulled off her biggest caper yet, one that captured headlines around the world, this time in the Republic of Ireland just south of Dublin.

On April 26, at about 9:30 PM, Rose and Eddie had driven their silver Ford Cortina station wagon to County Wicklow, near Blessington, accompanied by two men from Gallagher's own makeshift Active Service Unit. They parked the Cortina in an unlit patch by Russborough House, a majestic Palladian stately house, and went over their plan one last time. The men gathered their tools: knives, screwdrivers, tape, nylon stockings, rubber gloves, and pistols.[1] Rose did not don a mask but wore a disguise just as deceiving, climbing from the station wagon in heavy makeup, a black wig, and a fashionable blue tweed skirt suit with heels. She strode along a gravel path and called at the side door of Russborough House while the three men stealthily trailed behind. The door was answered by a manservant, James Horrigan, and the fourteen-year-old son of the butler, Patrick Pollard.

Rose addressed the pair in suspicious French, and, because Horrigan understood her when she said *voiture* and could see her Ford on the grounds, he assumed she had suffered car troubles. But before they could provide her with assistance, they were swarmed by Dugdale's three accomplices, who stormed in from both sides of the door. Horrigan and Pollard were both violently struck by the men. Horrigan recalled, "They held something against my neck and told me it was a gun. They threatened to shoot."[2] Pollard was grabbed by the scruff of the neck and ordered by the invaders to lead the gang to the owners of the house: Sir Alfred and Lady Beit.

Sir Alfred Beit was a tall, handsome, and enormously wealthy man. His uncle, the first Alfred Beit, had learned the diamond business in Holland and went from there to South Africa, where he discovered that

Cape diamonds were as good as any in the world. With a loan from his father, he built his own diamond company, dealing also in South African gold. These ventures earned him a great fortune, and with it he set out to build a world-class art collection. With the assistance of art historian and curator Dr. Wilhelm Bode, the first Sir Alfred acquired masterpieces through established dealers, including both Agnew and Colnaghi in London. When he died at just fifty-three in 1906, he left £2 million to charities in England, Germany, and South Africa, and his art collection to his brother, Otto Beit, Sir Alfred's father. Otto added generously to the collection, choosing well and purchasing masterworks by such renowned artists as Gainsborough, Velázquez, Goya, and Frans Hals, among others. Otto left the paintings to his son, who sold some of the lesser works and replaced them with pieces he liked. Sir Alfred would later advise, "A sterling rule to observe when selling works of art if you do not actually need the money for living purposes, is to replace immediately by buying other works of art more to your own taste."[3]

Sir Alfred Beit entered politics as a younger man and was a well-liked Member of Parliament until he lost his seat in 1945 and moved to South Africa, where he was described as "fiercely anti-apartheid." Beit was regarded as a kind, friendly man. The writer James Lees-Milne said that Beit was "forthright and fun to be with. Insatiably curious, ever-seeking knowledge, yet serious conversation with him usually ended in peals of laughter, especially when the jokes were turned upon himself."[4]

In 1939, at the age of thirty-five, Sir Alfred had married the former Clementine Mabel Kitty Freeman-Mitford, sixteen years his junior, after proposing to her under Goya's *Portrait of Doña Antonia Zárate*. Lady Beit was a cousin to the famous Mitford sisters, and with Unity Mitford she had traveled to Munich in 1937. There, she was introduced to Adolf Hitler, with whom they attended the Bayreuth Festival for ten days. Her cousin Deborah Mitford later said that Clementine had "struck up a close friendship with an SS officer." In her later life, Lady Beit made no mention of the aforesaid escapades. She had also once dated Winston

Churchill's son, Randolph. Her pedigree was indeed such that she was firmly attached to the British aristocratic establishment. [5]

Where Sir Alfred was warm and engaging, Lady Beit was described as "a plumpish figure with a settled facial expression that bordered on the sour." Any amusement, it was said, "derived more often from the way she said things rather than her actual words."[6] She was, in other words, an exemplar of the stuffy British nobility. However, in the ways that opposites attract, the Beits enjoyed what appears to have been a very long and happy marriage filled with incredible treasures and luxury in perhaps the finest home in Ireland. Homan Potterton, who would become the director of the National Gallery of Ireland, said that the Beits were not royalty, but "they may have considered themselves . . . royalty in Ireland."[7] Potterton wrote that turning down an invitation from Lady Beit was a faux pas, but quoted famed photographer Cecil Beaton's experience at a Beit dinner party: "Never has a more boring evening been endured by ten elderly people. I could think of nothing to ask anyone throughout the wasteful evening. The twenty eggs, the chicken and tarragon, and raspberries had been cooked in vain. The bills for décor might as well not have been incurred. Poor Alfred, he is so kind and nice, and Clem too, but ouch! the emptiness."[8]

In 1952, unhappy with the racist national policies of South Africa, the Beits moved to Ireland, where they purchased the Russborough House as a showcase for Sir Alfred's world-class art collection. The mansion, whose dimensions are said to make it the longest house in the country, was designed by the great Irish architect Richard Cassels in 1741. Irish painter and author James Reynolds, who was fascinated by architectural design, would tell of a visitor asking where one would go to see the best example of Irish Palladian architecture and getting the response, "If ye want a feast, see Russborough." Reynolds himself said of the place, "To my mind Russborough House has architectural sweep, beautifully considered proportions, stimulating and original details, inside and out and the 'the fine romantic air' hovering over all." In addition to the Beit paintings, the mansion was outfitted with statues from Herculaneum and Sicily and two shiploads of mahogany direct from Santa Domingo.[9] Every bit of Russborough House features exquisite detail and beauty, making it all the more a paradoxical setting for a brutal robbery.

The frightened, fourteen-year-old Pollard led the armed men, as instructed, to the Beits, who were sitting by the fire in the library beneath the room's elegantly detailed and ornate ceiling, listening to records on the gramophone. Suddenly, the door burst open, and men flashing pistols barged into the room and ordered the Beits to lie flat on the floor with their heads down, their faces in the fine rug. At first, Lady Beit thought it joke or a hoax, but she soon learned it was all very real when one of the men put his knee on the small of her back. Sir Alfred, a veteran of the Second World War, made the mistake of looking up at one of his attackers, who struck him in the head with the butt of a gun, drawing blood from the seventy-one-year-old that poured onto his wife's hand and sleeve. All the while, the intruders were yelling what Lady Beit described as "communistic" insults at Sir Alfred, calling him a "capitalist pig" and accusing him of "walking on the working classes."[10] These were claims consistent with Dugdale's view of the upper class, people of the Beits' sort. She would say of them, "You have to bear in mind that the wealth that existed in Russborough House was the wealth that had been derived from South Africa by the exploitation of the black people, the enslavement of the black people."[11] The Beits were the perfect targets.

Meanwhile, young Pollard was also forced to lead the invaders to find other staff members. Understandably, he did as he was told, even bringing them to a seventeen-year-old maid who was, at that moment, in the bath. An armed man kicked the door and ordered her to dress quickly, warning that he'd kill her if she didn't come out. Ultimately, all the staff members were brought to the library to join the Beits and Horrigan. Each victim was bound and gagged with nylon stockings, their arms and legs secured behind their backs. As the invaders secured the humble Russborough House staff, they apologized to them, saying, "Sorry about this, but it's got to be done." It was a sign of respect for the working class, though just minutes before they had forcefully struck and threatened Horrigan and Pollard.

Rose once again took the lead, just as she had at the theft from her family's estate. Caroline Dugdale, her mother, was involved in an art gallery in Paris before the war and also painted watercolors, and it was through her that Rose likely acquired a discriminating eye for pictures.[12] She set about calmly but quickly moving through the lushly appointed rooms of the Russborough House, using her knowledge to pick those paintings that were the most noteworthy and most valuable. The likes of Gallagher and the other muscle they brought along would have had no idea which paintings to take and which to leave. Rose pointed out the best of them to her cohorts, who, at her instruction, removed the larger works from their frames and took the smaller ones as they were. It wasn't that she knew the precise values, she would say later in life, but those that were well-known.[13] In all, she chose nineteen paintings. As Sir Alfred recounted, "The woman . . . was the leader of the whole operation, and knew what she was about."[14] Though Lady Beit saw her only briefly, she recalled that Dugdale "made a curious impression on me, of authority and command. It is difficult to explain, but she gave the impression of being a strong character.[15]

Dugdale and her accomplices made quick work of it. They bundled the paintings together, an awkward job given their various shapes and sizes. Then they separated the house members into separate rooms, checked the nylon binding to ensure that no one could get loose, and made their exit. The whole affair took no more than ten minutes. Unlike the rest, Lady Beit, who was more angry than afraid, was forced off toward the basement. She later recalled looking behind as she was pushed from the library to have one last glimpse of her dear Sir Alfred, helplessly trussed in the spot where he had proposed decades earlier. She believed she'd never see him again. "I was convinced that, like the unfortunate Romanovs, I was to be shot in the cellar," she remembered.[16] Lady Beit was made to go downstairs to lead one of the men to the family's money, which he believed was kept in the basement. Though the thief brandished a knife at her and warned that Sir Alfred would be harmed if she didn't cooperate, Lady Beit informed her captor that there was no money. With little time available to argue with her, she, too, was bound hand to foot. "This is punishment for you, you bloody pig," her tormenter sneered at her. "Punishment you deserve."[17]

The thieves placed all nineteen works in the back of the station wagon and piled into the car for a getaway that had been carefully planned. Stolen cars were deposited in predetermined locations. They drove the Cortina seventy miles to County Tipperary, where they climbed into a second car and drove to Ennis, in County Clare. Once there, they took a third stolen car 130 miles across to Gorey in County Wexford, where they abandoned it.

Shortly after 10:00 PM, Beit noted that a "silence had descended on the house." Correctly assuming the thieves had departed, he called out to those in the other rooms. After about thirty minutes, one of the staff managed to free himself. He grabbed a knife and cut the others loose. They pressed the push-button alarm system to notify the police, and Beit, his clothes spattered with blood from his head wound, rang 999, the emergency number, and reported the incident to the garda at Naas.[18] Fortunately, the thieves' attempt to cut the phone lines at Russborough House had failed. Next, an anxious search for Lady Beit commenced with great haste, the staff deeply concerned that she had been kidnapped or, worse, killed. Her husband, certain that she had been taken hostage, was soon relieved to find her upset—but unharmed—in the basement.

With his wife safe and the police on their way, Sir Alfred and the staff surveyed the loss. It was an unnerving scene. A number of empty frames were strewn on the floor, others leaned gently against an elegant sofa and chair. The walls were not bare—many paintings remained. But the leftovers were the ones that hadn't passed muster with Dugdale's discriminating eye. The best pieces left gaps that created an

unmistakable lack of symmetry on the gorgeous wallcoverings of Russborough House.

The staff summoned a doctor, and he arrived quickly, before even the
police, and administered first aid to the cuts received by Sir Alfred and
James Horrigan.[19] Then the Beits called Dr. James White, the director of
the National Gallery of Ireland, where they served as board members,
to seek his advice about the art that was missing as well as that which still
remained.[20]

The garda division at Naas was led by twenty-eight-year-old, and
newly promoted, Chief Superintendent Sean Feely. He took the passenger's seat as one of his constables sped to the crime scene. When they
arrived at Russborough House, he told his charge, "This could be big."
Feely told journalist Matthew Hart that when he called headquarters
and told them that the paintings which had just been stolen were worth
a million pounds, the reply from his incredulous superiors was, "There's
not a million pounds worth of paintings in the whole of Ireland." Feely
replied, "OK, make it half a million."[21] Little did the gardaí know that
they were speaking in terms of vast understatement.

The heist at the Russborough House, investigators would soon learn,
was the biggest property theft of its day. Rose Dugdale had chosen
well. According to Sir Alfred, "She stole . . . all the most important and
the most valuable" paintings,[22] a fact that was the direct result of her
breeding and education. They were works that could fit in any respected
museum in the world, and many of them would be among the jewels
of any collection. The timing had been perfect, too, as eleven of the
paintings she'd chosen had returned to the Russborough House only
a week before from the National Gallery of Ireland in Dublin, where
they had been held for safekeeping while the Beits visited South Africa.[23]
Rose bypassed the newer, more modern paintings that Sir Alfred had
purchased[24] and had her henchmen take four paintings by the Venetian Guardi (two views of St. Mark's Square and two small paintings

listed as *Smooth Caprice*); a small picture of a pond with a swan by the nineteenth-century British painter and sculptor Edwin Landseer, whose lions adorn Trafalgar Square; and two works by famed British painter Thomas Gainsborough, *Portrait of Madame Bacelli* and a small landscape. She chose an additional landscape by the Belgian artist Henry van de Velde titled *Calm Sea with a Boat*. Dugdale wisely had them take a painting by the premier Spanish master of King Philip the IV's court, Diego Velázquez, titled *The Servant*, and his later countryman Francisco Goya's beautiful *Portrait of a Woman in a Black Dress*. The Goya, a painting of Doña Antonia Zárate from the early nineteenth century, is considered one of the artist's greatest works.

If these ten represented the entire haul from that April evening, the robbery would rank among the great art heists of the ages. But Rose Dugdale was hardly done, and she turned her eye toward nine Dutch masterworks that stole all headlines. She confidently pointed to Paulus Moreelse's *A Lady Wearing a Ruff*, and Lady Beit took that as an opportunity to say, "Oh, they are taking the Vermeer," with the hope that she might trick them into leaving the Beit's actual Vermeer behind. Then two companion works by Gabriël Metsu, *The Letter Writer* and *The Letter Received*. Jacob van Ruisdael's *Cornfield*, described as "an unrestrained piece of pastoral lyricism" was thought to be Rose's favorite of the bunch,[25] a lovely landscape with obvious similarities to the Yarty Farm of her happy youth. Then there were three works by Peter Paul Rubens: *Head of a Monk*,* *Head of a Cavalier*, and *Sketch of Venus and Jupiter*. *The Lute Player*, a work by the Dutch master Frans Hals, alone worth more than the initial estimate of Chief Superintendent Feely, was also carefully selected. But it was the first painting[26] Rose had chosen that grabbed the most attention—*Woman Writing a Letter with Her Maid* by Johannes Vermeer.

---

* In 2015, *Head of a Monk* was rejected by Christie's over doubts of its authenticity. Art historian Dr. John Loughman has stated that the extensive literature on Rubens contains no mention of the work and that "no one knows this painting." Michael Parsons, "Questions over Authenticity of Russborough Paintings," *The Irish Times*, June 16, 2015, retrieved February 9, 2020, https://www.irishtimes.com/culture/art-and-design/visual-art/questions-over-authenticity-of-russborough-painting-1.2250594.

Like *The Guitar Player*, stolen just a few weeks earlier, *Woman Writing a Letter with Her Maid* is enormously valuable, catapulting the total value of the art stolen from Russborough House to above the £8 million range. "It is more important, more rare and more desirable than the two paintings—the van Gogh and the Turner—that have reached the $10 million plateau," Old Master dealer Eugene V. Thaw said at the time, comparing it to the highest sale prices of the age.[27] The theft of this painting at this time came with an historic twist. Three centuries earlier, Vermeer's widow, Catharina Bolnes, had removed *The Guitar Player* and *Woman Writing a Letter with Her Maid* from her home to settle a debt of three years' worth of bread with her baker. Now, with *The Guitar Player* still missing from Kenwood House, the two paintings were once again coupled in an unfortunate situation.

*Woman Writing a Letter with Her Maid* presents the viewer with yet another mystery and is regarded as one of Vermeer's more challenging works to interpret. As is typical, we do not know the identity of the beautiful woman busily writing at the table. What appears to be a crumpled letter rests on the recognizable tiled floor in front of the table and invites the viewer to ponder its relevance. Is it an angrily discarded letter, just received by the lady, that prompts her instant response? Did it belong to the unknown person who had been sitting in the now empty chair opposite the letter writer? As Vermeer expert Jonathan Janson points out, the fact that the maid has neither repositioned the chair nor picked up the discarded paper and accompanying stick of wax indicates that the mystery person has just recently departed the room.

Both the lady and her maid are positioned in front of a large painting, the biblical scene *Finding of Moses*, in this case attributed to Peter Lely, a Dutch contemporary of Vermeer's. While the meaning of the painting in this setting is difficult to interpret, the positioning of the two women tells a story. Janson describes a division between the two. The maid directs her attention out of the room toward the window, attempting "to isolate herself from the uncomfortable situation" and stands with her arms folded, her thoughts kept to herself. The lady's thoughts, too, are her own, as she busily works on her reply. Interestingly, the two figures never converge in Vermeer's composition.[28] What can be assumed is that the lady is writing about an affair of the heart, as letters in Dutch paintings typically represent love and relationships.[29]

*The Guitar Player* and *Lady Writing* share what Arthur Wheelock calls Vermeer's "experiment with a centrifugal composition," in which he draws the focus away from the center of the paintings.[30] Both also include an unseen character. Like the person who has just left the room in *Lady Writing*, *The Guitar Player* leaves the viewer to guess who the musician is looking at and playing for (or with). But for all its intrigue, *Lady Writing* answers at least one question: because it was packaged by Vermeer's widow with *The Guitar Player* when she removed it from her husband's collection, we can be reasonably sure that there is no pendant piece to the latter work. Vermeer intended for us to wonder who her companion was.

After accompanying *The Guitar Player* when it left the Vermeer household, *Lady Writing a Letter with Her Maid* soon went its own way, changing hands in Holland at least nine times after being given to the baker Van Buyten. By the late nineteenth century, it was in Vienna, then quickly sold to an owner in France, where it remained until the first Sir Alfred Beit purchased it from the Paris art dealer Kleinberger in the early 1900s. The second Sir Alfred took it with him to Ireland when he moved to Russborough House in 1952, where it hung for twenty-two years. Where it was at the moment was anyone's guess.

The garda quickly determined that the investigation into the Russborough House heist would require much more than the services of Feely and his constable alone. Police investigators flooded into the area, along with the media, as the story spread like a virus from quiet County Wicklow to the wire services around the world, taking front pages by storm. The volume of art taken was such that it was impossible to overstate the loss.

Police found that in addition to the paintings, the thieves had taken three brass clocks, a box containing £50, a Kodak camera, photos, and even a shoe rack. Sir Alfred remembered that the woman in charge had milled about his desk, and it was determined that his address book was also taken.[31] These random ancillary objects were of little consequence—it was the recovery of the paintings on which everyone was focused.

To that end, investigators from multiple garda stations went immediately to work. A command center was established at the garda post in Blessington under the auspices of Chief Superintendent Anthony McMahon. The usual overtures were made to the ports of entry and exit to keep watch for the four thieves and the masterpieces that had been taken. In addition, police officers swept through four hundred houses, barns, and cottages throughout the county looking for witnesses and clues—anything to help them solve the case. The pressure was intense: the government seat in Dublin considered the fact that the biggest theft in the world had occurred on their soil a national embarrassment.[32]

Gardaí quickly determined that three cars were stolen in various locations around Ireland shortly before the heist: the silver Ford Cortina, a green Cortina 1300, and a blue Triumph 2000. Then, on the afternoon following the robbery, the getaway car was found. John Ryan, from Cashel, County Tipperary, was on his own grounds in Kilshenane, tending to his cows and calves, when he noticed that a gate had been left open. He inspected and found a car parked in the mud with its front wheel stuck in a ditch. The car had no license plate, and he couldn't see inside because the windows had frosted in the cool country air. "I stayed away from it for fear of somebody being in the car," he recalled. "It came into my head that perhaps some of the Jehovah's Witnesses were in there because they were in the neighborhood at the time." Ryan went home, had breakfast with his wife, and milked his cows. Then, before heading to the creamery with the milk, he finally called the police about the suspicious car. Police rushed to the scene. "They were on site before I came back to the house," Ryan said.[33]

Inside the Cortina, police found an important clue: a driver's license bearing the name Vanessa Kelly of 174 Mortello Est., Portmarnock. The license gave investigators the break they needed. They knew that Vanessa Kelly was an alias sometimes used by Bridget Rose Dugdale. They made an official request for the license application, and on April 29 the documents were received from the Department of Automotive Registration in Dublin. On them, they found Dugdale's fingerprints. In the car, they also found a small fragment of a frame from one of the smaller stolen works. Later, the Ryan family found music programs that belonged to Sir Alfred Beit on their property in the vicinity of the car.[34]

Even before investigators had received the registration documents, suspicions of Dugdale's involvement leaked from investigators to the media. News of the heist was barely a day old and the fingerprint examinations weren't even complete when *The Observer* reported that "police believe the armed gang's leader, a woman of about 30 with a French accent, may have been engaged in extremist political activity in Britain." The allusion was obvious. The description of her cohorts was weak: "Three men . . . in their twenties, one short and stocky with a moustache and another even shorter and blonde,"[35] who spoke in "entirely Irish accents" of Waterford and possibly Northern Ireland.[36] That wasn't much to go in terms of the muscle, but when it came to the female leader, it took little imagination to connect Rose to the heist.

The report prompted the police to quickly try to discount her involvement, probably to try to keep her from going too deeply underground and for fear of inhibiting the ransom demand they knew was to come. On April 29, the day after the report of the female extremist from Britain, police downplayed the possibility that Dugdale was the leader of the armed gang at Russborough. *The Guardian* reported, "A senior police officer said that there was 'no question' of Dr. Dugdale being sought in connection with the robbery," stating that the thieves' repeated statements about the Beits being "capitalist pigs" and "exploiters of the works of the world" could merely have been a smokescreen to throw off investigators. They told the *Irish Times* that they had shown photos

of Dugdale to staff members who said "positively" that the leader of
the gang was not her.[37] Furthermore, Sir Alfred joined the police and
suggested that the motive was not political, saying that he believed the
woman was "associated with an international art gang" and that the
men with her were "purely hired thugs." However, he seemed to contradict himself by adding that he believed that the theft of *The Guitar Player*
from the Kenwood House (which had a well-known political motive)
"unquestionably started the whole thing."[38]

The truth was that the police already knew better. An investigator
who examined the registry documents police requested found another
interesting connection to Dugdale. An application in the files showed
that a form included a handwritten date in which the day, month, and
year were separated by colons, rather than the more common periods or
slashes.* He had seen this just recently: police in Northern Ireland circulated a report that showed that the woman behind the bombing at Strabane—whom they believed to be Rose—had dated a hotel register that
same unique way.[39] Forensic examination removed any conjecture—the
form was handled by Dugdale posing as "Vanessa Kelly."[40]

Meanwhile, the press, like the police, were anticipating a ransom
request, so attention naturally turned to the value of the paintings.
James White from Dublin's National Gallery was asked for a valuation.
As the person recently responsible for the more valuable pieces of the
Beit Collection, and the director of the nation's top museum, he was in a
unique position to speak authoritatively, and he set the total at £8.5 million. For his part, Sir Alfred was less specific. "You will have seen some
fancy valuations," he said, "and their guess is as good as mine. With the
rising cost of things today it is impossible to say what their worth is until
you come to sell them."[41] In a televised interview outside Russborough
House with RTÉ, he stated, "All I can say to you is the most important
ones amongst them were insured for important sums, but I'm not prepared to say for how much or what particular ones." Then Beit, wearing

---

* Indeed, a letter written by Dugdale years before to Mount Holyoke College and in the
possession of the author is dated 4:IV:62.

a smart checked suit and fashionable tie, with Lady Beit standing silently at his side, turned from the dollar value to the intrinsic, personal value of what was taken from him: "They were the apple of our eye. I mean, they represent a collection started by my forebears towards the end of the last century and which we have cherished now for over eighty years, and, from my point of view of course, no money can compensate for the loss of these beautiful objects." [42] As he spoke those last words, Sir Alfred looked firmly into the television camera.

Still, there was the unpleasant business of ransom to address. As police canvassed the area and pieced together information found from the various cars stolen for the gangs' getaway, the London insurance adjustor firm Cunningham, Hart and Co., announced a large reward of £100,000 for information leading to the recovery of the nineteen paintings. This was not, however, a buyback, partner Anthony Hart announced. "We are not interested in doing deals with thieves," he said with resolve. "The reward is being offered for the recovery of the paintings and the conviction of the thieves."[43] The offer was the first sign of how money might change hands if the masterpieces could be recovered, as the Beits had already indicated that they would not pay a ransom. Sir Alfred had announced almost immediately that he was not willing to pay for the return of the art, and when asked if he understood that this could mean the paintings might instead be destroyed, he was wistful: "It might almost come to that."[44]

Meanwhile, the police dragnet across the countryside for the paintings and their captors was in progress when, on May 3, exactly one week after the heist, a letter arrived addressed to James White at the National Gallery, postmarked from Belfast. Accompanied by pages from Sir Alfred's diary to prove authenticity,[45] it read:

All matters must be confidential. To our terms. The four hunger strikers, sisters Price, Feeney and Kelly to be returned immediately to the rest of their prison terms in Ireland. When this is done, these will be returned: *The Woman Writing a Letter; The Woman in the Black*

*Dress; The Letter Reader; The Cavalier; The Mulattu.** When this request
is granted, the remained of the pictures will be returned to you
on the payment of 500,000 pounds. Details of how this money
will be paid will be provided when the first phase of the matter is
completed. There will be no further contact between us. If you do
not comply with these two conditions by Tuesday 14th of May, all
pictures will be destroyed.[46]

In the meantime, Garda Sergeant Pat O'Leary was in Rosscarbery
to begin a search of the area. It was a good fit for him—he knew this
part of the country well, having begun his career in a nearby garda divisional headquarters. The morning after the ransom letter was received
in Dublin, Sergeant O'Leary, thirty-three, joined Billy Creedon, a fellow
officer who had an intimate knowledge of the area,[47] and began the
routine police work of a door-to-door search of homes and farms in the
thinly populated area.

In the early afternoon of that first day of canvassing, the pair knocked
at the door of yet another farmhouse. Situated on a picturesque cliff in
West Cork, it overlooked High Island, Low Island, and straight down the
coastline. The owner, Con Hayes, answered, and the police asked him
the same questions that their fellow officers had been asking hundreds
of people across the nation for over a week: Have you seen a suspicious
British woman in the area? Hayes said that he and his wife had in fact
rented a cottage to a Mrs. Merrimee from London. Hayes informed the
officers that her accent wasn't British, but foreign. She had come home
quite late on the night of the heist, Mrs. Hayes recalled, but she told
the owners that she and her husband had "met some friends, went to
the pub and had some drinks."[48] Con Hayes gave them directions to
the place she and her husband rented, just a hundred or so yards away.
The police partners drove over to the small cottage, and when O'Leary
knocked at the door, it was answered by Dugdale, who had heard the car

---

* *The Mulattu* was an alternative title for the Velázquez painting at the time.

door shut. Wearing dirty jeans and a messy sweater, Rose answered the door and maintained her cover. "I came out in my little wig and I tried to speak French to let on that I was a foreign tourist," she recalled. "But . . . apparently it didn't convince them."[49] She was right. O'Leary said, "She answered in very broken English . . . I remember standing in the yard and looking at her and thinking it might be her. Your sixth sense will tell you that."[50] O'Leary had also recalled "something peculiar" about the face in the photo that had been circulated among the police, and in this woman he saw the same look.[51]

O'Leary, believing he saw a curtain in the cottage's window move, wisely ended the conversation. He and his fellow unarmed gardaí investigating the case knew that Dugdale's confederates were heavily armed and very dangerous. A gun could have been trained on them at that very movement. Any move to try to arrest her on the spot would have been imprudent, and possibly fatal. So as not to alert Dugdale or the other person in the cottage to his suspicions, he and his partner acted nonchalantly. "I didn't drive off right away, because you wouldn't want to alarm them," he said. "We sat there for a minute or two, pretending just to chat, then I turned the car and went back down the road."[52] O'Leary returned to Creedon in the police car and remembered the orders he had been given: any officers who located the robbers must call for help. The officers were not even provided a radio; they would have to travel back to their station to make a confidential call.

After the police drove off, Rose walked from her cottage to speak with Con Hayes, who was at his barn. She said to him, "I had visitors today, like some forces. What did they want?" Hayes replied that they were members of the local gardaí and it was probably about the stolen paintings. Dugdale replied, "Oh yes, I read about those in the papers." At that point, Rose asked if she could again Hayes's car. He gave her the keys, and she drove off.[53]

Back at their post in Rosscarbery, O'Leary and Creedon hurriedly contacted divisional headquarters and reported their findings to

Superintendent Thomas Barrett. Arrangements were made for a police gathering point, and a large group of uniformed and plainclothes gardaí, armed themselves with automatic weapons in preparation for a major arrest of a dangerous gang. O'Leary determined that Con Hayes's black Morris Minor had left and headed for Glandore at around 2:00 pm. Within an hour, as Rose was staring out at Sherkin Island off the pier at serene Baltimore, the contingent of heavily armed police, joined by some military men, were speeding to get to the Hayes farm before she returned.

O'Leary suspected that she wouldn't be gone long, and he and the large team of gardaí awaited her return[54] along the road to the Hayes farm, while others went to her empty cottage and were let inside by the landlord. Within, they found the three brass clocks that had been stolen from the Beits, as well as a Swiss passport belonging to another woman and Sir Alfred's diary, with several pages torn from it. They also saw that all four beds in the home had been slept in, and found several pairs of men's trousers and suits in different rooms around the house. It was clear—all four members of the gang had used the home.[55]

Shortly before six o'clock, Rose decided it was time to leave the serenity of Baltimore and return to the cottage, where she suspected that police might be awaiting her. She had always known the day would come when she would be made to account for her militancy. She had expected worse from her trials after the raid on her family estate. But now, she was the ringleader of the biggest heist in history and wanted on a number of serious charges related to Strabane, gun-running, and an armed hijacking. Nevertheless, she continued on the road to Glandore.

By six o'clock, the black Morris Minor was spotted en route back to the cottage. Police pulled onto the road behind Dugdale as she went past and followed her to the cottage in what was essentially a low-speed pursuit. "She didn't make any move to drive away," Sergeant O'Leary remembered.[56] Rose said, "I could see the roof of a car down under the brow of the hill, and it was quite clear that we were being surrounded . . . that the cops were around to look for us or to arrest us."[57] Police approached her carefully as she climbed from the automobile and took her keys. Rose remained calm, still speaking in broken English and maintaining her French cover.

"Are you Rose Dugdale?" the police asked.

"That's for you to find out," she replied.[58]

When she was told by police that they were going to search the house, she replied, "I believe you have a warrant." But the superintendent informed her that he didn't need one, as permission was granted by the owner, Con Hayes.

Rose acknowledged that she was responsible for what was in the house, telling the police, "I rented it myself." Then police asked for keys to the bedroom doors, as she had left them locked behind her. She handed them over, and behind the first door they unlocked were three of the stolen Beit paintings: Rubens's *The Cavalier*, Goya's *Portrait of a Woman in a Black Dress*, and Velázquez's *The Servant*.[59] Meanwhile, an officer opened the Morris Minor and found three large bundles wrapped in red paper. Inside were the rest of the stolen paintings.

Rose Dugdale was arrested for the theft at the Russborough House. "She wasn't offensive at all," O'Leary recalled. "I think she realized the game was up."[60] Before the police took her away, Rose, ever mindful of the struggles of the working class, turned to Con Hayes and said of the rent she owed, "I hope to make good the remainder of the money."[61] She was then transported to Bridewell Garda Station in Dublin, under heavy garda and army escort, including a parade of squad cars and six jeep loads of soldiers. Rose ducked beneath a blanket held by a detective in the back of a police vehicle.[62]

## THIRTEEN
### *Proudly and Incorruptibly Guilty*

Eighteen of the recovered Russborough House paintings were transported by armed guards to headquarters in Dublin, while one, the Vermeer, was taken to Blessington for identification by Sir Alfred Beit himself. He looked at the precious canvas with a sense of great relief and confirmed for a police technical services officer that it was indeed his painting. On May 6, ten days after it was stolen, *Lady Writing a Letter with Her Maid* was handed over to James White at the National Gallery, along with the rest of the stolen art, for treatment by paintings conservators.

On that very same day, Detective Sergeant Peter Jones, of the Flying Squad at Scotland Yard, acting on an anonymous tip, drove to a cemetery in St. Bartholomew the Great's Churchyard in London's financial district. He scoured the grounds, and there, propped up against the back of an old headstone, he found a small package wrapped in newspaper that had been tied closed with string. Inside, just as the tipster—and, earlier, Nella Jones—had promised, was *The Guitar Player*. Despite some slight moisture on the precious painting, detectives announced that the masterpiece was "in quite good condition." Kenwood House's curator, John Jacob, instantly recognized the original seventeenth-century stretcher and the wooden dowels along the edge of canvas as authentic. "It's beginning to show signs of damp," he said with an air of certainty, "but it can be made good." He added, "The people who took it obviously didn't know how to look after a painting of this delicacy and it will take some weeks to restore it."[1] Like the Beit paintings, it would be turned over to the care of trained art conservators who would correct the dampness and minimize its effects. Police found no evidence at the scene or in the package to aid their investigation into who had been holding the stolen Kenwood House Vermeer, and curiously stated that they were certain that the tipster could be of no further help to the police. They did not reveal how they had come to this suspicious conclusion, but no one was ever arrested for the crime.[2]

Meanwhile, news of the recovery of the Beit paintings spread throughout the media, each headline some variant of the Associated Press's "Millionaire's Daughter Held as Irish Art Theft Solved" and "Rich Girl Rebels: A Classic Case."[3] It made for excellent copy. Rose's comments at the sentencing phase of her earlier court appearance for the theft at Yarty Farm appeared in newspapers from London to Los Angeles, as armchair psychologists considered her motivations. Her story relegated word of the recovery of the Kenwood House Vermeer to lesser notice in later pages.

The fallout from the thefts of the two Vermeers included demands from the public for cultural property to be better secured. Sir Hugh Leggatt wrote in *The Guardian*, "Clearly there is a vital need for international cooperation on the problems of security of works of art and the rejection of any pressures that may be brought to bear in connection with them." As to the recent spate of ransom demands connected to art theft, he opined, "Organisations throughout the world should declare publicly that under no circumstances will they yield to any financial demands whatsoever from those who have stolen artistic treasures."[4] Member of Parliament Ernie Money wrote, "It is to be hoped that the Governments of Britain and Eire, where treasures in public and private collections and their guardians may continue to be at risk, will not take the present situation very seriously indeed and will adopt every active and effective step to safeguard both against what we hope is a transitory but very real and very vicious menace."[5]

Kenwood House curator John Jacob, who better understood the realities and limitations of working in a museum environment, was asked after the recovery of *The Guitar Player* by an interviewer, "What are you going to do about security?" He was much more pragmatic than the editorial writers, saying, "Well, we are improving our security, obviously." But he added, "This is an historic building; we have to watch that we don't destroy the amenity in making people more secure."[6]

Police continued their dragnet for the three criminals who had accompanied Rose Dugdale at the Russborough House. From the Hayes family, they knew that the man purported to be Mr. Merrimee had stayed in the rented bungalow. They had seen him sitting in the car when Rose came to rent the cottage, his face intentionally obscured by a newspaper. They also saw him approaching the rental on a motorcycle, but this time a helmet prevented them from getting a look at his face. Most recently, the reports in Donegal were that when Rose had departed the property soon after the visit by Officers O'Leary and Creedon, her husband was in the passenger seat of the Morris Minor. At least three witnesses in and around Baltimore saw her accompanied by a man while she was gone from the cottage, with one making note of her trademark speedy driving style. One even saw the man get out of the car and enter a supermarket to buy a bottle of wine. But none of the witnesses were able to provide a useful description.

Con Hayes said that he estimated his car had been driven about seventy miles during the few hours Rose was speeding around with the unidentified man and the sixteen masterpieces.[7] Her mysterious actions raise more questions than answers. Later in life, Dugdale provided a vague description of her activities, leaving out key details and the names of her companions: "We managed to load a number of paintings into the car in order to try to take them somewhere else because we had a call from the guards, and I think we probably were a bit suspicious." So, ostensibly, she had left the three paintings back at the rental because she couldn't fit them in the Morris Minor with the other sixteen. She added that she wasn't certain whether she had been found out, but she "had a place in mind to leave some of the paintings safely, and, unfortunately, that didn't work out, so I had to drive the paintings back, and I did so."[8] Still, it's hard to imagine that nowhere in that vast open land could she find a place to stow the paintings better than back at the cottage, given very real possibility that the police were on to her. And if indeed the passenger in the car with her had been Eddie, why did he allow Rose to travel alone back to what was—at best—an uncertain fate at the cottage?

Investigators had hoped to elicit answers to these questions from Rose as she sat in the police station for her interrogation. But in the early hours after her arrest, police wouldn't confirm that their arrestee was actually Bridget Rose Dugdale because they hadn't obtained official acknowledgment from her that this was a fact. This was a major case—the biggest in history—and the garda had to make sure every step was done correctly, methodically, and beyond dispute. They would not build their case upon assumptions. But throughout, after she was told of her right to remain silent, Dugdale played the militant well, steadfastly refusing to provide her name or confirm her identity. For three days she carried on with the ruse, willing only to say, "I did not commit any crime." She would not even remove her brunette wig.[9] It was a method that Gerry Adams himself had employed when he was arrested, reasoning that the longer he could delay an investigation beyond his identity, the more difficult it would be for police to make a case against him.[10]

Dugdale maintained her stoic silence when transferred under heavy guard to Mountjoy Prison in the center of Dublin, the very prison from which IRA Chief of Staff Seamus Twomey, Kevin Mallon, and two others had escaped via helicopter just six months earlier. On her second day there, a prison matron gave a guard a telegram to be delivered to her. The guard recounted that the message was addressed to Dr. Rose Dugdale. "I went to her cell where she was writing a letter," the guard said. "I told her that I had a telegram and I handed it to her. She looked at the address and took the paper out of the envelope. I asked her if she was accepting the telegram and she replied that she was."[11] It was the closest thing to a confirmation the authorities could muster.

Undaunted, investigators went about the work of meticulously reconstructing her complicity in the crime by analyzing every bit of evidence they uncovered in the cottage and in the stolen cars. They even identified the blue tailored skirt suit she had worn at Russborough House.[12] Police also found something else important during their investigation: along with Dugdale's, the fingerprints of a man named Thomas McFeely were discovered inside the rented cottage. McFeely, twenty-five, a blocklayer, had been arrested just days before along with a companion, Desmond O'Connor, twenty-one, by the gardaí, and the pair were later accused of being members of the IRA before the Special Criminal Court. Soon after his arrest, the gardaí visited McFeely at Portlaoise Prison and told him that Dugdale had been captured. In the true Republican manner, he replied that he had nothing to say. He also refused to appear in a lineup before the victims from Russborough House, as was his right. McFeely was never charged with participating in the art heist.[13]

Another suspected IRA man's name was on the garda radar. Harry Duggan, the Provo whose father had been told his son was killed in paramilitary activities—but had, in fact, merely faked his death and assumed the identity of Michael Wilson—is believed to have been involved in the heist. Duggan was said to have been tagging along with Dugdale, Gallagher, and another man for a major operation.[14] When Dublin police fingerprint experts traveled to confer with Scotland Yard, the alleged dead man was wanted for questioning in relation to multiple crimes, the Russborough House heist among them.[15]

Given the demands for the release of the Price sisters and their cohorts, Rose Dugdale's status as a committed and wanted Republican sympathizer, and the discovery of McFeely's fingerprints in the holiday cottage, police naturally suspected that the IRA was behind the Russborough House heist. But despite the aforementioned connections, the Beit robbery was not a sanctioned IRA operation. While his unit was working with some contact with the IRA council,[16] Gallagher was known to be a maverick, dissatisfied with the hierarchy of the Provisionals and their chain-of-command policies, and more than willing to act on his own wild impulses. And while Dugdale was steadfastly committed to the cause, no one was willing to lay claim to her. The *Irish Times* opined, "No Irish separatist should have any illusion about the British Government's attitude to art treasures which were not directly related to its own treasury. There seemed to be, at the very least, muddled thinking, and it did not seem to many to be muddled Irish thinking,"[17] the latter point perhaps a dig at Dugdale's British nationality.

Sources in Dublin reported that no IRA operation would involve openly renting a cottage in a locale where strangers would be instantly recognized. Instead, the IRA would have taken one of the Beits hostage (as Sir Alfred himself had expected) and gone underground in the city.[18] In fact, some in the Republican movement were downright angered and even somewhat embarrassed by the heist. According to one high-level IRA source, "People like Dugdale, who are in revolt against their upbringing and perhaps feel a bit guilty about their comfortable situation in life, should stay out of our business and leave the fighting to the people who know what they are doing."[19]

David O'Connell, the senior officer on the Provisional Army Council, was described as "furious" about the Beit robbery. He felt that the heist was stealing headlines from the actual hunger strike, which had been making some headway in recent months. Though the Dugdale caper had the tactical purpose of aiding the Price sisters, O'Connell knew full well that the British government would not trade terrorists for paintings, regardless of their value. And from an operational perspective, the roadblocks he encountered throughout Ireland were not good for the business he and his men meant to conduct. They interfered with highly secret talks between senior IRA officials and a well-known Unionist politician from Ulster planned for the day after the heist.[20] In a television interview, he strongly denied any connection between Rose and the Provos. O'Connell said:

> Well, Dr. Dugdale was not a member of the Republican Movement. She was known to personnel in the Movement. She had been to Derry way back in the days of the Civil Rights and so forth. From what one knows she was a very dedicated person, one with deep convictions . . . However, it is a known fact that the IRA was not involved in procuring any of those [Beit] paintings.

"Was she ever a member of the Provisional IRA?" O'Connell was asked.

"No, she was not, no."

"Did she ever want to become a member?"

"I couldn't say so, if she had expressed any desire to become part of the movement. As I say, she was not unknown to us."

"Did you know her?"

"Not personally, no," said O'Connell, who reportedly had met her some years earlier.

"Well, where was she in terms of the Movement?"

"Well, she was on the fringe."

"Was she much talked about before the robbery?"

"Not really, no. She wasn't, no."[21]

O'Connell's claim of Rose's obscurity in Irish circles was backed up decades later by the former mayor of Limerick and Labour Party politician, Frank Prendergast. "No one knew who she was until the Russborough House robbery came to light," he said. "It was a huge media story. That was the first time we had heard anything about her." Prendergast even recalled resentment among the everyday Irish citizenry. "The ordinary community here disliked Rose. They didn't accept her. She came from a privileged background in England. She was a former professor. It's believed her parents were affluent people from the aristocracy. She must have had an independent Republican outlook on life. I don't know how she became immersed in Irish Republicanism," he recalled, adding, "but she was very serious about it."[22]

Serious indeed—enough to refer to the IRA as "our army" and to describe herself as an "Irish freedom fighter." But these were likely careful semantics. Journalist Marina Warner, who profiled Dugdale after the Russborough House heist and trial, said that Rose had "appointed herself to this role."[23] She added that though Rose won "unofficial comradeship" with the Provisionals, in her absence she was the subject of their mockery.[24] Rather than being a member itself, it seems that Rose's only connection to the IRA was Eddie Gallagher, and Eddie and the Provisionals held each other at arm's length. But in a very real sense, it didn't matter whether Dugdale was an official Provisional—she might not have been theirs, but their cause was certainly hers.

Defending the movement was at the forefront of her mind when she first encountered her Garda inquisitor, Detective Chief Superintendent Anthony McMahon. Her first words to him were pure Republicanism: "Do you consider yourself a good Irishman, or do you agree you have betrayed your country?"[25] Strong if not curious words from a British woman indeed, but McMahon was unaffected. He had been through enough tough interrogations to take insults in stride. And he knew that he had her in a spot from which she could not squeeze free. No judge was going to look the other way this time and issue a perfunctory slap on the wrist, as had happened at Exeter Crown Court after the raid on her parents' home. She had ventured into the very real world of what the authorities viewed as terrorism.

In all, Rose Dugdale was charged with ten counts under the Larceny and Firearms Acts related to the Beit heist and the bombing attack at Strabane in January. At her initial court appearance on May 7, she refused to speak. She would neither acknowledge her name nor reply when twice asked if she was seeking bail. Dressed in an open-necked blouse and a mauve cardigan under a green coat with shiny brass buttons and wine-colored slacks, she contemptuously refused to even turn her eyes to the bench. Only when the short hearing ended did she remark, "There are still four hunger strikers in England, and the British are still in occupation of a small part of Ireland, but not for long."[26]

Rose's father, Colonel Dugdale, yet further disheartened and exasperated by his daughter's latest exploits, told the media that he was without answers. "I've done everything I can for her. She knows perfectly well she could turn to me if she wanted to," he said. "The whole thing is tragic."[27]

Still, his daughter remained defiant. At her next court appearance at Dublin's Special Criminal Court on May 17, the judge declared that her trial would be held the following month, on June 24. A grim, frowning, unafraid Dugdale stood and leaned forward on the mahogany rail in front of her in the dock. Speaking in an affected brogue, she took the opportunity to admonish the Court as a bevy of police surrounded her: "I stand in absolute condemnation of the Government of Ireland, which, trading on the victories of our army in the North—"

The judge tried to interrupt, but it was pointless. This was her moment. She continued, "The Government of Ireland is wheeling and dealing with a government of murderers, assassins and torturers in London. This execrable government is torturing four of the bravest Irish people ever to walk this land . . . I propose to go on hunger strike until the demands of these four people are met. Consequently, I shall be in a considerably weakened state by the date you envisage."[28]

When she finished, the judge, who remained unaffected, reiterated the June 24 date. As the police stood to lead her down from the dock, Rose's demeanor suddenly changed. Her pale blue eyes sparkled, and she smiled as she raised a clenched fist and shouted to the courtroom, "Up the Provos, the People's Army!" One reporter noted that even some of the police cracked a grin at her fervor.[29]

Two weeks into Rose's own hunger strike, when it was reported that she would only take tea, coffee, and water, a spokesman for the Department of Justice assured the press, "There is no reason to believe she is very ill or very weak."[30] The same could not be said of the four Irish prisoners back in England, as the state of their health had become dire. Dolours Price wrote her mother at the end of May 1974 that "physically we are pretty worn out, even to walk to the loo drains us and the least movement leave may heart pounding and beating like a drum. Every day passes and we fade a little more, but no matter how the body may fade our determination never will. We have geared ourselves to this and there is no other answer."[31]

But all was not lost. Just as David O'Connell had believed, there appeared to be some softening of the British government's stance regarding the movement of the Price sisters to Armagh Prison in Northern Ireland. The Home Secretary, Roy Jenkins, with whom the decision rested, was said to have an "open mind" on the transfer, a strategic and pronounced change in the government's position. Suddenly, there was a glimmer of hope for the survival of the Price sisters, Gerry Kelly, and Hugh Feeney.

Then, fate dealt a grim hand in their favor. Michael Gaughan, an Irish prisoner and Republican movement organizer, who had been on a hunger strike for two months, died at Parkhurst Prison on the Isle of Wight on June 3. Though the official cause of death was pneumonia, his family maintained that he had died as the result of a force-feeding tube having pierced his lung, allowing food to become lodged within.[32] Gaughan's death was a major development in controversy over hunger strikes by Republicans in British jail cells and forced the British government's hand over its treatment of Irish inmates demanding to be treated as political prisoners. At Gaughan's funeral, David O'Connell defiantly gave the graveside oration despite the heavy presence of police and his status as a very wanted man. The director of public prosecutions wisely discouraged police from arresting IRA marchers at the services for fear of an angry backlash. O'Connell was not apprehended.[33]

Gaughan's death had important implications for the Price sisters, Feeney, and Kelly. On June 7, when Home Secretary Jenkins again showed his hand by publicly stating they would come to serve the majority of their sentences near their homes in Northern Ireland, the four ended their hunger strike. Though no date for their transfer back to the North was provided, they had received what they had demanded— an assurance that they would be treated as political prisoners and allowed to serve their time at home in the North. For the Price sisters, it meant they would be sent to Armagh Prison, where they would be the third generation of women in their family to be incarcerated in the ancient jail.

Word of the cessation of the hunger strike spread fast and wide, and Rose Dugdale also ended her solidarity hunger strike upon hearing the news. The Department of Justice released a simple statement: "Dr. Rose Dugdale this morning resumed eating food."[34] No word of thanks for her efforts was extended by either the Price sisters or their compatriots—not publicly, anyway. But Rose was not in this for thanks or recognition. As Walter Heaton had explained, she wasn't one for personal relationships; rather, the greater goal of a united Ireland was where her sights were set.

One June 24, 1974, Rose Dugdale stood trial for the heist at Russborough House. She was tried alone—no accomplices had been apprehended, and she had no interest in cooperating with the police. Though the hunger strike had ended a few weeks earlier, its effect on her was clear. She was gaunt, with circles under her eyes. Her skin appeared gray, her breath labored.[35] But she was ready for her turn onstage and appeared happy, wearing a smart blue suede jacket over a white blouse and smiling at friends in the public gallery.[36]

The trial itself was somewhat pro forma. The prosecution had all the evidence it needed, having recovered the paintings in Rose's possession, and finding supporting evidence solid enough to build an airtight case against her. Their confidence was such that they even dropped the art theft charge, feeling it unlikely they could fully prove that she was at Russborough House that night. Yet though a guilty verdict was the obvious outcome, the trial provided Dugdale with a theater in which to perform her dyed-in-the-wool role of revolutionary. When asked how she pleaded, she declared herself "proudly and incorruptibly guilty!"

From the very start, it was apparent that she wished to utilize the trial for political purposes, a tactic that she learned and admired via other revolutionary movements. Her attorney was Myles Shevlin, a legal adviser to the Provisionals. Shevlin, perhaps sensing that his client wasn't seeking the sort of defense customarily provided in a case of this magnitude, asked the court for permission to be released from his duties. Rose interjected, saying to the judge, "I beg you, I beg you to let me speak briefly in explanation." But the judge would have none of it, steadfastly informing her, "This is not the appropriate time."[37]

While before the Special Criminal Court, Dugdale made every attempt to put her disrespect for the government on full display, refusing to wait patiently for "the appropriate time." Throughout her court appearances, she often sat with her feet up on the rail. She interjected loudly and derisively, such as when Chief Superintendent McMahon testified about her background and upbringing in Britain. She challenged McMahon's testimony. "Anything that occurs to an English person in England has no relevance to the proceeding of this so-called court in the Republic of Ireland," she said, mixing up the traditional IRA parlance of "the so-called Republic of Ireland."[38] When McMahon continued, she again interjected, "That information has been obtained from somewhere. I wish to know where it was obtained. The right of this gentleman to give this evidence is dependent on where and by what means the information was obtained."[39] But when she was given the opportunity to conduct a cross-examination of the witness, she used her time not to contradict his testimony but to point out contemptuously that "an Irishman must go to discover what the English Government had chosen to do with the freedom fighters in Ireland." The court, as required, asked Rose if she would like to give evidence or call witnesses. She wished for neither. She had already entered a guilty plea. Now she wanted the stage. She had been awaiting this moment for some time, and had carefully prepared to deliver what would essentially be her manifesto:

> I have answered your question of this morning—proudly, incorruptibly guilty. I stand proudly here as the perpetrator of a calm political act to change the corporate conscience of a Cabinet. There will be, and there could be, no trial today. There is no court of justice that I can see, and there is no crime that I can apprehend, for where is the right of this court, your right, to put us on trial, to intern us and deprive us of our freedom to fight for Ireland and the freedom of the Irish people? You have no such right. I hold that the whole people of Ireland have and are solely entitled to the wealth of this land which they labored to produce. The wealth of this land may not be appropriated from them. It neither belongs to the Englishman nor his Orangeman Carsonite lackey, nor his Green Tory lapdog in Dublin.[40]

Rose was parsing her words carefully. While she spoke of "us" when referencing freedom fighters, she was careful not to insinuate that she was part of those whose labor produced Ireland's wealth. Along these lines, she continued:

> No, I am not on trial. I don't count, despite your efforts to prove otherwise with the Garda, the military and their armor surrounding this court. What you had hoped to have on trial today is the justice of our cause, to absolve you in the treachery of your ways and the

treachery of the ways of this Government. We will not stand idly by, said our great Republican bipartisan Government, just before the British went out to murder 13 Republicans in Derry, but it seems you were prepared to collaborate with the English as they tortured six brave Irish prisoners* in English jails and murdered one Michael Gaughan.

Dugdale went on to make the odd claim that the IRA "has defeated the military power of Britain in what she claims to be on her own streets." She pointed criticism at politicians like John Hume (who would later be a co-recipient of the Nobel Peace Prize), whom she claimed did nothing but "cry out to the English who had ruled Ireland for 800 years in unrivalled barbarity and cruelty," asking them to keep the British Army in Ulster. She warned that the British should "fear the people of Belfast who have gained nothing but poverty and death from their enslavement by the British Government." The people of Ireland, she said, were giving their lives that others might be free, yet were being betrayed. She closed with an angry flourish:

> Yes, I am guilty and proudly so. If guilty has come to describe one who takes up arms to defend the people of Ireland against the British tyrant who would deprive the people of this land of their wealth, then I am guilty. But you stand accused and are found guilty in the judgment of the people of Ireland who must suffer under English rule. Here you are guilty of treacherous collaboration, and you stand accused and guilty of betraying some of the bravest men and women who in the history of this country have gone out to fight for the right of Ireland to be free.

"You cannot defeat us ever," she said coldly. "The tyrant will be brought down. Victory is with the army of the people."

---

* In addition to the Price sisters, Gerry Kelly, and Hugh Feeney, Dugdale was now including Gaughan and Frank Stagg, who later died in February 1976.

Returning to the matter at hand—her sentence—she told the court, "For how long you sentence me has no relevance to anything and no importance. I regard it with the total contempt that it deserves."

All the while, the judge fixed his gaze on a side wall in the room, paying no mind to the defendant's oratory.

Journalist Marina Warner reported that though Dugdale's speech read well, the delivery, perhaps affected by the earlier hunger strike, was "excruciating to hear." She added that it was "labored, repetitive, and disjointed."[41] The *Times* of London called it "almost incoherent." But Rose had accomplished what she had set out to do. She paid no mind to the facts of the Russborough House case, offering neither excuses nor apologies. She never touched on the topic of the paintings other than to repeat that she was indeed guilty. Rather, her soliloquy was focused solely on what she saw as tyrannical British rule in Ireland aided by an Irish government uninterested in protecting its own people. As she sat back down in the dock, she again put her feet on the rails and nonchalantly flipped through the newspaper. She had barely enough time to make it to the back pages: the three-judge panel returned in just forty-five minutes and sentenced Rose Dugdale to nine years in prison. She turned immediately to the crowd of sympathizers, one of whom, a woman, had shouted abuse at the police, and gave a clenched-fist salute.[42]

Immediately after the trial, she was escorted back to Mountjoy Prison under the heavily armed security presence that had surrounded her since her capture. Once she was processed out of Mountjoy, she was then taken to a waiting helicopter for transit to Limerick Prison, where she would serve her sentence. The helicopter arrived at her new home under continued strict security. Police and prison officials, worried about another embarrassment, conducted drills to practice the chopper landing during the days leading up to her arrival. To their great relief, it went off without a problem.

Ever a magnet for controversy, Rose's speech had caused a stir with censors for the national public service media of Ireland, RTÉ. The network
refused to broadcast three specific parts of her speech, arguing that they
contravened a controversial law aimed at preventing material considered
to promote the aims of any organization "which engages in, promotes,
encourages, or advocates the attaining of any particular objective by violent means." The first offending statement was her claim that there was
no crime, "for where was the right of the court to deprive [her compa-
triots] of their freedom to fight for Ireland?" The second, that Rose said
the Republic owed its very existence to the fact that others had fought
and died for this principle. The third was perhaps the most objection-
able to the censors: "We have the right to take up arms in reclaiming the
wealth of Ireland for her own."[43]

The decision to ban sections of Dugdale's statement caused an
outcry from Irish journalists concerned with the stifling of relevant,
important news coming out of an Irish courthouse, especially during
such a high-profile case. The censorship was widely criticized in the
Irish Republic. One editorial argued that though "the philosophies put
forward in her defence by Miss Dugdale are questionable to say the
least . . . any censorship of an accused's explanation must be regarded
as unethical." Besides, it argued, "what has happened now . . . is that
Miss Dugdale's remarks have been given an importance out of all proportion to their worth."[44] The *Irish Press* agreed, saying "It was surely
an error of judgment that the brief extract from what she said should
have been excised or censored under the vague shadowy umbrella of
the directive issued to RTÉ." However, they called it a "misuse [of] language in a way in which no native English speaker should be guilty" for
her to have described her crime as a "calm political act."[45]


Rose still had to answer charges for the bombing at Strabane, and on
November 25, 1974, she was back in court for that trial. A month earlier,
she had made a brief preliminary appearance in court shortly after a

visit at Limerick Prison from her parents, who said their daughter's situation was "a very painful subject" but that prison conditions were good.
Rose remained silent in the dock, again refusing to answer even the most
basic questions. Nevertheless, she made news at the short appearance.
This time, it was what she was wearing: along with her suede jacket and
pink open neck smock blouse and slacks, Rose was sporting a simple gold
wedding ring.[46]

There was no husband present, however, when she entered the dock
to answer for her crimes at Strabane earlier that year. As soldiers armed
with machine guns surrounded the courthouse and officers from Special
Branch searched people entering the building, Dugdale entered her plea:

> I stand here today in shame and in anger at what is being done to
> the people of Ireland. The army of the people of Ireland, which
> will shortly free this land for once and for all of the English tyrant
> does not plead before traitors and abject slaves, who are traitors to
> the cause for which hundreds have died over the past 800 years and
> for which men at the moment are lying down their lives. I refuse to
> plead. I refuse to recognize the right of this court to bring me here
> to answer any charge.[47]

At the Strabane trial, Rose was not alone in the dock. The two young
toughs from the bombing, Patrick Treacy and Eamonn McNulty, also
stood trial for their crimes. The pair, twenty and eighteen years of age,
respectively, followed Dugdale's lead like she was their personal Joan of
Arc, refusing to recognize the court and enter pleas. Default "not guilty"
pleas were entered on behalf of all three. It mattered little—the government's case against them was rock-solid. Highly credible witnesses
provided detailed and damning testimony. A priest from Ards Friary
who had happened upon the men loading the bombs onto the helicopter
testified to what he'd witnessed. Fingerprint expert Detective Inspector
William Byrne told the court that a palm mark found on the road map
left behind in the chopper came from Rose's right hand. He also found

McNulty's prints on the ordnance survey map and Treacy's at the hotel.[48] An explosives expert, Lieutenant Colonel James McDevitt, testified as to the makeup of the bomb. He stated that he found a length of cortex detonating fuse extended through a hole in the lid of the milk churn. Inside the churn were fourteen sticks of the explosive gelamix as well as some nitrobenzene. All told, he approximated the bomb to be about one hundred pounds. Perhaps most interestingly, the device was shockingly amateurish—a sign that the bombing at Strabane was not an official IRA operation. Lieutenant Colonel McDevitt told the prosecutor that in his view, lighting the fuse would not have been an effective method to ignite the bomb. Rather, it needed an electrical detonator or time fuse detonator.[49]

The most compelling witness was the helicopter pilot, Captain John Hobday, who was both victim and eyewitness. He had met with "Stephanie Grant" on multiple occasions, and he had little doubt as to her guilt. He told the court exactly what had happened nine months earlier with exacting detail. At one point, as Captain Hobday testified, Rose suddenly interrupted, complaining that she was being held "like an animal in cage" and that visitors from England who had traveled over to Ireland to see her were not allowed access during the previous lunch break. As to the fact of the case, her only protest was to question the propriety of the court considering Hobday's evidence from Strabane, which she said was outside the court's jurisdiction. To ensure a fair trial, the judge adjourned to consider her claim, but it was soon denied.[50]

It took little time for the court to find Rose and her two underlings guilty on all five charges related to the helicopter hijacking at Donegal, as well as the related guns and explosives charges. After the verdict was read, and as had now become practice, Rose burst into a political speech. She said that the people of Britain did not know why their sons were dying in Northern Ireland, and that they should demand withdrawal lest the war there escalate "in violent and savage retribution."

The judge tried in vain to interrupt, arguing that throughout the trial he had been lenient with her, but she went on. Finally, the judge ordered

the gardaí to remove her from the dock. As they neared her, McNulty
and Treacy defiantly stood between them and their mentor like the apos-
tles at Gethsemane. It was a sweet gesture of loyalty from the young
men, but it was easily overcome by the trained officers, who took control
of Rose and led her to a cell beneath the courthouse.[51]

Sentencing came later that morning. McNulty and Treacy were given
six years in prison, with lesser charges to run concurrently. Dugdale was
given a much stiffer sentence of nine years in prison, but, mercifully,
the judge ordered that the nine years be served concurrently with the
Russborough-related charges. She would have a longer criminal record,
but she wouldn't serve any extra time for it. Again, she was offered the
opportunity to speak, but her earlier removal to a cell had dampened her
spirit. She replied, "You prevented me from speaking. You insisted on
hauling me from the dock with a lot of wasted breath."[52]

While the sentence was something of a break for Rose, not everyone
was pleased with the judge's decision. One Ulster politician complained
that the sentence made a farce of the Irish government's efforts to be
tougher on terrorists by letting Dugdale go virtually "scot free."[53] But
the fact was that Rose certainly was not going free. She was again transported under heavy security to Limerick Prison where she would spend
the rest of her thirties. There would be no more hearings, trials, or
speeches. Instead, she would ostensibly spend her days staring at the
sky through iron bars, chatting with fellow prisoners, and waiting for
the years to pass until she could again fight against British colonialism.
And her lover—the man whose ring she wore—was yet to be caught or
charged for his role in the crimes they had committed together.

ABOVE: Rose Dugdale photographed in the flat she shared with Walter Heaton. *From the author's personal collection.* BELOW: Russborough House in County Wicklow, Ireland. The home of Sir Alfred and Lady Clementine Beit, and the scene of Rose Dugdale's Vermeer heist. *2020 Joanna Barry, joannabarry.com.*

ABOVE: Rose Dugdale raises a defiant fist in Tottenham. Just days later, she would depart for Northern Ireland. LEFT: Rose's parents Lt. Col. James and Caroline Dugdale make their way to Exeter Crown Court, where their daughter stood trial for an art theft at their country estate. *Both from the author's personal collection.*

LEFT: Walter Heaton and Rose Dugdale raise their fists in solidarity with the Soledad Brothers, three African-American inmates charged with the murder of a white prison guard in California. *From the author's personal collection.* BELOW: The helicopter used by Rose Dugdale and her accomplices in the bombing at Strabane. *Photo by Victor Patterson.*

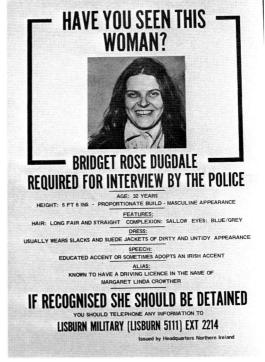

ABOVE: Empty frames litter the otherwise elegant setting of the Russborough House after a group led by Rose Dugdale stole 19 paintings including *Vermeer's Lady Writing a Letter with Her Maid*. *From PA Images / Alamy Stock Photo*. RIGHT: The wanted poster issued for Rose Dugdale by the British Army in Northern Ireland. *Photo by Victor Patterson.*

ABOVE: Eddie Gallagher is escorted by Special Branch officers from the siege house at Monasterevin where he and Marion Coyle surrendered to Irish Police. *Both from the author's personal collection.* BELOW: Rose Dugdale's son Ruairi is taken to court in Dublin to see his father Eddie Gallagher stand trial for the kidnapping of Tiede Herrema. He is held by his guardian, Betty O'Neill.

*The Love Letter* (oil on canvas), Johannes Vermeer (c. 1669–70). Stolen from the Brussels Fine Arts Palace in Belgium in 1971 and recovered less than a month later. *From Rijksmuseum, Amsterdam, The Netherlands / Bridgeman Images.*

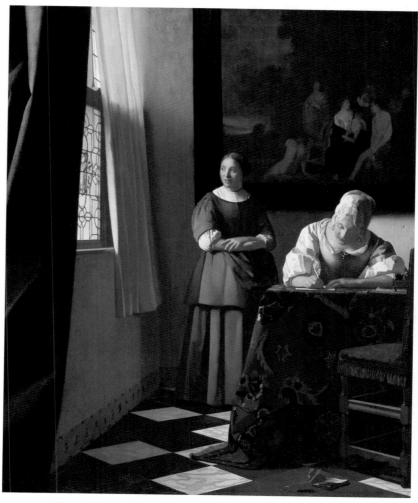

*Woman Writing a Letter with Her Maid*, Johannes Vermeer (c. 1670).
Stolen from Russborough House in 1974 and recovered soon after.

*The Guitar Player* (oil on canvas), Johannes Vermeer (1632–75). Stolen from Kenwood House in 1974 and recovered shortly after The Russborough House paintings were recovered. *From The Iveagh Bequest, Kenwood House, London, UK / © Historic England / Bridgeman Images.*

# FOURTEEN

## A New Life on the Inside

W hile Rose was shuttling between court appearances and her cell at Mountjoy Prison, Eddie Gallagher remained a very active paramilitary, building on a reputation for wild and daring exploits that earned him the moniker "Mad" Eddie Gallagher. He was said to be serving as an adjutant under an important figure in the early days of the Provisionals, Brendan Hughes of County Tyrone. A former Provisional source described Hughes as a militant "who later did his own thing and was basically an armed robber with no political affiliations."[1]

Gallagher continued to conduct military operations without the approval of the IRA's leadership.[2] One August evening in 1974, Eddie and a friend, Richard Behal, went to a pub in Portlaoise, where they drank until closing and left with two women they knew from Republican circles. They all climbed into Behal's car to visit a friend, but they didn't get far. Before they could leave, Eddie had a gun pointing at his face through his window. At the other end of it was a Special Branch officer who, along with his partner, sent the girls away. "Mad" Eddie put up a fight with the police that resulted in both his and Behal's arrest.[3] He was charged with unauthorized possession of a revolver with the intent to endanger life and assaulting a garda.[4]

Gallagher, who had previously served time in Curragh Prison for IRA activity, was this time incarcerated at Portlaoise Prison, not far from where he was arrested. The facility was considered one of Ireland's most impenetrable prisons[5] and housed a large number of IRA, including Kevin Mallon, who had been recaptured after the helicopter escape from Mountjoy with Seamus Twomey and sentenced to twelve months for IRA membership. Eddie immediately joined a group of eighteen other IRA men in a plot to break out of the prison that had been in the works for nearly two months. The group was chosen among the 150 Provisionals at Portlaoise "because they have vital links in the campaign in the North," and because of the length of their sentences, a source told Kieran Patton of the *Irish Press*. There was no point in breaking out men whose releases were imminent.[6] Gallagher wouldn't have to worry about getting used to his paper-thin mattress—the escape would happen on only his second day in Portlaoise.

On August 14, 1974, at just around noon, the prisoners enacted their daring plot. They attacked the prison guards in their wing, and after what was described as a "short severe struggle," they over-powered the unarmed officers and took their keys and some compo-nents of their uniforms. With the guards subdued and keys in hand, the nineteen men were able to access an adjoining flat roof from which they could jump to the ground. There were still two obstacles between them and freedom. As they ran to the first—a gate at the governor's residence—an officer in an observation post saw them and sounded the general alarm. Officers grabbed weapons and hurried to posts from which they could fire, but when they aimed in, they saw a number in the cluster wearing the familiar tunics and hats of prison guards. Unsure if some among the group were their brother officers giving chase, they were forced to hold their fire lest they hit friendly targets.[7]

The nineteen prisoners stopped at the gate at the governor's resi-dence and detonated an explosive charge that had been smuggled into the facility. The blast opened the gate. One guard on the opposite side of the wall was fooled by the uniform disguises and yelled to them, "No prisoners came out this way," before realizing what had happened. The escapees repeated that measure when they got to the second gate at the exterior wall. Again, the explosives worked. The armed prison officers were by now sure that all the men—including those in uniform—were escapees, mainly because the prisoners' shaggy hairstyles were starkly different from the regulation haircut of the guards.[8] They opened fire, but fortunately for the IRA prisoners, none of the bullets met their targets. The escape, which took just minutes, went perfectly.

The nineteen made their way to the nearest road where they began hijacking passing cars. A sixty-three-year-old factory worker was out for a Sunday drive with his wife when one of the men, whom he took for a prison guard, ran up to the car and waved for him to stop. "The man with the cap and guard uniform ran to my door and ordered me out while the others jumped in the back and told my wife to leave," the shocked man recalled. His wife was pushed to the ground as the car sped off. Another couple were on their way to a wedding when they were run off the quiet road. The escapees treated the driver roughly, dragging him from the car and kicking him in the stomach after throwing him to the ground. His wife was pushed into a ditch.[9] A Bass ale van and a Health Board minivan were also taken over. The escapees drove to Mountmellick in central Ireland, and witnesses told police that they were headed north toward Tullamore.[10]

Hundreds of officers mobilized to give chase, but their pursuit was made more difficult when ten pubs in the area received bomb threats just after the escape that required local police attention.[11] A Provisional source told the *Irish Press*'s Patton that senior Provos held a meeting to plot how to get the escapees to safety,[12] and the calls were undoubtedly made by accomplices to distract and limit the responding gardaí. Despite the frantic efforts of police, the men were long gone, and, once again, the Irish government had suffered another embarrassing escape from one of its penitentiaries. In the wake of the helicopter escape from Mountjoy, the government in Dublin, including the Irish prime minster, Liam Cosgrave, had assured the public that they would shore up security. In fact, just a month before the escape, defenses at Portlaoise had been significantly tightened, with a 60 percent increase in joint garda-army patrols and intensified searches of visitors.[13] Yet, somehow, gelignite had been smuggled into the place government officials believed the most secure in which to hold IRA men, even making its way to a special wing for political prisoners.[14]

Of the nineteen men who escaped, Eddie Gallagher and Kevin
Mallon were the most notorious. There were suspicions emerging that
Eddie was connected to Rose Dugdale, but no one went on the record
to confirm this. When it became clear that he was one of the escapees,
authorities at Limerick Prison implemented a tight watch on Dugdale
out of fear that an attempt to break her out might be imminent.[15]

There was no secret, however, about Kevin Mallon's reputation. Not
only had he been involved in the infamous helicopter escape just six
months earlier alongside senior IRA figures, but the thirty-six-year-old
fugitive was believed responsible for planning a series of bombings in
London. He was considered one of the six most wanted men in the
North.[16] In October 1974, Mallon was identified by a police officer
when he and a protégé, twenty-year-old Marion Coyle, attempted
to enter a dance in Portlaoise. As the officer apprehended Mallon, a
struggle ensued, and Mallon yelled to Coyle, "You have a gun, use
it!" Marion, an IRA member who had a reputation for her militant
loyalty to the Movement, pulled out a Beretta pistol and tried to shoot
the officer, but the gun misfired. She was grabbed by a second officer
and brought into the dance hall and arrested. Incredibly, at trial later
that month, Coyle was acquitted by the Special Criminal Court due
to the failure of some of the officers to positively identify her. Coyle,
who refused to acknowledge the court, represented herself admirably
in front of Mr. Justice Pringle, the same judge who would preside over
Rose Dugdale's trial for the bombing at Strabane just weeks later.[17]
That wasn't Coyle's only connection to Dugdale. She had since become
associated with the renegade Active Service Unit headed by none other
than Eddie Gallagher.

It's not a coincidence that both Mallon and Gallagher had been
arrested in the vicinity of Portlaoise Prison. The men were committed
to efforts to break prisoners out of the jail, and just seven weeks before
their own escape, police had found an eighty-foot tunnel that extended
from the shrubbery outside of a psychiatric hospital to beneath a road
and cottage, intended to meet a manhole in the prison yard. The time

they spent near the prison also provided them with an intimate understanding of the route out of Portlaoise to freedom after the jailbreak.[18]
Indeed, breaking fellow Provisionals out of prison became something
of an obsession for Gallagher. He would later tell journalist Eamonn
McCann that he and Kevin Mallon had "made a pact to help each other
escape if we were imprisoned."[19]

In 1974, journalist and documentarian Tom Mangold conducted extensive research for a BBC-1 documentary and subsequent article on Rose
Dugdale's incredible odyssey from privileged youth to her incarceration
at Limerick Prison. His piece ended with the claim that she was "now
the most famous woman prisoner in Limerick" and asked what would
come next for her. "Attempt a daring escape? Go in for a hunger strike
or two?"[20]

Mangold's suspicions that she wouldn't sit quiet would prove to be
accurate, if not understated. She was already winning some sympathy
for her exploits. Back in the United States, the *New York Post* wondered
whether she was merely a well-intentioned "Robin Hood for the IRA."[21]
Lisa Lansing, her old friend from Mount Holyoke wrote, "I have to con-
fess that I'm sorry they caught her."[22]

Little did any of them know that Mangold's hypotheticals would
become reality, or that she would quickly be back to making international news. In December, not feeling herself and untrusting of prison
officials, she chose an unconventional method of pregnancy testing:
"I discovered by smuggling out a bottle of urine and putting it to be
tested and discovering the answer . . . from my solicitor who's now
dead, and he wrote me a letter saying the answer to your . . . question
is 'definitely yes.'"[23]

Despite a thorough and intrusive search upon being processed into
Limerick Prison, no had noticed that she was with child. Philip Bray, a
prison officer at Limerick, remembered that he was "at a loss to explain
how no one spotted that Rose Dugdale was four months pregnant when

she was admitted," adding that "the first the prison authorities knew of the situation was when the contractions started."[24]

Dugdale's parents were also taken by surprise by the news and met it with a measure of skepticism. When she had last appeared in court seventeen days earlier, Rose hadn't appeared to be pregnant, perhaps due to the loose clothing she had worn. Questioned by the media about the reports of the pregnancy, her mother, Caroline, said, "We just don't know anything about it. I am supposing that it is a hoax for publicity—it won't be the first one she has played on us. When my daughter sees fit to tell us perhaps we shall know what is happening."[25] One can forgive Mrs. Dugdale for her skepticism, given Wally Heaton's provocative but false claim a year earlier that Rose was carrying his child.

The discovery of her pregnancy and imminent delivery set prison and government officials into a frenzy. Dugdale described the Limerick doctors as "hardly medical practitioners" who had "panicked because they didn't want to let me out."[26] Rose was a high-risk inmate and arranging to move her to a proper medical facility on short notice presented a complex logistical problem and security nightmare. Security surrounding her incarceration had already been estimated to cost an additional £3 million over the life of her sentence.[27] When the prison doctor at Limerick called in a gynecologist, who immediately suggested that Rose be moved to the local maternity hospital, the recommendation was refused after a cabinet meeting held by Prime Minister Liam Cosgrave on December 12. The cabinet declared that Rose would "be allowed to give birth to her baby in Limerick prison but, if the gynaecologist in charge, Dr. Holloway, should consider that in order to cope with medical complications or difficulties, recourse to hospital facilities is necessary, the mother and/ or child may be removed to the hospital in Limerick." They also ordered that the garda and army be alerted to stand by in case security cover was needed.[28]

Privately, the Irish government decided that the Justice Department spokesman should only say publicly, "I do not myself know anything about this matter, and I do not propose to make any enquiry about it since it is the practice of prison authorities not to give information about the personal affairs of persons in their custody."[29] The government would do all it could to avoid having to make any comment on the matter at all. It was a wise decision. There was no easy answer as to how to deal with a famous prisoner with dangerous allies who was about to give birth.

Given the government's decision that the delivery of Dugdale's baby would take place behind bars, the local hospital's "flying squad" scrambled to construct a makeshift maternity ward inside the penitentiary, bringing into Limerick Prison the materials and equipment that would be used for any other attended birth on the outside.[30] Rose remembered, "They needed to construct a maternity ward within the jail, so they put two cells together and erected a couple of very bright lights in the corners." Though she does not remember whether she was administered an anesthetic,[31] she told an interviewer that she was handcuffed to the bed during labor.[32]

Rose's baby, a son she named Rauirí, was born happy and healthy on December 12, 1974. The prison's visiting committee members described him as "exceptionally beautiful and placid," and the prison announced that both mother and child were "very well looked after" and treated "with great humanity."[33] Rose remarked of her newborn, "He's going to be a guerilla."[34]


Almost immediately, because of the unusual nature of the delivery and the mayhem that was Rose's life, questions naturally emerged as to who the child's father was. Bouquets of flowers from unnamed well-wishers arrived at Limerick Prison to celebrate the birth.[35] Within days, rumors were swirling that he was one of the nineteen IRA Provisionals who had recently escaped from Portlaoise Prison and had remained a fugitive.[36] And, to add to the mystery and speculation, she was already wearing a wedding ring. But she provided no answers. Meanwhile, in an English prison, Walter Heaton was crestfallen. His lover and soulmate had become pregnant after a mere three months away from him, and her pledge to avenge him would never be fulfilled. She didn't even bother to mention him in her long, rambling courtroom speeches.

Heaton said, "The first I knew of her being pregnant was when I was in Wandsworth prison. A letter came through her solicitor giving me what turned out to be just 24 hours' notice of the birth, but I didn't know who the father was at the time." In her letter to Wally, Rose wrote that she was sure Walter would understand. Her confidence was misplaced. "I didn't at first," Heaton said. "I was hurt and filled with jealousy and indeed hatred, but these emotions go, and we carried on writing to each other."[37]

For the first time in years, Rose Dugdale's focus was now on something other than revolution, if only momentarily. The arrival of little Rauirí brought her an unexpected joy. "Having a baby in jail made a great pleasure of being in jail, of the jail experience," she said, reminiscing on that time in an interview late in her life. "There was always the child in the cell. He was a lovely child, and he would smile, wake up smiling, always smiling cheerfully. It's not as if he understood that he was in jail. So, it made a big difference I suppose for all of us prisoners, but as well for myself."[38]

Rose knew that the pleasure wouldn't last for long. It was clear to her that the government was not about to release her from prison simply because she had given birth, and she also knew that her son could not live in prison with her. Limerick prison guard Philip Bray said that the rules there were simple: "A new mother is allowed to keep her child while she is feeding it, but once the baby is weaned, it is removed from the prison."[39]

Rose prepared herself for the coming adjustment to life without Rauirí, contemplating how a prison upbringing was no sort of infancy for her son. In a rare show of domestic sentimentality, she was wistful: "It wasn't much of a life for him, anyway. I mean, he wouldn't see an animal, he wouldn't see a car."[40] She made secret arrangements through

Eddie Gallagher for their son to find a proper home with loving care-takers. After all, Eddie was a fugitive actively fighting the Loyalists and in no way prepared or able to care for a baby. But still, as Rose said, "he was the father of the child and it was very important that he had some part in seeing the child." Eddie "discovered a family out in Meath where they had two adopted kids and would be happy to care for a third one, and they cared for the child."[41] Little Rauirí's caretakers were Repub-lican lorry driver John O'Neill and his wife, Betty, of Blackstone Estate in Navan, County Meath.[42]

Rose's repeated reference to her newborn as "the child" as opposed to "my son" or his given name was telling. There was no question that she cared for Rauirí, but she lacked the motherly instinct that unconsciously leads a woman toward affection as opposed to detachment. "I have to say that my own childhood and subsequent life meant that I was not very maternal and didn't really do the job terribly well," she would admit decades later.[43]

It would later be revealed that Ruairí's godparents were also com-mitted Republicans. For godmother, Provo Marion Coyle, the protégé of Kevin Mallon and a friend of Eddie Gallagher's, was chosen. Inter-estingly, Martin McGuinness was named godfather. McGuinness (who claimed to have left the IRA by 1974)[44] was one of the most important figures in the Republican Movement for the better part of three decades, having traversed an odyssey that led him from being a senior member of the IRA in Derry, to chief of staff for the Provisionals, and then to minister of Sinn Féin, where he played a key role in the peace process.[45]

In later interview about her time in prison, Rose self-consciously made it clear that she was up to the rigors and tribulations of incar-ceration. Eager to portray herself as a battle-hardened militant, she would reflect on her time at Limerick Prison, "I wasn't counting the days to my release."[46] It's a striking comment coming from a mother who had given birth soon after imprisonment only to have the infant wrest from her and sent away. She did acknowledge that when she first arrived and found there were no other Republican prisoners, she felt some isolation, even when comrades eventually landed at Limerick.[47] Born with an unmistakable intellectual curiosity, she used the end-less idle hours and solitude to brush up on histories of Ireland and nineteenth-century Russian novels.[48] In time, the acclaimed author Iris Murdoch, who knew Rose from Oxford, wrote to the Irish ambas-sador to Great Britain, urging the government to make more books available to her. She offered the somewhat elitist argument that Rose "wishes to study but cannot, a terrible extra punishment to an intel-lectual person." She added, "Condemned to reading thrillers, in the company of uneducated IRA ladies, she is most likely to emerge an embittered urban guerilla." One suspects that if Dugdale had seen this letter by Murdoch, she'd have been incensed by the characteriza-tion of the female Republicans. However, "embittered urban guerilla" certainly wasn't derogatory to Dugdale; rather, it read like her vision for the ideal epitaph. Murdoch also made it clear in her letter that she disapproved of Dugdale's crimes. "Needless to say I detest her actions and views," but, she added, "this loss of serious reading is a grave matter, not least because any hope of 'a change of heart' lies in the possibility of reflection."[49]

In fact, Rose and her sister prisoners at Limerick already had access to a wide range of reading materials. She submitted to prison authorities a list of books she wished to have available, and the requests were granted. She could also choose from a prison collection stocked by the City Public Library and was allowed to buy one newspaper of her choice each day. She could also purchase *Hibernia Magazine*, *The New Yorker*, and *Scientific American*.[50]

The vast hours spent reading are not at all to suggest that she became a docile prisoner, studiously surrounding herself with literature and intellectual pursuits in her cell. Complacency was never Rose's nature, and she was as difficult and insistent a prisoner as she had been an advocate at the claimants union, forcefully slamming her fist on the desks of bureaucrats. Steve Coughlan, Limerick's representative in the Irish Parliament, called her "one of the most demanding prisoners ever . . . living better than some in a top-class hotel." He added that Dugdale was "a grave embarrassment to the prison authorities and the Irish Government."[51] In one notable instance shortly after she gave birth, she made a formal request to prison authorities that they construct a squash court "to provide for her physical development." Such requests for what he deemed "special treatment," especially on the heels of the controversial accommodations she received when she gave birth to Ruairí, riled Coughlan and others.[52] Complications over her incarceration were such that rumors that the Irish government was considering deporting Dugdale back to her native Britain hit the newspapers.[53]

Her protests weren't limited to sport and recreation. When she came to believe that letters and presents sent to her by friends outside the prison to celebrate her son's birth were being banned, Dugdale began her second hunger strike in late April 1975, accepting only liquids in protest.[54] Her health suffered so much that security officials mounted a round-the-clock watch on her condition and were said to have prepared a plan to transport her from Limerick Prison by helicopter to a hospital if it worsened.[55] Word of her fast spread to Portlaoise Prison, where Republican prisoners there staged a short hunger strike is solidarity and out of concern for her health.[56] The Committee for the Defence of Women Political Prisoners, comprised of representatives of ten radical, Republican, women's, and civil rights organizations, also announced in a circular that they would demand an improvement in conditions for Rose, stating that she had been refusing visits because of the "barbarous circumstances" under which they were allowed.[57] Dugdale finally ended the strike after a grueling thirty-four days, during which she lost a significant amount of weight, when Limerick authorities made assurances to her that all mail items would be delivered.[58]

Passive protest wasn't the only sort of trouble Rose made for prison officials. Later in her term, she and other Republican women threw a pot of boiling water at a guard over what they complained was their lack of privacy while fixing snacks. She and her cohorts barricaded themselves against responding guards and had to be forced out of the kitchen with water hoses.[59] More seriously, and though she had not yet had a visitor, prison officials discovered in February 1975 that a hacksaw blade had been somehow smuggled into the prison to her. Rose had used the blade, which officers found among her possessions, to begin cutting through a bar in her cell. Authorities also found that a bar in the women's bathroom had been cut out, and that discovery, combined with the sighting of two men with Republican ties parked in a car near the bathroom, raised suspicions that there was a serious movement afoot to break her out of jail.[60] The media, keen to rumors as to who had fathered Dugdale's child, reported that a "27-year-old Provo of Bally-bofey, Co. Donegal . . . was seen in Limerick recently. He's on the run after bursting out of Portlaoise Prison."[61] They were now all but naming Eddie as Rose's partner and hinting that he might have been behind the escape attempt.

Provisional prison escapes and attempts at such were, by 1975, nothing new for Irish prison authorities. They were well aware that high-profile Republican inmates were especially likely to be the subject of breakout plans. So, there was heightened attention on Dugdale. But she presented something of a special case, as credible sources insisted that there was no liaison between Rose and the Provisionals. The *Irish Times* reported that "her links are closer with the Official wing of the movement, but even those members have shown little interest since she was taken to Limerick Prison last May."[62] Nevertheless, law enforcement authorities remained suspicious. In May, when a British colonial chief justice was the subject of an attempted kidnapping, some speculated that it could have been part of an attempt to win her release. And when bombs were discovered and safely removed from three Limerick hotels a few days after, investigation naturally included possible ties to the town's most famous inmate.[63] The Provisional IRA denied any connection to the plot.[64] But even behind bars, Rose Dugdale remained a source of consternation for government officials. There would be more to come.

# FIFTEEN
## Love and Marriage

As an official inquiry into the hacksaw found in Rose Dugdale's cell was announced, there was much bigger news dominating the British and Irish media. On the evening of February 9, 1975, the Provisional Irish Republican Army announced an indefinite stoppage of its offensive military action in Northern Ireland and Britain to begin the following day. The British secretary of state released an optimistic statement, saying, "A genuine and sustained cessation of violence can be the basis of a more constructive and peaceful future for Northern Ireland."[1] Though it seemed an important step forward after years of intense violence and loss of life, it wasn't universally popular. From prison, Gerry Adams was vehemently opposed to the truce, describing it as injurious to the IRA.[2] Veteran senior Provo and Sinn Féin politician John Kelly agreed, telling *Frontline* in an interview, "I think it disrupted the Republican movement and . . . it achieved nothing and people felt betrayed by it and they felt uneasy by it . . . and there was a lot of infiltration at that time by the British intelligence into the IRA. And that, all of that combined to make people very wary of the . . . situation."[3]

Eddie Gallagher, never one to support leadership, fiercely opposed the IRA cease-fire and remained committed to conducting his militant and sometimes dramatic operations without their authority.[4] Given the lack of enthusiasm on the part of many important Provos of the era, it didn't seem like a risky position. But Mad Eddie had a way of pushing boundaries.

In reality, Gallagher didn't really care what the prevailing sentiment of the IRA was at the moment. His personal loyalties would dictate his actions. In January 1975, his friend, Kevin Mallon, was yet again arrested following his escape from Portlaoise. For the police, it was an important rearrest. Mallon, a twenty-year veteran of the Troubles, was considered by British authorities to be the IRA's top explosives man and was suspected in a bombing that had killed twenty-seven in Britain. Police found him in the fashionable Dublin suburb Foxrock not long after he had met with Protestant churchmen to negotiate a cease-fire in December. His arrest despite these efforts was considered by Republican leaders a bad-faith move on the part of the Dublin government.[5]

With Mallon back behind bars, Gallagher was keenly aware of the vow the pair had made with each other—if either were to be imprisoned, the other would work to break him out. His fraternal commitment to Mallon was shared by Marian Coyle, but it didn't compare to his love and longing for Rose Dugdale. She had captivated him completely— Rose was the sort of woman who could instill an adoring devotion in her mate, and to Eddie she was both lover and leader. Even Walter Heaton still held her in high regard late into his life despite her having completely abandoned him. While Wally eventually resigned himself to letting her go, the much younger but equally passionate Gallagher could not abide being without her.

Eddie would have to devise a plan to get them both out of prison. But he faced a dilemma: the two inmates were held in separate institutions. Moreover, though he had no compunction at all about the use of violence, there was an unwritten rule amongst the Provisionals not to harm or kill Irish prison officers. He told Eamonn McCann, "After every escape or escape attempt, prison security was tightened until it became impossible to free prisoners without killing guards . . . Against that background, we couldn't justify an escape attempt which could cause the death of an Irish guard, warder or soldier." So, Gallagher decided, "New tactics were needed."[6]

Eddie was committed to nothing less than the simultaneous release of his friend and his lover. He knew exactly what to do, and that he'd have to do it watching his back, because it would be an operation that ran afoul of long-established Republican rules. Therefore, he decided to keep his plan quiet, recruiting only Marion Coyle and a small band of trusted members of his Active Service Unit to help, and that he would not seek approval from leadership. In a later interview with Eamonn McCann, Gallagher said, "At one stage we just refused to tell them what we were about to do, in case we were ambushed when we arrived to do our job."[7]

Coyle was no alien to danger and was intensely loyal to her mentor, Mallon. She would take very little—if any—convincing. Further, as a member of Gallagher's dissident ASU, she had already earned his trust, and her mettle had been tested in ways that defied her young age. Thanks to his suspected role in a number of bank robberies and his status as a fugitive, Gallagher was high on the Garda list of wanted criminals, so he couldn't wait long to act. The time was now.

In 1975, the Ferenka, Ltd. Factory in Limerick was the biggest employer in the county. With upward of 1,400 workers, the steel cord plant was an essential part of the lives of virtually everyone in the small town of Annacotty where it had been built. But operations for the Dutch company were rarely smooth. Even before Ferenka opened its doors, construction of its new plant was interrupted by a labor strike. Later, picketers marched on the building over electrical contractors used at the jobsite. But despite the dustups, the *Irish Times* was rife with advertisements for jobs with the new employer, and thanks to Ferenka, a 1973 story in the *Irish Times* proclaimed, "Survey shows job opportunities best in Limerick."[8] It was a time of hope in a place longing for prosperity.

By the spring of 1975, however, Ferenka's production was already stumbling and 160 workers were made redundant. The managing director in Limerick, Dr. Tiede Herrema, presented a plan to contain redundancy, including a two-week shutdown and a retraining program that would stop the bleeding.[9] It wouldn't bring back the lost workers, but it would keep the firm on course into autumn, when production was forecasted to increase.

Herrema was a popular figure in Limerick—a middle-aged gentleman with an athletic build and bearing that had served him well as a Dutch resistance fighter facing off against the Nazis during World War II. Despite having been captured and brutally interrogated before spending time in a concentration camp for prisoners of war in Poland, he wore a constant, genuine smile.[10] He was a warm man with gentle eyes and a friendly Dutch accent, and he and his wife, Elisabeth, had grown very fond of Ireland and its people.

On the morning of October 3, 1975,[11] Herrema pulled out of his garage to make his way to an early work meeting to show a group of Americans around the Ferenka plant. He was less than two hundred yards from his home on Montaleen Road when he was flagged down and ordered to stop by a police officer who approached his vehicle and asked, "Are you Dr. Herrema?" Puzzled, he answered, "Yes, I am." The police officer drew a gun and ordered him out of the car. The Dutchman complied and was forced into the back seat of a Ford Cortina and blindfolded. This wasn't an arrest; it was a kidnapping.

His captors, mistaking him for a German, asked him the name of the German ambassador to Ireland. "I'm Dutch," Herrema replied, to the surprise of his interrogators. Herrema, who had been in tight spots decades during the war, was completely unaware as to why he was being kidnapped. "They were frightened," he sensed, noting that his kidnappers were two men and a woman, all seemingly as anxious as he.

Finally, after about forty-five minutes, the car came to a full stop. Herrema could hear the sounds of animals and realized that he had likely been brought to a farm. He was dragged from the car and shoved into a small, uncomfortable room in a safe house in Mountmellick near the Slieve Bloom Mountains. He was pushed onto a bed, and his hands and feet were bound; then he was left alone in the dark. Even blindfolded, he could tell that the room was dusty and dirty, and an ugly odor overwhelmed his heightened olfactory senses. Hungry and unaware of his surroundings and totally at the mercy of his unknown tormentors, he thought about what might be next.

The kidnappers then showed their hand, placing a phone call that would provide investigators a clue as to their identity. Speaking with the Dutch embassy, the gang made its demands to attaché Eric Kwint: Dr. Herrema would be killed within forty-eight hours if three Republican prisoners were not released. The caller then provided the prisoners' names: Republican James Hyland, a hedge cutter by trade and a fellow member of Gallagher's rogue ASU, and Gallagher's friend and key Provo Kevin Mallon, both of whom were incarcerated at Mountjoy Prison, and Rose Dugdale, of Limerick Prison. It was later suspected that Hyland's name was thrown in to clumsily try to divert attention from the obvious connections between Gallagher and Dugdale and Coyle and Mallon.[12]

Dugdale's name was no surprise to authorities. They suspected—with good reason—that the hacksaw blade discovered in her cell had been sent by Gallagher. But there was yet a better indicator that her freedom was the basis for the plot. Less than two weeks before Herrema was taken, Special Branch had learned that a woman visiting Rose was found to be carrying a letter from Eddie Gallagher that told her to be "ready." The note stated that a kidnapping to secure her release would be executed and that they would soon be reunited.[13]

Herrema noted that throughout the ordeal, while kidnapper Marian Coyle remained cold and silent, her partner Eddie Gallagher was markedly nervous. The stress on him manifested itself in intense, almost unbearable neck pain. Mad Eddie had good reason to be so tense. Not only was there a nine-thousand-man strong nationwide manhunt in progress, the biggest in the nation's history, that might lead to his capture or even death, a group far more dangerous than the Garda was in hot pursuit—the IRA.

The *Irish Press* reported that an attempt to kill Gallagher had been made in Kerry just prior to the kidnapping and that both Gallagher and Coyle had been "disowned by the Provos for not adhering to the rules of the organization."[14] The *Sunday Independent* reported that the pair had been placed on a "Provo death list for the misappropriation of funds,

accounting to more than £300,000."[15] Moreover, from its very beginning, the Provisionals had been opposed to kidnapping as a policy, and
in a statement about the Herrema affair, the Irish Republican Publicity
Bureau said, "We have been asked to state that neither the Republican
movement nor any of its members had any involvement in the kidnapping of Mr. Herrema. Furthermore, it is not the policy of the Republican movement to differentiate between Republican prisoners in seeking
their release."[16]

Provisional IRA sources told an *Irish Times* reporter that they had
been looking for Gallagher for a month before the kidnapping and
said that he had left the group several months earlier over his dis-
satisfaction with the cease-fire. He and other "dissidents," the source
said, had formed a "maverick" group and friction between it and the
Provisionals was growing.[17] It wasn't just friction at issue, however.
Eddie was believed to be refusing to give any money to the Provo
leadership from the bank robberies he was said to have committed.[18]
As a result, an IRA gang of twelve heavily armed men was reportedly
"scouring the country for former Provo Eddie Gallagher," who, they
believed, had gotten his hands on £200,000 taken in a bank job in
Navan during the summer. A source told journalist Noel Smith that
Gallagher was an optimist who remained focused on his objective,
regardless of his resources: "He never gives up once he sets his mind
on doing something and in this case that something is springing Rose
Dugdale."[19]

Optimism, however, was not what Tiede Herrema was hearing
from his captors. He feared that he would be killed by his captors, one
of whom refused to speak to him and the other, Gallagher, showing
flashes of anger and violence brought on by his anxiety. At one point,
Gallagher struck Herrema in the mouth with his revolver, breaking
one of Herrema's teeth. He would often sadistically press the barrel of
his gun to Herrema's head to let him know that he held his life in his
hands.[20] Herrema remained calm and humanized himself by engaging
in conversation with Gallagher, who especially liked speaking about

politics with him. From the discussions, it was clear that Eddie's views had been molded by Dugdale. Herrema wrote in his diary, "He's very emotional. He seems to be intelligent, but he has no school education. He uses a lot of slogans and terms about politics and Marxism but he doesn't really know what it means, I think."[21] Still in his twenties, the farm boy Gallagher was in the development stage of his intellectual awakening, knowing just enough about his cause to be a militant but not enough to be an expert. Rose was not only his lover and the mother of his child, but clearly his teacher and guru as well. In fact, Herrema noted that Gallagher didn't speak of his newborn child at all. Aside from politics, he spoke most often of Dugdale. His strong feelings for Rose were at the forefront of his mind, even under incredible stress.[22]

As Herrema lay on the bed, still bound and blindfolded, he could hear the radio in the next room as Gallagher monitored the news. He heard the demands that Gallagher and Coyle had made, and the call for Dugdale's release must have made perfect sense to him. He also heard that the kidnappers had demanded that his Ferenka plant be shut down.[23] The company complied, ordering a closure of the plant that kept its 1,200 workers home with pay. Eddie would later tell a close friend that he had been offered $2 million to release their employee.[24] But it wasn't money that he wanted; it was Dugdale.

While he would not stand in the way of the Ferenka offer, Prime Minister Cosgrove was not nearly as willing to accede to the kidnappers' demands. He had endured the embarrassing escape of too many Republican prisoners from Irish penitentiaries. Moreover, when his intelligence team heard rumors of a possible plot to kidnap government ministers in the months prior to Herrema's seizure, his Cabinet had agreed at the risk of their own lives that there could be no capitulation in the face of even the most serious demands.[25] The Minister for Justice, Patrick Cooney, made clear the government's position. "The Government has no choice," he said, reasoning that any concession would "place the State in jeopardy." Instead, Mr. Justice Cooney appealed to the people of Ireland to come forward with information that might lead officers to the location of Tiede Herrema.[26]

Meanwhile, the massive manhunt continued. IRA sympathizers grew weary of the repeated searches that Gallagher and Coyle had caused with their unsanctioned exploits. In a statement, Sinn Féin said it believed "that the abduction serves no useful purpose and we call on those responsible to release him."[27] Herrema's wife and children pled for his freedom. Trade union leaders called off a planned strike and led workers on a march through Limerick denouncing the kidnapping and calling for the freeing of their boss. And the Provisional IRA repeated it denials that it had anything to do with the matter.[28] Sensing growing pressure, Gallagher and Coyle decided to change locations. They traveled to 1410 St. Evin's Park, Monasterevin, in County Kildare, where a sympathizer, Michael Hall, allowed them to hole up within his home while he and his wife stayed elsewhere.

Shortly after Eddie and Marion changed venues, the police caught a break. A vehicle registered to Eddie was spotted in Tullamore, just fifteen miles from Monasterevin. Police took one of the vehicle's occupants, Brian McGowan, to Portlaoise for questioning that lasted two days. The seriousness of the matter and the chosen locale suggest that the interrogation was no friendly affair. McGowan was released and as one of the lead investigators drove him home, McGowan made statements about Gallagher and the kidnapping that led to his rearrest.[29] The next morning, officers from Special Branch raided the house in St. Evin's Park. Ironically, they had already searched the home the day before, but a quick-thinking Gallagher had hurried the group into the attic and kept Herrema quiet by threatening his life. This second visit was anything but quiet. Three shots were fired, followed by an eighteen-day standoff featuring threats, floodlights, snipers, a small army of police, and around-the-clock news coverage.

The nation sat transfixed by Gallagher's desperate gambit to free his lover. For her part, Rose was reportedly "dejected and silent" when she heard the news. Limerick officials granted her no special privileges, forcing her away from the dramatic events on television at 8:30 PM with the rest of the prisoners.[30]

Her parents were asked to speak with their daughter and request that she intervene. Her father told the press, "The Mayor of Limerick rang me and said would I speak to Rose on the telephone to try and get her friends to spare the life of this man. Of course, I could not refuse."[31] Colonel Dugdale added, "My wife and I spoke to her on the phone and did all we could for about five or ten minutes."[32] But his headstrong daughter would have none of it, believing that Gallagher's actions were justified. She remembered, "The screws came to me and asked me to talk to someone on the phone, I think essentially to get me to persuade Eddie to release Tiede Herrema. Of course not. I didn't have a one-to-one conversation [with Eddie], but I wouldn't have had one anyway and they wouldn't have allowed it. I wasn't interested in trying to argue against the intent of the operation, which I mean was fair play to anyone who was involved in it."[33]

Negotiations between Eddie Gallagher and the police dragged on for days. There were requests from Gallagher and Coyle for fresh clothes, food, and aspirin for their headaches and stress-related pain. Herrema even took to massaging a severe ache in Eddie's neck that caused him great distress. Finally, with the Irish government unwilling to budge on the release of even Rose Dugdale alone, Eddie and Marian Coyle surrendered, dropping their weapons from the second-story window that had been their refuge. The entire affair had lasted a total of thirty-six days—the longest such affair in Irish history.

Before leaving, Gallagher handed Herrema a bullet as a souvenir, remarking that it had been meant for him. Remarkably, the Dutch industrialist, just freed from his ordeal, held no ill will toward his kidnappers. He called them "problem children" that he imagined could have been his own.[34] In the decades to follow, Herrema would speak of Gallagher in only warm terms, with an unusual amount of empathy and forgiveness. He and his wife were later honored with honorary Irish citizenship and never lost their affinity for the country and her people. Two years later, the Ferenka plant closed.

Eddie Gallagher's trial would garner headlines, but only because of the enormity of the affair, and not because of any lengthy polemics. He and Marian Coyle mounted a defense that argued they had no choice but to try to free Rose Dugdale from captivity. Eddie made an unsubstantiated and fantastical claim that his son, Ruairí, had been born with two broken arms because of the brutal treatment his mother had allegedly suffered while pregnant. Marion claimed that Rose had been slashed in the face while imprisoned. Both claims were easily refuted by prison doctors.

In the end, the judge handed down harsh sentences for the kidnappers: Gallagher would serve twenty years for his crime, and Coyle fifteen. Spectators jeered and whistled at the sentences while some scuffled with the police. Eddie was threatening in his remarks to the judge, Dennis Pringle. Referring to a failed bomb the judge had received in the post at the start of the trial, Gallagher shouted, "Hey, Pringle, the letter bomb was a warning you did not heed." He added, "You have been sentenced, Pringle."[35]

Despite these ominous words, there would be no harm done to Pringle. Eddie would serve his sentence at Portlaoise Prison and Rose would remain at Limerick, where she was soon joined by Marian Coyle and making headlines yet again. There was the report that Ruairí's guardians, the O'Neills, had purchased a new luxury home and car three miles from their former house, with money gifted to them by her. "Rose wanted me to buy a farm or start my own business" said John O'Neill. "But I didn't want that, so she said: 'If you want a house buy a house. If you want a car, buy one.'" He added that for Dugdale, "money doesn't seem to be any problem." Reportedly, the money came to O'Neill through an Irish solicitor, and Mrs. O'Neill said that "some people might be suspicious, but Rose still has money." She also reported that there seemed to be a warming between Dugdale and her mother, who were writing to each other regularly. Mrs. Dugdale even painted a watercolor of Rauirí, and she and the colonel sent Christmas gifts.[36]

Rose wasn't done making demands of prison officials. In 1977, she and Eddie began petitioning the Irish government to allow them to marry while still in prison. Through their solicitor, Gordon Hayes, they argued on their behalf as well as their son's for a declaration that they were entitled to marry and that the Minister of Justice had violated the constitution in omitting to provide facilities for the marriage.[37]

It was a wild request: no such accommodations had ever been afforded prisoners in Ireland before. In August 1977, after eight months of trying, the Minister for Justice, Gerry Collins, that he had no personal objection to allowing the couple to marry, provided security could be arranged. His decision was believed to have been based on a recent Irish policy of relaxing prison conditions.[38] He would later add that he made the decision for the sake of their child's future.[39]

A year after they had begun making requests, the couple's wedding day finally arrived midmorning on January 24, 1978. Gallagher was transported into Limerick Prison under heavy guard by the army and officers of Special Branch, including one who was handcuffed to the prisoner. Wearing a blue suit, Gallagher met his bride, who was described as "radiant"[40] in her black velvet jacket and corduroy trousers. She sported a lovely white rose on her lapel and had also cut her hair. Their son was there with them—the first time the three of them were together as a family—and during the ceremony he often called out, "Mammy, Daddy," to his parents. The couple exchanged vows and silver rings, valued at £50 each and purchased by Ruairí's guardian, Betty O'Neill, who served as Rose's matron of honor. Eddie's brother Pat (who was also being held on a firearms charge) stood as his best man. Pat Gallagher reported, "Rose and Eddie embraced and kissed." He added, "There were no tears, but their meeting was an emotional affair and they were obviously very happy for their short time together."[41]

In addition to the ring, Eddie gave Rose the only wedding gift he could. Handing his bride a few sticks of chewing gum, he told her "these are my only worldly possession."[42] By 1:45 PM, Eddie was headed back to Portlaoise. The Catholic priest who had officiated the wedding remarked, "It seems against all natural laws that they were not allowed together for a while."[43]

Despite the brevity of their time together and the incongruous accommodations, the wedding was a success for Rose and Eddie. They had gotten their wish from the government, and were now joined in holy matrimony. The only damper on the event was the fact that Dugdale's parents were not in attendance. Caroline Dugdale told reporters weeks before the ceremony that though they still maintained "a great deal of affection" for their daughter, "nothing would induce us to go to this wedding."[44]

Both Eddie Gallagher and Rose Dugdale would remain behind bars in separate facilities, while their son lived with guardians. It was just the sort of odd domesticity one would expect from Dugdale, who had begun her adult life railing against the idea of being set up with a suitable husband during the debutante season. No marriage could have been as far afield from the aristocratic dreams her parents had held twenty years earlier than the one she had just entered.

# SIXTEEN

# *The Afterlife*

In October 1980, Rose Dugdale left Limerick Prison a free woman. She had served six years, the required two-thirds of her nine-year sentence. She had promised parole officials that she would settle matters with her parents, and that played an important role in the decision to release her.[1] It wasn't an idle promise—in fact, Rose and her parents had already reconciled. Caroline Dugdale reported as early as 1978 that she, Colonel Dugdale, and her daughter were "very friendly on a domestic level. We get letters from time to time. Although our politics are completely at odds, we just try to keep the door open. It's all we can do, and I'm sure any parent would do the same."[2]

By August 1980, media outlets were reporting that Dugdale would be freed sometime in October, and suspicions about the exact date of her release began when reporters learned that John O'Neill and Ruairí had been seen leaving Limerick Prison with a suitcase. O'Neill told the press that Dugdale would be let out the following Wednesday, but he returned a short while later and was allowed to drive into the prison facility. When he pulled out again, reporters were certain they'd see Rose in the car, but there was no sign of her. Ever the guerrilla, she had hidden in the trunk.[3]

Once it was revealed that Dugdale had indeed been released, the pursuit was on to determine where she had gone. O'Neill's car was followed by both reporters and detectives to Dublin, where she had settled.[4] Though she would later say that her time in prison was not "anything like a sufferance that a lot of people would think,"[5] one reporter described her as "looking the worse for wear."[6] Another remarked that she appeared "robust but pale," and "more gaunt" and walking with "stooping shoulders."[7]

Despite appearances, Dugdale was energized. "I've come out feeling much more strongly than when I went it," she told journalist David Beresford.[8] Indeed, she wasted no time getting back into revolutionary activities. This time she appears to have stayed within legal parameters, most likely due in large measure to the constant surveillance under which she found herself. She told *Gara* magazine, "The secret police constantly monitored my house until the 90s, and anyone visiting was at risk of being held and identified. But that didn't stop me from continuing with my militancy and all those years I continued with my work on all fronts of the Republican movement."[9]

Indeed, while rumors were circulating that she would run a Donegal pub as a socialist workers' cooperative,[10] she was again a full-time activist. Less than a month after her release, she joined the staff of *An Phoblacht*, a journal published by Sinn Féin.[11] Given her intellect and writing skills, the publication allowed her to the chance to use her education to further her cause.

That's not to say she stayed behind the scenes. She was a frequent speaker at marches, such as the numerous H-Block protests,* where she told the crowds that the men on hunger strike in Long Kesh were "inspired by a dream and a resolve that one day [Ireland] would be rid of all foreign influence. The British Government would let these men die," she said, unless the people made their voices heard "by going out onto the streets."[12] At another H-Block rally in Tuam, a curious and sympathetic crowd turned out to hear her speak.[13]

No longer was Rose merely a community advocate and behind-the-scenes gunrunner and financier. Her exploits and those of Eddie Gallagher had made her something of a celebrity, and her notoriety gave

---

* Republican prisoners in HM Prison Maze's H-Blocks staged protests when, in January 1976, the British government rescinded their Special Category Status as paramilitary prisoners. The removal of this status meant that the Republicans would be treated as common criminals rather than political prisoners. In response, Republican prisoners refused to wear prison uniforms and started the "Blanket protests," which evolved into the "Dirty protests" wherein Republican prisoners refused to shower or remove their human waste, instead smearing it on the walls of their cells.

a broader bully pulpit from which to spread her message of anti-capitalism and staunch Republicanism. It wasn't always productive. When she concluded an H-Block address in Donegal with "Victory to the hunger strikers, victory to the Provos," many felt that she had undermined the H-Block committee's efforts to stress its objectivity and neutrality.[14]

While Rose Dugdale found new ways to remain committed to Irish Republicanism, the family that she had started while incarcerated didn't quite fit with her new life. Besides, she was never one for the happily-ever-after story. Her relationship with Eddie Gallagher was short-lived. "Well you can't really continue a relationship when one is in jail and the other is in jail as well," she told RTÉ's John Murray. "It doesn't breed good relationships and it's very hard to share the ideas of the kind of Ireland that we're trying to build in those circumstances." It didn't get any easier when she was released and he still faced about a decade in Portlaoise. She added, "Of course we remain on friendly terms."[15]

Soon after Eddie Gallagher was released from prison in March 1990, after serving fourteen years of his twenty-year sentence, Rose sent Ruairí, now a teenager who had lived with his mother and attended school in Dublin, to spend time with him. It wasn't an easy adjustment. "Rory got to know Eddie a bit in the immediate years when he got released," she recalled to Murray. "You mustn't forget that he'd done a very long sentence and has had some awful effects that has done on a lot of prisoners."[16]

Though Ruairí maintained a close relationship with his mother throughout her life, Rose stayed true to her first love: activism. She set her sights on the heroin epidemic gripping Dublin at the time, joining the Concerned Parents Against Drugs campaign to force drug dealers out of local areas. While its intentions were plainly good, the group was the subject of controversy when it was suspected that the IRA was behind beatings meted out as punishment to dealers. Dugdale recalled that a conflict arose between supporters: "If the movement in Dublin at the time had decided that . . . the drug pushers needed to be confronted with weapons and the IRA was the ideal organization to do that . . . I think that would have been a very forced decision. I think that probably Sinn Féin, under some guise of the Republican movement, might have thought that this was a people's struggle and we needed to get involved in it and be seen to lead it."[17] The differing perspectives damaged the anti-drug crusade.

The most lasting effort Rose undertook was to join Sinn Féin veteran Jim Monaghan on leading the educational wing of the organization. Late into her life, she was active in attending and hosting seminars, and even though she was never fully accepted by the IRA, she continued to support the group. Reflecting on her life, she said in a rare television interview, "I think there is a sense in which it's the armed struggle I wanted to be a part of and that is always something that you have to learn, you have to learn how to do it, just as a class struggle, you have to learn how to do that, and it doesn't necessarily come instinctively to anyone of any class. And it wasn't that I wanted to become a member of the working class because I was never going to do that, but it seemed to me that I wanted to be good at helping that struggle to move forward."[18]

The April 10, 1998, Good Friday Agreement between the British and Irish governments, as well as the eight political parties of Northern Ireland, finally brought peace to Northern Ireland and an end to the Troubles. Rose saw it as a victory for the IRA. She told John Murray, "I think what the IRA achieved in the handling of the negotiations and the starting the negotiations, I mean they fought a war against the Brits and they fought them to the negotiating table and that is amazing. And they negotiated a deal that maybe wasn't satisfactory all the way across the board but that really isn't the point. They managed to succeed in establishing the structures of power in the North which could enable us to move on from the conflict."[19]

Well into her seventies, she can be seen in her wheelchair happily attending parades with Gerry Adams, the legendary and controversial Sinn Féin leader. The image strikes a stark contrast with Dolours and

Marion Price, who both late in life regarded Adams with contempt for a compromise with which they disagreed. Moreover, Dolours provided journalist Ed Moloney with interviews in which she names Adams as having ordered the murder of Jean McConville, the mother of ten alleged to have been killed for assisting British troops in Northern Ireland. When Dolours died suddenly at the age of sixty-two in 2013, her claims became public, casting Adams as a villain to some despite his Herculean efforts for peace. More than forty years after Rose stole Vermeer, she would be at stark odds with the woman whose battle she tried to fight.

In her golden years, Rose has become something of an icon in Ireland. She is occasionally honored at small community ceremonies in Dublin for her lifetime of dedication to the people of Ireland, as well as her work for Sinn Féin's educational branch. In 2010, Ogrha Shinn Féin, the youth wing of Sinn Féin, said of her, "Rose remains a personification of revolution. She had the option of a comfortable life . . . Yet she followed her instinct and threw her lot in with the revolution . . . when we honour the female activists who have participated in our struggle, we salute Rose Dugdale, as one of the very finest of that company. A revolutionary to her very core."[20]

To her mind, there could be no finer praise. In interviews, she is adamant that she has absolutely no regrets about the course she chose. She was not plagued by post-traumatic stress, as Dolours Price was. She remembers, and maybe even longs for, the time she spent as a militant, taking direct action to the extreme. In 2007, at a Sinn Féin conference, as she stood to back a motion, Rose Dugdale declared, "I'm here in support of the revolution—I mean the resolution."[21] Like old habits, revolutionaries don't die easily.

# EPILOGUE

Rose Dugdale will forever be remembered for the Russborough House heist, and for good reason. We are a world obsessed with size and accomplishment, and she pulled off the biggest heist of her age and was the first—and still only—woman to do so. The incredible story of that heist and the reasoning behind it have become somewhat obscured by the later thefts from the Russborough House. But the work of Martin Cahill and his gang, who in 1986 repeated her feat and copied her acumen in selecting paintings, does not lessen her audacious and notorious achievement. In fact, there can be no doubt that she was the impetus for Cahill's clever caper. Though his criminal intelligence was legendary, it's unlikely that he would have understood the immense value of the Beit Collection, for even the garda had been taken aback by it upon word of the Dugdale heist.

A mystery that does remain, however, was whether Rose was also the mastermind of the Vermeer theft at Kenwood House. Unless she comes forward now, in the autumn of her life, to answer this question (a question this author submitted to her, without response, through a trusted intermediary), we will likely never have a definitive answer. However, it is your humble author's opinion that she was indeed behind the heist of *The Guitar Player* prior to the Russborough House theft. The evidence for this conclusion, though circumstantial, is convincing, and the similarities between the heists at Kenwood and Russborough Houses are striking.

First and most important is the combination of the timing and the cause. In both cases, valuable art was stolen with the stated intent of forcing the British authorities to honor the demands of the hunger-striking Price sisters and their compatriots. The four staged their protest with the primary purpose of forcing their transfer from prisons in Britain to cells in Northern Ireland where they could serve out their terms as political prisoners. The heists were within just two months of each other, and right at a time when the condition of the Price sisters was increasingly precarious and, as a result, a major news story on an almost daily basis. The timing of the heists was also interesting in that the Kenwood House theft was committed on the very evening that Rose officially became a fugitive, perhaps giving her reason to quickly launch plans to trade a masterpiece for the transfer of the noteworthy Republican prisoners. That the tip that led to the recovery of *The Guitar Player* came just a day after the recovery of the Russborough paintings was also suspicious. Even the ransom demands made by the Kenwood thieves lead to hints that perhaps Rose was involved. First, the comment by the Irish caller about making love above the painting while it was under the bed perhaps hints at Eddie's passion for his lover. Moreover, the ransom letter that was sent to the *Times* of London was rumored to match the writing style of Rose Dugdale.*

This latter claim is part of a fascinating investigation conducted by the acclaimed novelist Luke Jennings, author of the *Villanelle* series of books. Jennings spoke with the now-deceased curator for Kenwood House, John Jacob, who said that the ransom notes sent for both the Russborough and Kenwood heists were the same. Even more interestingly, Jennings interviewed retired detective Arthur Pike, who had led the hunt for *The Guitar Player*. Pike, who began his conversation with Jennings "happy to reminisce about the case," became abrupt when asked about Dugdale. "I'm not at liberty to discuss any matter relating to Dr. Dugdale," he said tersely. Pike did, however, confirm that there were aspects of the Kenwood case that had never been revealed and, even as late as 1999, were off-limits. Pike has since passed away.

---

* Throughout 2018 and 2019, attempts were made by this author to obtain a copy of the ransom letter sent to the *Times* for *The Guitar Player*, to no avail. Kenwood House officials ultimately stated that they were not in possession of the letter and directed inquiries to New Scotland Yard and the *Times*. An archivist at the *Times* was unable to produce a copy, and a public records request to NSY has, to date, been unfruitful.

Jennings raises an interesting theory: since Dugdale was under surveillance for gun smuggling at the time, might the Security Service have allowed her to operate with the hope that she might lead them to senior figures, such as fugitive Provisional chief of staff David O'Connell? When Jennings ran it by an ex-MI5 official, he received "a polite clearing of the throat" in response.[1]

Moreover, after each heist, the IRA disavowed any connection to the theft. While official IRA denials were not uncommon following notorious crimes and attacks, they were not the rule, and it is important to note that the repudiations came via unnamed Republican sources speaking to reporters, not simply from politicized press releases.

The ransom requests were similar not just in the demands related to the hunger strikers but also because a clear condemnation of capitalism as an evil system was featured. Rose was by no means the only anticapitalist involved with Republicanism, but this theme, presented loudly in the ransom demands, was repeated often during the Beit theft and, of course, throughout Dugdale's entire life.

The choice of Vermeer as the target points to an educated thief. The most frequently stolen masters are Rembrandt and Picasso, and that is because their names are so widely known, even to those lacking a formal education. But Vermeer speaks to a slightly more refined thief. *Lady Writing a Letter with Her Maid* was reported to be the first work targeted by Rose when it was stolen from the Beit Collection, and *The Guitar Player* was the only piece taken from Kenwood, despite its proximity to a very well-known Rembrandt. And the fact that the artnappers of *The Guitar Player* were cultured enough to send just a sliver from the tacking edge of the painting, rather than employing the more brutish approach of sending a painted segment of canvas, indicates a heightened appreciation for the masterpiece.

Furthermore, Kenwood House and Russborough House both had the sort of history that would likely inspire Dugdale to strike them. The Guinness family, which owned Kenwood House for some time, had a history of loyalty to the British crown, and in 1913, Lord Iveagh donated

£100,000 to the Ulster Volunteer Force's arms fund, prompting a boy-cott of Guinness products by Irish nationalists.[2] And Rose's gang of thieves made no secret of their disdain for the wealth Sir Alfred Beit's family accumulated, in her view, on the backs of South Africans. These are the sorts of facts that a voracious student like Rose would know.

There are countless important works of art spread through museums in the United Kingdom and Ireland, but the thieves in both heists chose to target these famous houses holding fine art instead of the more well-known and better-guarded national galleries and similar institutions.

Finally, the modus operandi was similar in that these were evening thefts rather than the slightly more common smash-and-grabs that are pulled off at public institutions while they are open. Phone lines were cut at Kenwood House and attempted to be cut at Russborough House. And upon review of the heists, the deputy leader of the Greater London Council, which was responsible for Kenwood House, remarked after the Russborough House heist, "I think there was a connection."[3]

The theft of a Vermeer is, without question, a remarkably noto-rious crime, and Rose Dugdale's fame for the Russborough House heist is deserved. But stealing two Vermeers is the stuff of criminal legend, requiring a combination of cunning, taste, and gall unsurpassed in art theft history. Remarkably, it is probable that Rose Dugdale pulled off such a coup. This, combined with the art theft from her family's home, establishes her as a true outlier and major figure in the annals of crim-inal history.

# AUTHOR'S NOTE

In 2018, I sent word to Rose Dugdale through a close contact of hers that I desired to interview her at length in Ireland and at her leisure for this book. The intermediary met my overture with goodwill and great optimism for cooperation. Sometime later, however, came a call from my emissary: Rose needed "permission" from Republicans to participate, and they had refused. It seemed that they knew that, in addition to being a writer, I am also an investigator, and thus believed that there could be some risk to her—or others—if she cooperated. My contact referenced elderly Republicans facing arrest for decades-old crimes as a result of contemporary interviews.

Though he refused to elaborate, it is my belief that the reason Dugdale could not cooperate was because of the controversy caused by the interviews done with IRA member Dolours Price by journalist and documentarian Ed Moloney. The interview had been released just months before in a fascinating documentary titled *I, Dolours* and implicated living persons in capital crimes. In addition, interviews conducted as academic research into the Troubles through the Belfast Project, under the auspices of Boston College, had just years earlier been obtained by the Police Service of Northern Ireland and used to prosecute individuals for earlier crimes. The attention that these interviews brought had, I believe, a chilling effect on the likelihood of Republican figures to cooperate with interviewers in the present day.

# BIBLIOGRAPHY

Archer, Peggy. "Scorn of a Rebel," in Ronald Duncan, *Facets of Crime* (Plymouth, UK: Bossiney Books, 1975).

Artaraz, Kepa. *Cuba and Western Intellectuals Since 1959* (New York: Palgrave Macmillan, 2009).

Bailey, Anthony. *Vermeer: A View of Delft* (New York: Henry Holt, 2001).

Bogdanor, Vernon, *The People & the Party System: The Referendum and Electoral Reform in British Politics* (Cambridge, UK: Cambridge University Press, 1981).

Brady, Conor. *The Guarding of Ireland—The Garda Síochána and the Irish State 1960–2014* (Dublin: Gill & Macmillan, 2014).

Bray, Philip, with Anthony Galvin. *Inside Man: Life as an Irish Prison Guard* (Dublin: Gill & Macmillan, 2008).

Burrough, Bryan. *Days of Rage: America's Radical Underground, the FBI, and the Forgotten Age of Revolutionary Violence* (New York: Penguin Books, 2015).

Carter, April. *Direct Action and Liberal Democracy* (New York: Routledge, 2010).

Demaris, Ovid. *Brothers in Blood: The International Terrorist Network* (New York: Charles Scribner's Sons, 1977).

Fanon, Frantz. *The Wretched of the Earth* (New York: Grove Weidenfeld, 1963).

Hart, Matthew. *The Irish Game: A True Story of Crime and Art* (New York: Walker, 2004).

Jackson, Richard, Lee Jarvis, Jeroed Gunning, and Marie Breen-Smyth. *Terrorism: A Critical Introduction* (London: Red Globe Press, 2011).

Jones, Nella, and Mandy Bruce. *Nella: A Psychic Eye* (London: BCA, 1992).

Kefe, Patrick Radden. *Say Nothing: A True Story of Murder and Memory in Northern Ireland* (New York: Random House, 2019).

Kerr, Gordon, and Phil Clarke. *Hostages: Dramatic Accounts of Real-Life Events* (Canary Press ebooks, 2011).

Lasky, Melvin. *On the Barricades, and Off* (Livingston, NJ: Transaction, 1987).

MacCarthy, Fiona. *Last Curtsey: The End of the Debutantes* (London: Faber and Faber, 2006).

Mahoney, Harry Thayer, and Marjorie Locke Mahoney. *Ireland Defined: Espionage through the Ages* (Baltimore: Academica Press, 2001).

McGuire, Maria. *To Take Arms: My Year with the IRA Provisionals* (New York: Viking Press, 1973).

Meltzer, Albert. *I Couldn't Paint Golden Angels* (Chico, CA: AK Press, 2001).

Miller, Ian. *A History of Force Feeding* (New York: Palgrave Macmillan, 2016).

Montias, John Michael. *Vermeer and His Milieu: A Web of Social History* (Princeton, NJ: Princeton University Press, 1989).

Moysey, Steve. *The Road to Balcombe Street: The IRA Reign of Terror in London* (Binghampton, UK: The Haworth Press, 2008).

Mulvenna, Gareth. *Tartan Gangs and Paramilitaries: The Loyalist Backlash* (Liverpool: Liverpool University Press, 2017).

Pateman, Trevor, ed.. *Counter Course: A Handbook for Course Criticism* (Middlesex: Penguin Books, 1972).

Potterton, Homan. *Who Do I Think I Am?: A Memoir* (Kildare: Merrion Press., 2017).

Ross, Colin. *Death of the Docks* (London: AuthorHouse UK, 2010).

Smith, Evan, and Matthew Worley, eds. *Waiting for the Revolution: The British Far Left from 1956* (Manchester: Manchester University Press, 2017).

Wheelock, Arthur, Jr. *Jan Vermeer* (New York: Albradale Press, 1981).

White, Robert William. *Ruairí O Bradaigh: The Life and Politics of an Irish Revolutionary* (Bloomington: Indiana University Press, 2006).

# ENDNOTES

## introduction

1. Harry Thayer Mahoney and Marjorie Locke Mahoney, *Ireland Defined: Espionage through the Ages* (Baltimore: Academica Press, 2001), p. 110.
2. Oliver Harvey, "Celtic Fan Was IRA Terrorist," *The Sun* (UK), January 10, 2009, retrieved November 11, 2019, http://ifyouknowtheirhistory.blogspot.com /2009/03/celtic-fan-was-ira-terrorist.html.

## chapter one

1. "Business News in Brief," *The Guardian*, September 9, 1950, p. 9.
2. Marina Warner, "The Revolution of Rose Dugdale," *The Sunday Times Magazine*, August 18, 1974, p. 11; and Fiona MacCarthy, *Last Curtsey: The End of the Debutantes* (London: Faber and Faber, 2006), p. 253.
3. MacCarthy, *Last Curtsey*, p. 253.
4. Joseph Mancini, "Playing Robin Hood for the IRA?," *New York Post*, May 11, 1974, p. 21.
5. MacCarthy, *Last Curtsey*, p. 254.
6. Laurence Marks, "How Dr. Dugdale Abandoned Rhetoric for Revolution," *The Observer*, June 30, 1974, p. 4.
7. Marks, "How Dr. Dugdale Abandoned Rhetoric for Revolution."
8. Tom Mangold, "The Case of Dr. Rose Dugdale," *Encounter* 44, no. 2 (February 1975): 18–27.
9. Mangold, "The Case of Dr. Rose Dugdale," p. 18.
10. Rose Dugdale, interview by John Murray, *The John Murray Show*, RTÉ Radio 1, January 5, 2012.
11. Rose Dugdale, interview by John Murray, *The John Murray Show*.
12. Iñaki Irigoien, "Renunci a una vida de lujo la lucha armada antiimperialista en Irlanda," *GARA*, March 11, 2012, retrieved from https://gara.naiz.eus. Translated by the author.
13. Irigoien, "Renunci a una vida de lujo la lucha armada antiimperialista en Irlanda."
14. Ibid.
15. "Obituary: Jane Fawcett," *The Economist*, June 4, 2016, retrieved July 6, 2019, https://www.economist.com/obituary/2016/06/04/obituary-jane-fawcett.
16. "What Is Dalcroze?," Dalcoze Society of America, updated May 9, 2019, retrieved July 6, 2019, https://dalcrozeusa.org/about-dalcroze/what-is-dalcroze.
17. MacCarthy, *Last Curtsey*, p. 249.
18. MacCarthy, *Last Curtsey*, p. 252.

19. Warner, "The Revolution of Rose Dugdale," p. 11.
20. Irigoien, "Renunci a una vida de lujo la lucha armada antiimperialista en Irlanda."
21. Fiona MacCarthy, "Recalling the Lost Era of the Debutantes," *The Telegraph*, March 16, 2008, retrieved July 8, 2019, https://www.telegraph.co.uk/news /uknews/1581822/Recalling-the-lost-era-of-the-debutantes.html.
22. Mangold, "The Case of Dr. Rose Dugdale," p. 19.
23. MacCarthy, "Recalling the Lost Era of the Debutantes."
24. Ibid.
25. Rose Dugdale, interview by John Murray, *The John Murray Show*.
26. Rose Dugdale interview, *Mná an IRA* (TG4 Ireland, 2012).
27. MacCarthy, *Last Curtsey*, p. 14.
28. Rose Dugdale, interview by John Murray, *The John Murray Show*.
29. MacCarthy, "Recalling the Lost Era of the Debutantes."
30. Review of *William Morris: A Life for Our Times*, quote by A. S. Byatt, Allen & Unwin Book Publishers, retrieved November 12, 2019, https://www.allenandunwin.com /browse/books/general-books/biography-autobiography/William-Morris-A-Life -for-Our-Time-Fiona-MacCarthy-9780571255597.
31. MacCarthy, *Last Curtsey*, pp. 243, 251.
32. MacCarthy, *Last Curtsey*, p. 248.
33. MacCarthy, "Recalling the Lost Era of the Debutantes."
34. People Staff, "A Rose Comes with the Art," *People*, May 20, 1974, retrieved November 12, 2019, https://people.com/archive/a-rose-comes-with-the-art-vol -1-no-12.
35. MacCarthy, "Recalling the Lost Era of the Debutantes."
36. Mangold, "The Case of Dr. Rose Dugdale," p. 19.
37. Ibid.
38. Rose Dugdale, interview by John Murray, *The John Murray Show*.
39. Rose Dugdale interview, *Mná an IRA*.
40. Matthew J. Reisz, "Fiona MacCarthy: The Last Debutante," *The Independent*, October 6, 2006, retrieved on July 6, 2019, https://www.independent.co.uk/arts -entertainment/books/features/fiona-maccarthy-the-last-debutante-418834.html.
41. Rose Dugdale, interview by John Murray, *The John Murray Show*.
42. Reisz, "Fiona MacCarthy: The Last Debutante."
43. Irigoien, "Renunci a una vida de lujo la lucha armada antiimperialista en Irlanda."

## *chapter two*

1. "Dugdale—The Reluctant Debutant," *Irish Press*, June 26, 1974, p. 1.
2. Mangold, "The Case of Dr. Rose Dugdale," p. 19.
3. Tom Lambert, "Englishwoman Trips on Revolutionary Road," *Los Angeles Times*, June 29, 1974, p. 6.
4. Irigoien, "Renunci a una vida de lujo la lucha armada antiimperialista en Irlanda."
5. "The Reluctant Debutante. *Newsweek*, May 20, 1974, p. 63.
6. Warner, "The Revolution of Rose Dugdale," pp. 11–12.
7. Rose Dugdale, "A Radcliffe Bibliography," *The Bankers' Magazine*, March 1962, pp. 218–23.
8. Oxford Correspondent, "Student Council at Oxford?," *The Guardian*, Feburary 8, 1961, p. 7.

9. Peter Ady, letter to Elizabeth Green, February 12, 1962.
10. Mary Ogilvie, letter to Elizabeth Green, January 18, 1962.
11. Ibid.
12. Rose Dugdale, letter to Elizabeth Green, January 19, 1962.
13. "Dugdale—The Reluctant Debutant."
14. Lambert, "Englishwoman Trips on Revolutionary Road."
15. Sorcha Berry, "Dublin Volunteers Dinner Dance 2011 Honouree Rose Dugdale," *An Phoblacht*, September 9, 2011, retrieved July 23, 2019, https://www.anpho blacht.com/contents/1093.
16. "History," Mount Holyoke, retrieved July 9, 2019, https://www.mtholyoke.edu /about/history.
17. Iris Murdoch, letter to Elizabeth Green, February 14, 1962.
18. Mary Ogilvie, letter to Elizabeth Green, January 18, 1962.
19. "G," letter to Elizabeth Green recommending Dugdale, March 4, 1962.
20. Elizabeth Green, letter to Rose Dugdale, March 30, 1962.
21. Rose Dugdale, letter to Elizabeth Green, April 4, 1962.
22. Christian Kay, Press Release, August 21, 1962.
23. "Dr. Dugdale Was Mount Holyoke College News Intern 12 Years Ago," *Holyoke Transcript*, May 8, 1974, p.12.
24. Mancini, "Playing Robin Hood for the IRA?"
25. Martin Lauer, "Suspect in Record Robbery Former Mt. Holyoke Student," *The Springfield Union*, May 8, 1974, p. 26.
26. Lauer, "Suspect in Record Robbery Former Mt. Holyoke Student."
27. Ibid.
28. Mancini, "Playing Robin Hood for the IRA?"
29. Lisa Lansing, "Weird Orchard among Daisies," *The Berkshire Eagle*, May 20, 1974, p. 12.
30. Peter Ady, letter to Elizabeth Green, February 12, 1962.
31. "MPs Fight to Save Equity from Bill," *The Guardian*, January 29, 1971, p. 14.
32. Mangold, "The Case of Dr. Rose Dugdale," p. 20.
33. Ibid.
34. David Beresford, "The Prison Graduate," *The Guardian*, November 5, 1980, p. 17.
35. Bridget Rose Dugdale, "Proper Names" (PhD diss., Bedford College, 1970), p. 2, retrieved February 9, 2020, https://repository.royalholloway.ac.uk/file/170d1551 -326c-4a0e-9250-d17e431b61b1/1/10098174.pdf.
36. Dugdale, "Proper Names," p. 48.

## chapter three

1. Jed Stout, "Black Power Tailored for Reds: Hoover," *The News* (Paterson, NJ), January 5, 1968, p. 6.
2. Rose Dugdale, interview by John Murray, *The John Murray Show*.
3. Irigoien, "Renunci a una vida de lujo la lucha armada antiimperialista en Irlanda."
4. Bryan Burrough, *Days of Rage: America's Radical Underground, the FBI, and the Forgotten Age of Revolutionary Violence* (New York: Penguin Books, 2015), pp. 63–64.
5. "1968: 'I Remember Being Terrified,'" BBC "On This Day," retrieved July 9, 2019, http://news.bbc.co.uk/onthisday/hi/witness/march/17/newsid_4090000 /4090886.stm.

6.  Donald Macintyre, "My Part in the Anti-War Demo That Changed Protest Forever," *The Observer*, March 11, 2018, retrieved July 9, 2019, https://www.theguardian.com/world/2018/mar/11/battle-of-grosvenor-square-50-years-vietnam-protest-donald-macintyre; "1968: Anti-Vietnam Demo Turns Violent," BBC "On This Day," retrieved July 9, 2019, http://news.bbc.co.uk/onthisday/hi/dates/stories/march/17/newsid_2818000/2818967.stm.
7.  Rose Dugdale, "Economic Theory in Class Society," in Trevor Pateman, ed., *Counter Course: A Handbook for Course Criticism* (Middlesex: Penguin Books, 1972), p. 159.
8.  Dugdale, "Economic Theory in Class Society."
9.  Mangold, "The Case of Dr. Rose Dugdale," p. 20.
10. Andreas Whittam Smith, "The Paris Riots of May 1968: How the Frustrations of Youth Brought France to the Brink of Revolution," *Independent*, May 6, 2018, retrieved July 6, 2019, https://www.independent.co.uk/news/long_reads/may-1968-paris-student-riots-demonstrations-sorbonne-nanterre-de-gaulle-a8335866.html.
11. Roger Scruton, interview by Peter Robinson, "How to Be a Conservative," *Uncommon Knowledge* podcast, July 19, 2017.
12. Dugdale, "Economic Theory in Class Society," p. 160.
13. "Mna on IRA," Sean O Briain, Jan 5, 2012, YouTube video, 24:57:00.
14. Merwin Sigale, "Mixed Reasons Take 19 Americans to Cuba," *The Miami News*, July 19, 1968, p. 25.
15. Sigale, "Mixed Reasons Take 19 Americans to Cuba."
16. UPI, "Rations, Draft Mar Cuban Anniversary," *Press and Sun Bulletin* (Binghamton, NY), January 3, 1968, p. 35.
17. Reuters, "Cuba Sets 9th Victory Celebration," *Fort Lauderdale News*, January 1, 1968, p. 44.
18. Kepa Artaraz, *Cuba and Western Intellectuals Since 1959* (New York: Palgrave Macmillan, 2009), p. 121.
19. Ruben Salazar, "Castro Training Rebel Students from Abroad," *The Los Angeles Times*, August 11, 1968, p. 31.
20. Mangold, "The Case of Dr. Rose Dugdale," p. 20.
21. Ibid.
22. Artaraz, *Cuba and Western Intellectuals Since 1959*, p. 121.

## chapter four

1.  AP, "Black Takeover at Two Colleges," *The San Francisco Examiner*, February 27, 1970, p. 18.
2.  "Protests Reach Sedate Oxford," *The Daily Times* (Salisbury, MD), June 9, 1968, p. 4.
3.  Rose Dugdale interview, *Mná an IRA*.
4.  "Students Occupy U.K. Campus to Protest Secret Dossiers," *Calgary Herald*, February 28, 1970, p. 53.
5.  Rose Dugdale, interview by John Murray, *The John Murray Show*.
6.  Rose Dugdale interview, *Mná an IRA*.
7.  Kitty Holland, "Bernadette McAliskey: 'I Am Astounded I Survived. I Made Mad Decisions,'" *The Irish Times*, September 22, 2016, retrieved July 11, 2019, https://www.irishtimes.com/life-and-style/people/bernadette-mcaliskey-i-am-astounded-i-survived-i-made-mad-decisions-1.2798293.

8. "Charge of Bias on Ulster," *The Guardian*, November 1, 1971, p. 22.
9. Harold Jackson, "Stormont MPs Begin Hunger Strike at No 10," *The Guardian*, October 20, 1971, p. 20.
10. Documentary footage, *Mná an IRA*.
11. Rose Dugdale interview, *Mná an IRA*.
12. Beresford, "The Prison Graduate."
13. Holland, "Bernadette McAliskey: 'I Am Astounded I Survived. I Made Mad Decisions.'"
14. Rose Dugdale interview, *Mná an IRA*.
15. Ibid.
16. Warner, "The Revolution of Rose Dugdale," p. 12.

## chapter five

1. Associated Press, "Railroad Strike Chokes London," *Sioux City Journal*, March 1, 1973, p. 9.
2. Vernon Bogdanor, *The People & the Party System: The Referendum and Electoral Reform in British Politics* (Cambridge: Cambridge University Press, 1981), p. 63.
3. "Opposition Attempts to Widen Questions in Ulster Border Poll," *The Guardian*, November 22, 1972, p. 8.
4. Andrew Mack, "No Way Out," *The Ottawa Citizen*, March 9, 1973, p. 7.
5. Colin Baker, "Northern Ireland Referendum to Be in War-Like Scene," *The Daily Messenger* (Canandaigua, NY), March 7, 1973, p. 1.
6. UPI, "Terrorists Blast Polls in Belfast," *The Honolulu Advertiser*, March 5, 1973, p. 2.
7. UPI, "Bombs Tear Dublin Center," *The Pocono Record* (Stroudsburg, PA), December 2, 1972, p. 1.
8. "On Equal Footing," *The Irish Times*, March 7, 1973, p. 13.
9. Michael McInerney, "Full Briefing for Coalition Leaders," *The Irish Times*, March 8, 1973, p. 1.
10. Michael E. Miller, "In Ireland, Bloody Sunday's 'Communal Wound' Reopened on Eve of St. Patrick's Day," *The Washington Post*, March 16, 2019, retrieved June 29, 2019, https://www.washingtonpost.com/history/2019/03/16/ireland-bloody -sundays-communal-wound-reopened-st-patricks-days-eve.
11. Peter Deeley et al., "Yard Is Told There May Be More Car Bombs," *The Observer*, March 11, 1973, p. 1.
12. David Gray and James MacManus, "A Taste of Ulster's Violence," *The Guardian*, March 9, 1973, p. 1.
13. Michael Stern, "London Police Kill 2 Attacking Embassy," *The New York Times*, February 21, 1973, p. 3.
14. Gray and MacManus, "A Taste of Ulster's Violence."
15. Deeley et al., "Yard Is Told There May Be More Car Bombs."
16. Edwin Roth, "A Bomb Shatters Complacency," *The Vancouver Sun*, March 14, 1973, p. 4.
17. Alvin Shuster. "Britain Holds 10 in Two Bombings." *The New York Times*, March 10, 1973, p. 65.
18. Roth, "A Bomb Shatters Complacency."
19. Ibid.
20. Gray and MacManus, "A Taste of Ulster's Violence."
21. Alvin Shuster, "Wartime Again," *The Ottawa Journal*, March 9, 1973, p. 21.

22. Shuster, "Wartime Again"; "SYND 8-3-73 Terrorist Bombing in London," AP Archive, July 21, 2015, YouTube video, 4:30, https://www.youtube.com /watch?v=JY57Ikn0n-Q.

23. James Downey and Denis Coghlan, "Ten Arrested in London after Car-Bombs Kill Man and Injure 243 People," *The Irish Times,* March 9, 1973, p. 1.

24. Shuster, "Wartime Again."

25. Downey and Coghlan, "Ten Arrested in London after Car-Bombs Kill Man and Injure 243 People."

26. *I, Dolours,* directed by Maurice Sweeney (Dublin: Element Pictures, 2018), streaming.

27. Colin Smith, "The Sisters of Terror," *The Observer,* November 18, 1973, p. 15.

28. Smith, "The Sisters of Terror."

29. Ibid.

30. *I, Dolours.*

31. Ibid.

32. Ibid.

33. Ibid.

34. Gareth Mulvenna, *Tartan Gangs and Paramilitaries: The Loyalist Backlash* (Liverpool: Liverpool University Press, 2017), p. 65.

35. *I, Dolours.*

36. Ibid.

37. Ibid.

38. Ibid.

39. "Something of How It Feels in Belfast," *The Irish Times,* March 9, 1973, p. 1.

40. Patrick Radden Keefe, *Say Nothing: A True Story of Memory and Murder in Northern Ireland* (New York: Random House, 2019).

41. Rosie Cowan, "'I Have No Regrets,'" *The Guardian,* March 12, 2003, retrieved November 17, 2019, https://www.theguardian.com/world/2003/mar/13 /gender.uk.

42. *I, Dolours.*

43. Smith, "The Sisters of Terror."

44. Ibid.

45. Ibid.

### chapter six

1. Trevor Pateman, ed., *Counter Course: A Handbook for Course Criticism* (Middlesex: Penguin Books, 1972), p. 7.

2. Irigoien, "Renunci a una vida de lujo la lucha armada antiimperialista en Irlanda."

3. Dugdale, "Economic Theory in Class Society," p. 159.

4. Dugdale, "Economic Theory in Class Society," pp. 159–65.

5. Dugdale, "Economic Theory in Class Society," pp. 179–81.

6. Evan Smith and Matthew Worley, eds., *Waiting for the Revolution: The British Far Left from 1956* (Manchester: Manchester University Press, 2017), p. 37.

7. Mangold, "The Case of Dr. Rose Dugdale," p. 21.

8. Denis Coghlan, "Bridget Rose Dugdale's Road to Limerick Jail," *The Irish Times,* October 13, 1980, p. 7.

9. Coghlan, "Bridget Rose Dugdale's Road to Limerick Jail."

10. Walter Heaton, interview with the author, September 3, 2019.

11. Coghlan, "Bridget Rose Dugdale's Road to Limerick Jail."
12. Mark Curtis, "The War in Malaya, 1948–60," February 13, 2007, retrieved July 14, 2019, http://markcurtis.info/2007/02/13/the-war-in-malaya-1948-60.
13. Joe Glenton, "Marine A-Style Killings Have Always Been a Feature of Britain's Dirty Wars—Ever Heard of Batang Kali?," *HuffPost*, November 12, 2013, retrieved July 17, 2019, https://www.huffingtonpost.co.uk/joe-glenton/marine-a -style-killings-h_b_4422160.html.
14. "Supreme Court Admits British Troops Committed 'Mass Murder'—Malaya Massacre Lawyer," *RT*, November 25, 2015, retrieved July 14, 2019, https://www .rt.com/uk/323434-batang-kali-malaya-massacre.
15. Walter Heaton, interview with the author, September 3, 2019.
16. Mangold, "The Case of Dr. Rose Dugdale," p. 21; Warner, p. 12.
17. Coghlan, "Bridget Rose Dugdale's Road to Limerick Jail."
18. Marks, "How Dr. Dugdale Abandoned Rhetoric for Revolution."
19. David MacDonald, "Bridget Rose Dugdale Known as the Angel of Tottenham," *The Ottawa Journal*, June 3, 1974, p. 24.
20. Warner, "The Revolution of Rose Dugdale," p. 13.
21. Mangold, "The Case of Dr. Rose Dugdale," p. 21.
22. "Direct Action in London (Editorial)," *The Guardian*, August 22, 1973, p. 10.
23. April Carter, *Direct Action and Liberal Democracy* (New York: Routledge, 2010), p. 3.
24. Marks, "How Dr. Dugdale Abandoned Rhetoric for Revolution," p. 4.
25. Warner, "The Revolution of Rose Dugdale," pp. 13–14.
26. Marks, "How Dr. Dugdale Abandoned Rhetoric for Revolution," p. 4.
27. Mangold, "The Case of Dr. Rose Dugdale," p. 21.
28. Warner, "The Revolution of Rose Dugdale," p. 13.
29. Mangold, "The Case of Dr. Rose Dugdale," p. 22.
30. Mangold, "The Case of Dr. Rose Dugdale," p. 21.
31. "Dugdale—The Reluctant Debutante."
32. Marks, "How Dr. Dugdale Abandoned Rhetoric for Revolution," p. 4.
33. John Charles Marsland II, *We'll Help Ourselves: The English Working-Class Struggle to Remake Itself, ca. 1968–1985*, dissertation defended April 30, 2018, p. 59. Submitted to the Faculty of the Graduate School of the University at Buffalo, State University of New York, in partial fulfillment of the requirements for the degree of Doctor of Philosophy, Department of History. Retrieved July 12, 2019, https://ubir.buffalo.edu/xmlui/bitstream/handle/10477/77977/Marsland _buffalo_0656A_15685.pdf?sequence=1&isAllowed=y.
34. Coghlan, "Bridget Rose Dugdale's Road to Limerick Jail."
35. Irigoien, "Renunci a una vida de lujo la lucha armada antiimperialista en Irlanda."
36. Colin Ross, *Death of the Docks* (London: AuthorHouse UK, 2010), pp. 129–30.
37. Originally printed in *An Phlobacht* on September 9, 2011, archived on the Facebook page of Cairde na hÉireann, retrieved November 17, 2019, https://www .facebook.com/CNEScotland/photos/rose-dugdale-was-born-into-into-a -wealthy-family-in-devon-in-the-south-west-of-e/796883440390837.
38. Warner, "The Revolution of Rose Dugdale," p. 15.
39. Ibid.
40. Ibid.
41. Mangold, "The Case of Dr. Rose Dugdale," p. 23
42. Mangold, "The Case of Dr. Rose Dugdale," p. 22
43. Coghlan, "Bridget Rose Dugdale's Road to Limerick Jail."

44. Warner, "The Revolution of Rose Dugdale," p. 17.

45. Derek Brown, "Jail Is Price for Principles," *Times Colonist* (Victoria, BC), July 13, 1974, p. 5.

46. Maria McGuire, *To Take Arms: My Year with the IRA Provisionals* (New York: Viking Press, 1973), p. 4.

47. Mahoney and Mahoney, *Ireland Defined*, p. 163.

48. Coghlan, "Bridget Rose Dugdale's Road to Limerick Jail."

49. Ibid.

## chapter seven

1. Albert Meltzer, *I Couldn't Paint Golden Angels* (Chico, CA: AK Press, 2001). Online edition, retrieved July 26, 2019, http://www.spunk.org/library/writers/meltzer /sp001591/angels13.html.

2. Derek Brown, "The English Lady and the IRA," *The Guardian*, June 26, 1974, p. 13.

3. Danny Haiphong, "Cuba Is Fanon in the Flesh," *Pambazuka News*, June 3, 2015, retrieved July 27, 2019, https://www.pambazuka.org/governance/cuba-fanon -flesh.

4. Frantz Fanon, *The Wretched of the Earth* (New York: Grove Weidenfeld, 1963), p. 36.

5. Beresford, "The Prison Graduate."

6. Irigoien, "Renunci a una vida de lujo la lucha armada antiimperialista en Irlanda."

7. "Dugdale—The Reluctant Debutante."

8. David Brazil, "Cold, Committed and Naïve: The Rose Dugdale I Knew," *The Irish Press*, November 10, 1977, p. 3.

9. Warner, "The Revolution of Rose Dugdale," p. 13.

10. Mangold, "The Case of Dr. Rose Dugdale," p. 22.

11. Ibid.

12. Mancini, "Playing Robin Hood for the IRA?"

13. Mangold, "The Case of Dr. Rose Dugdale," p. 22

14. Warner, "The Revolution of Rose Dugdale," p. 13.

15. Mangold, "The Case of Dr. Rose Dugdale," p. 22.

16. Marks, "How Dr. Dugdale Abandoned Rhetoric for Revolution," p. 4.

17. Mangold, "The Case of Dr. Rose Dugdale," p. 23.

18. Coghlan, "Bridget Rose Dugdale's Road to Limerick Jail."

19. Mangold, "The Case of Dr. Rose Dugdale," p. 23.

20. Mangold, "The Case of Dr. Rose Dugdale," p. 24.

21. "10 Years for Man Who Informed on Dugdale," *The Irish Times*, Febuary 15, 1975, p. 7.

22. AP, "Million at English Derby," *The New York Times*, June 7, 1973, p. 59.

23. Peggy Archer, "Scorn of a Rebel," in Ronald Duncan, *Facets of Crime* (Plymouth, UK: Bossiney Books, 1975), pp. 18–19.

24. "Woman 'Made to Steal Paintings,'" *The Guardian*, October 9, 1973, p. 7.

25. "Art Case Woman Tells of Threats to Her Life," *The Times* (UK), October 17, 1973, p. 5.

26. "Oxford Don Says She Lied in Art Theft Case," *The Times* (UK), October 13, 1973, p. 2.

27. Coghlan, "Bridget Rose Dugdale's Road to Limerick Jail."

28. UPI, "'I Regard Them as Thieves,'" *The Vancouver Sun*, October 23, 1973, p. 1.

29. "Woman Says Her Father 'Hopes I Am Guilty So That I Can Get Psychological Care,'" *The Times* (UK), October 20, 1973, p. 2.
30. Matthew Hart, *The Irish Game: A True Story of Crime and Art* (New York: Walker and Company, 2004), pp. 10–11.
31. Hart, *The Irish Game*, p. 10.
32. "The Reluctant Debutante," *Newsweek*.
33. Melvin Lasky, *On the Barricades, and Off* (Livingston, NJ: Transaction, 1987), p. 71.
34. Walter Heaton, interview with the author, September 3, 2019.
35. Mangold, "The Case of Dr. Rose Dugdale," p. 23.
36. "Hunger Strike Threat over Art Robbery Charge," *The Times* (UK), July 6, 1973, p. 5.
37. UPI, "'I Regard Them as Thieves.'"
38. "Dr. Bridget 'Better Free,' but Must Pay £5,000 Costs," *The Guardian*, October 27, 1973, p. 7.
39. Coghlan, "Bridget Rose Dugdale's Road to Limerick Jail."
40. James Hughes-Onslow, "Time Gives Trivia a Place in History," *The Sydney Morning Herald*, July 6, 1983, p. 9.
41. The accounts of the courtroom proceedings at Exeter Crown Court are largely from the essay "Scorn of a Rebel" by Peggy Archer from *Facets of Crime*.
42. AP, "Art Treasures Recovered," *The Ottawa Journal*, May 6, 1974, p. 14.

## *chapter eight*

1. Lasky, *On the Barricades, and Off*, p. 70.
2. "Red-handed," *The Digger*, November 10–December 8, 1973, p. 2.
3. "The Reluctant Debutante," *Newsweek*.
4. Warner, "The Revolution of Rose Dugdale," p. 13.
5. Brazil, "Cold, Committed and Naïve: The Rose Dugdale I Knew."
6. "Refusal of Blood Test Earns Driving Ban," *The Guardian*, November 13, 1973, p. 7.
7. Warner, "The Revolution of Rose Dugdale," p. 15.
8. Ibid.
9. Marks, "How Dr. Dugdale Abandoned Rhetoric for Revolution," p. 4.
10. Walter Heaton, interview with the author, September 3, 2019.
11. Much of the information about the early years of Eddie Gallagher's life comes from Kieran Gill, "A Rebel in a Vacuum," *The Irish Press*, October 31, 1975, p. 7.
12. Nick Love, "Eddie Gallagher Was My Flat-Mate," *Leitrim Observer*, November 1, 1975, p. 1.
13. Love, "Eddie Gallagher Was My Flat-Mate."
14. Derek Dunne, "A Rough Deal," *Magill Magazine*, January 1986, p. 6. Archived via *1169 and Counting . . .* blog, retrieved October 5, 2019, https://1169andcounting. blogspot.com/search?q=eddie+gallagher+and+brendan+hughes.
15. Ovid Demaris, *Brothers in Blood: The International Terrorist Network* (New York: Charles Scribner's Sons, 1977), p. 363.
16. Dunne, "A Rough Deal," pp. 6–9.
17. Derek Brown, "Bomb Kills Officer," *The Guardian*, January 26, 1974, p. 26.
18. Coghlan, "Bridget Rose Dugdale's Road to Limerick Jail."
19. Warner, "The Revolution of Rose Dugdale," p. 17.

20. Eamoonn McCann, "Herrema's Kidnapper Explains His Motive," *Sunday Tribune*, October 23, 2005, archived on *The Blanket: A Journal of Protest and Dissent*, retrieved October 6, 2019, http://indiamond6.ulib.iupui.edu:81/emcc711058g.html.
21. McCann, "Herrema's Kidnapper Explains His Motive."

## chapter nine

1. The story of the Mountjoy Prison escape comes from: UPI, "Hijacked Copter Grabs IRA Chief from Prison," *The Times* (UK), November 1, 1973, p. 20; "IRA Mountjoy Helicopter Escape 31 October 1973," Shane Gallagher, retrieved August 16, 2019, YouTube video, 2:37, https://www.youtube.com /watch?v=t3mtMm5yiVU; "Helicopter Snatches Three Provisionals from Mountjoy," *The Irish Times*, November 1, 1973, pp. 1–6.
2. "Twomey Thought to Be Still in Dublin," *The Irish Times*, November 2, 1973, p. 1.
3. UPI, "IRA Hints Air Raid on Belfast," *The Tribune* (UK), December 29, 1973, p. 1.
4. Demaris, *Brother in Blood*, p. 364.
5. "Gerry's Holiday Hideaway That Was Once a Nerve Centre for Republican Leadership," *Independent*, August 17, 2019, retrieved August 18, 2019, https://www .independent.ie/irish-news/gerrys-holiday-hideaway-that-was-once-a-nerve -centre-for-republican-leadership-26853041.html.
6. "Jailed for Hijacking Copter from Donegal," *Strabane Chronicle*, November 30, 1974, p. 3.
7. "Jailed for Hijacking Copter from Donegal."
8. "Northern Ireland troubles | Strabane | IRA | British Army | 1974," ThamesTv, retrieved August 10, 2019, YouTube video, 12:27, https://www.youtube.com /watch?v=-JZJQ50XVdw.
9. Peter Hetherington, "Nothing but the Truth in Strabane," *The Guardian*, January 13, 1975, p. 11.
10. "Jailed for Hijacking Copter from Donegal."
11. Mangold, "The Case of Dr. Rose Dugdale," p. 25.
12. Rose Dugdale interview, *Mná an IRA*.
13. Rose Dugdale, interview by John Murray, *The John Murray Show*.
14. Rose Dugdale interview, *Mná an IRA*.
15. Rose Dugdale, interview by John Murray, *The John Murray Show*.
16. Ibid.
17. Ibid.
18. James Downey, "Cabinet Talks on Security After Hijack," *The Irish Times*, January 26, 1974, p. 1.
19. Coghlan, "Bridget Rose Dugdale's Road to Limerick Jail."
20. Brazil, "Cold, Committed and Naïve: The Rose Dugdale I Knew."
21. Mahoney, *Ireland Defined*, p. 117.
22. Rose Dugdale interview, *Mná an IRA*.

## chapter ten

1. Raymond R. Coffey, "IRA Blamed for Bus Deaths," *The Corpus Christi Caller-Times*, February 4, 1974, p. 2.
2. "Police Swoop on IRA Homes in NW," *The Guardian*, February 5, 1974, p. 2.
3. Ibid.

4. Peter Chippendale, "Carr Orders Alert to Block IRA Reprisals," *The Guardian*, November 16, 1973, p. 1.

5. AP, "U.K. Stand Caused German's Death," *Edmonton Journal*, January 29, 1974, p. 12,

6. Derek Brown, "UFF Campaign Goes on in Retaliation for 'Useless Killings,'" *The Guardian*, February 12, 1974, p. 4.

7. "Forced Feeding in Brixton Palace," *I, Dolours* Documentary Feature Film website, retrieved August 15, 2019, http://idolours.com/i-dolours/life_story/forced-feeding.

8. Ian Miller, *A History of Force Feeding* (New York: Palgrave Macmillan, 2016), p. 193.

9. *I, Dolours*.

10. Ibid.

11. Miller, *A History of Force Feeding*, p. 211.

12. Chippendale, "Carr Orders Alert to Block IRA Reprisals."

13. "Carr to Probe Prison Visits Refusal Claim," *The Irish Times*, January 7, 1974, p. 8.

14. "Bernadette protests," *The Irish Times*, February 7, 1974, p. 5.

15. "More bombs in Britain," *The Guardian*, February 6, 1974, p. 1.

16. *I, Dolours*.

17. Mac Giolla Cearr, "Hunger Strikers Seek Only to Serve Their Sentence in North," *The Irish Times*, January 21, 1974, p. 8.

18. Rose Dugdale, interview by John Murray, *The John Murray Show*.

19. Ibid.

20. Ibid.

21. Ibid.

22. Ibid.

23. Derek Brown, "Grave a Thin Cover for Duggan," *The Guardian*, December 15, 1975, p. 20.

24. Steve Moysey, *The Road to Balcombe Street: The IRA Reign of Terror in London* (Binghampton: The Haworth Press, 2008 ), p. 5.

25. Chippendale, "Carr Orders Alert to Block IRA Reprisals."

### chapter eleven

1. "Helicopter Bombing: Hunt for Woman," *Irish Press*, February 26, 1974, p. 4.

2. "Police Hunt Dr. Dugdale," *Irish Press*, Febuary 25, 1974, p. 3.

3. Anthony Bailey, *Vermeer: A View of Delft* (New York: Henry Holt & Co, 2001), p. 51.

4. Bailey, *Vermeer*, p. 15n.

5. Simon Jenkins, "What Vermeer's Guitar Player Taught Me about the Joy of Art," *The Guardian*, December 27, 2013, retrieved November 17, 2019, https://www.theguardian.com/commentisfree/2013/dec/27/vermeer-guitar-player-art-kenwood-house.

6. Bailey, *Vermeer*, p. 219.

7. Elizabeth E. Gardner, "Thoré's Sphinx," *Metropolitan Museum of Art Bulletin*, November 1948, p. 74.

8. AP, "$2 Million Vermeer Stolen in London," *The Boston Globe*, February 25, 1974, p. 1.

9. Emilie Gordenker, "Is Vermeer Still the 'Sphinx of Delft'?" Google Arts & Culture, retrieved on August 31, 2019, https://artsandculture.google.com/theme/YAKSAIB-SeBYIQ.

10. "Vermeer's 'A Lady Writing' Comes to the Norton Simon Museum," Norton Simon Museum, podcast, October 6, 2008.

11. Peter Schjeldahl, "The Sphinx," *The New Yorker*, April 8, 2001, retrievedNovember 17, 2019, https://www.newyorker.com/magazine/2001/04/16/the-sphinx.

12. Peter Schjeldahl, "Dutch Touch," *The New Yorker*, September 14, 2009, retrieved on November 17, 2019, https://www.newyorker.com/magazine/2009/09/21/dutch-touch.

13. Jonathan Janson, "Vermeer's Most Popular Paintings," retrieved August 31, 2019, http://www.essentialvermeer.com/popular_works.html#.XWrkAHdFyM-.

14. Arthur Wheelock Jr., *Jan Vermeer* (New York: Albradale Press, 1981), p. 9.

15. Carol Vogel, "Long Suspect, a Vermeer Is Vindicated by $30 Million Sale," *The New York Times*, July 8, 2004, p. 1.

16. Erica Trapasso, "Johannes Vermeer: The 36th Painting," *Artnet News*, August 19, 2013, retrieved August 31, 2019, https://news.artnet.com/market/johannes-vermeer-the-36th-painting-30525.

17. CPI Inflation Calculator, accessed August 31, 2019, https://www.officialdata.org/us/inflation/1675.

18. Bailey, *Vermeer*, p. 205.

19. "History of Kenwood," *English Heritage*, retrieved September 3, 2019, https://www.english-heritage.org.uk/visit/places/kenwood/history-stories-kenwood/history.

20. "Vermeer's Famed Guitar Player Stolen," *The News-Palladium* (Benton Harbor, MI), February 25, 1974, p. 7.

21. Dennis Barker, "Call Threat to Destroy the Vermeer," *The Guardian*, February 26, 1974, p. 26.

22. Luke Jennings, "Every Picture Tells a Story," *Evening Standard*, December 3, 1999, p. 17.

23. "Vermeer's Famed Guitar Player Stolen."

24. Ibid.

25. Nigel Gosling, "The Treasures of Kenwood House," *The Observer*, July 30, 1967, p. 20.

26. John Michael Montias, *Vermeer and His Milieu: A Web of Social History* (Princeton, NJ: Princeton University Press, 1989), p. 197.

27. Bailey, *Vermeer*, p. 115.

28. "Inventory of Movable Household Goods of Vermeer's Home at Oude Langendijk, Delft," Essential Vermeer 3.0, retrieved September 2, 2019, http://www.essentialvermeer.com/inventory.html#.XW0-_3dFyM8.

29. Nella Jones and Mandy Bruce, *Nella: A Psychic Eye* (London: BCA, 1992), pp. 31–33.

30. Barker, "Call Threat to Destroy Vermeer."

31. Senior Detective Arnie Cooke, Scotland Yard (ret.), telephone interview with the author, June 10, 2017.

32. Barker, "Call Threat to Destroy Vermeer."

33. "Vermeer Thefts: 1971—*The Love Letter*," Essential Vermeer 3.0, retrieved September 2, 2019, http://www.essentialvermeer.com/fakes_thefts_school_of_delft_lost_sp/vermeer_theft_01.html#.XW16HXdFyM8; UPI, "Belgium Recovers Stolen Masterpiece," *The Times* (UK), October 7, 1971, p. 1.

34. AP, "Reward Offered for Masterpiece, but British Rule out Huge Ransom," *Arizona Republic*, February 27, 1974, p. 2.

35. Jennings, "Every Picture Tells a Story."

36. "Reward Offered for Painting," *The Burlington Free Press*, February 27, 1974, p. 2.
37. Peter Deeley, "IRA Vermeer Deal Offered," *The Observer*, March 3, 1974, p. 1.
38. "Vermeer Theft Denial," *The Guardian*, March 8, 1974, p. 2.
39. Peter Deeley, "Offer to Vermeer Thieves," *The Observer*, March 10, 1974, p. 2.
40. Peter Chippindale and Lindsay Mackie, "Price Sisters Plea," *The Guardian*, March 11, 1974, p. 1.
41. AP, "Price Sisters Appeal for Return of Painting," *Green Bay Press-Gazette*, March 11, 1974, p. 1.
42. Peter Niesewand, "Vermeer 'a Part Payment,'" *The Guardian*, March 14, 1974, p. 7.
43. Jennings, "Every Picture Tells a Story."
44. Jones and Bruce, *Nella*, p. 35.
45. AP, "Vermeer Shred Tested," *The Kansas City Times*, March 14, 1974, p. 6.
46. UPI, "Kin of IRA Bombers Seeks Artwork Return," *The Morning News* (Wilmington, DE), March 18, 1974, p. 24.
47. Gareth Parry, "Vermeer Deadline Ticks Past . . . ," *The Guardian*, March 18, 1974, p. 1.

## chapter twelve

1. Details of the Russborough House heist come primarily from five sources: An interview with Sir Alfred Beit in the RTE archives "Paintings Stolen in Raid at Russborough House 1974," retrieved May 30, 2017, http://www.rte.ie /archives/2014/0425/611718-art-collection-stolen-from-russborough-house; Hart, *The Irish Game*; Warner, "The Revolution of Rose Dugdale"; "Rob $19M from Irish Mansion," *The New York Daily News*, April 27, 1974, p. 2; Staff Reporters, "Police Theory on Art Theft Gang," *The Observer*, April 28, 1974, pp. 1–3.
2. Dick Grogan, Jack Fagan, and Joe Joyce, "Paintings Worth Millions Stolen in Blessington," *The Irish Times*, April 27, 1974, p. 1.
3. Foreword to the exhibition catalogue, *National Gallery of Ireland Acquisitions 1986–1988* (1988).
4. Homan Potterton, *Who Do I Think I Am?: A Memoir* (Kildare: Merrion Press, 2017), p. 214.
5. Potterton, *Who Do I Think I Am?*, p. 215.
6. Ibid.
7. Potterton, *Who Do I Think I Am?*, p. 218.
8. Potterton, *Who Do I Think I Am?*, pp. 218–19.
9. Dorothy Quick, "Quick Look at Things," *The Central New Jersey Home News*, September 15, 1951, p. 4.
10. UPI, "Irish Seal Off Country After Greatest Robbery," *The Crowley Post-Signal*, April 28, 1974, p. 1; and Clementine Beit statement to Police, Beit Archive, Alfred Beit Foundation, Russborough, Co. Wicklow (April 28, 1974).
11. Rose Dugdale, interview by John Murray, *The John Murray Show*.
12. Warner, "The Revolution of Rose Dugdale," p. 11; "Luxury Home for Dugdale Baby," *Irish Press*, March 1, 1977, p. 1.
13. Rose Dugdale, interview by John Murray, *The John Murray Show*.
14. Dick Grogan, "Owner Describes Art Robbery of the Century," *The Irish Times*, April 29, 1974, p. 9.
15. Clementine Beit statement to Police, Beit Archive, Alfred Beit Foundation, Russborough, Co. Wicklow (April 28, 1974).

16. Potterton, *Who Do I Think I Am?*, p. 220.
17. Clementine Beit statement to Police, Beit Archive, Alfred Beit Foundation, Russborough, Co. Wicklow (April 28, 1974).
18. Grogan, "Owner Describes Art Robbery of the Century."
19. Speisialta, "An Stát v. Dugdale."
20. Grogan, "Owner Describes Art Robbery of the Century."
21. Hart, *The Irish Game*, p. 15.
22. "Paintings Stolen in Raid at Russborough House 1974."
23. "Police Theory on Art Theft Gang."
24. Ibid.
25. Warner, "The Revolution of Rose Dugdale," p. 11.
26. Combined Dispatches, "Rob $19 million in Art from Irish Mansion," *New York Daily News*, April 27, 1974, p. 2.
27. Michael Brenson, "About the Stolen Vermeer," *The New York Times*, May 23, 1986.
28. Jonathan Janson, "*Lady Writing a Letter with Her Maid*," Essential Vermer 3.0, retrieved September 16, 2019. http://www.essentialvermeer.com/catalogue/lady _writing_a_letter.html#.XX-b63dFyM8.
29. "Vermeer's 'A Lady Writing' Comes to the Norton Simon Museum."
30. Wheelock, *Jan Vermeer*, p. 146.
31. Tuairisceoir Speisialta, translated by Sarah D. Doherty, "An Stát v. Dugdale: Cuid a dó," *Comhar* 39, no. 12 (December 1980), pp. 25–30. Translated by Sarah D. Doherty.
32. Hart, *The Irish Game*, p. 15.
33. Speisialta, "An Stát v. Dugdale: Cuid a dó."
34. Ibid.
35. "Police Theory on Art Theft Gang."
36. Grogan, "Owner Describes Art Robbery of the Century."
37. Dick Grogan and Michael McConnell, "New Clues in Search for Paintings," *The Irish Times*, April 29, 1974, p. 1.
38. "Political Motive Doubted in Art Theft," *The Guardian*, April 29, 1974, p. 20.
39. Hart, *The Irish Game*, p. 16.
40. Speisialta, "An Stát v. Dugdale: Cuid a dó."
41. AP–Reuters, "Armed Raiders Get $20 Million in Masterpieces," *Calgary Herald*, April 27, 1974, p. 1.
42. Interview with Alfred Beit from RTÉ Radio 1 documentary *Kidnapped—The Herrema Diaries*, Alan Torney, director, December 11, 2005, retrieved November 17, 2019, https://www.rte.ie/radio1/doconone/2009/0617/646041-herrema.
43. AP, "Irish Trace Stolen Cars, $20 Million Paintings," *Longview (WA) Daily News*, April 29, 1974, p. 3.
44. Staff Reporters, "Police Theory on Art Raid," *The Observer*, April 28, 1974, p. 3.
45. Donal Musgrave, "Whole Art Gang May Have Used Co. Cork Cottage," *The Irish Times*, May 7, 1974, p. 5.
46. Speisialta, "An Stát v. Dugdale: Cuid a dó."
47. Pat Connolly, "No Better Ambassador for West Cork Gardai," *Southern Star (West Cork, Ireland)*, March 30, 1985, p. 7.
48. Warner, "The Revolution of Rose Dugdale," p. 18.
49. Rose Dugdale interview, *Mná an IRA*.
50. Hart, *The Irish Game*, pp. 20–21.

51. Connolly, "No Better Ambassador for West Cork Gardai."
52. Hart, *The Irish Game*, p. 21.
53. Speisialta, "An Stát v. Dugdale: Cuid a dó"; Jim Cluskey, "Gardai Hunt Art Case Man," *Irish Examiner*, May 6, 1974, p. 1.
54. Hart, *The Irish Game*, p. 22.
55. Musgrave, "Whole Art Gang May Have Used Co. Cork Cottage."
56. Hart, *The Irish Game*, p. 23.
57. Rose Dugdale, interview by John Murray, *The John Murray Show*.
58. Cluskey, "Gardai Hunt Art Case Man."
59. Ibid.
60. Hart, *The Irish Game*, p. 23.
61. "The Reluctant Debutante," *Newsweek*.
62. Cluskey, "Gardai Hunt Art Case Man."

## chapter thirteen

1. Ed Blanche, "Art Experts Begin Work on Recovered Vermeer Painting," *The Tennessean*, May 8, 1974, p. 14.
2. Dennis Barker, "Link in Art Thefts," *The Guardian*, May 9, 1974, p. 24.
3. AP, "Heiress Facing Theft Charges," *Dayton Daily News*, May 6, 1974, p. 1.
4. Hugh Leggatt, "Old Masters, New Hazards," letter to the editor, *The Guardian*, April 29, 1974, p. 10.
5. Ernie Money, "Old Masters, New Hazards," letter to the editor.
6. "SYND 8-3-73 Terrorist Bombing in London."
7. "An Stát v. Dugdale," translated by Sarah D. Doherty, *Comhar* 40, no. 2 (February 1981), pp. 18–24.
8. Rose Dugdale, interview by John Murray, *The John Murray Show*.
9. "An Stát v. Dugdale," February 1981.
10. Keefe, *Say Nothing*, p. 82.
11. "An Stát v. Dugdale," February 1981.
12. Ibid.
13. "An Stát v. Dugdale," February 1981; "2 Remanded in Custody on IRA Charges," *The Irish Times*, May 9, 1974, p. 10.
14. Moysey, *The Road to Balcombe Street*, p. 44.
15. Michael O'Flaherty, "Man Who Never Was," *Daily Express*, December 15, 1975; Moysey, *The Road to Balcombe Street*, p. 43.
16. Warner, "The Revolution of Rose Dugdale," p. 17.
17. Warner, "The Revolution of Rose Dugdale," p. 18.
18. Ibid.
19. Mahoney, *Ireland Defined*, p. 117.
20. Warner, "The Revolution of Rose Dugdale," p. 17.
21. From Mangold, "The Case of Dr. Rose Dugdale," p. 25; David O'Connell, quoted in *Mná an IRA*.
22. Frank Prendergrast on *Mná an IRA*.
23. Warner, "The Revolution of Rose Dugdale," p. 17.
24. Ibid.
25. Mangold, "The Case of Dr. Rose Dugdale," p. 26.
26. "Dugdale on 10 Charges," *Irish Press*, May 5, 1974, p. 1.
27. "Today's Quote," *Great Falls Tribune* (Great Falls, MT), May 13, 1974, p. 6.

28. Warner, "The Revolution of Rose Dugdale," p. 10.

29. Ibid.

30. "Dr. Dugdale Two Weeks on Hunger Strike," *The Irish Times*, May 31, 1974, p. 1.

31. Martin Cowley, "Jenkins Has Still 'Open Mind' on Price Girls," *The Irish Times*, May 31, 1974, p. 9.

32. Aengus O Snodaigh, "Take Me Home to Mayo: 25th Anniversary of Michael Gaughan's Death," July 1, 1999, from *An Phoblact*, retrieved September 17, 2019, https://republican-news.org/archive/1999/July01/01hist.html.

33. Simon Hoggart, "Prosecution of IRA Marchers Discouraged," *The Guardian*, June 11, 1974, p. 30.

34. "Dr. Dugdale Ends Hunger Strike," *Irish Press*, June 11, 1974, p. 6.

35. Warner, "The Revolution of Rose Dugdale," p. 10.

36. "Dugdale Trial Begins," *Irish Examiner*, June 25, 1974, p. 12.

37. Warner, "The Revolution of Rose Dugdale," p. 10.

38. "Dr. Dugdale Jailed for Nine Years," *The Irish Times*, June 26, 1974, p. 9.

39. "Dr. Dugdale Gets Nine Years," *The Irish Times*.

40. Transcripts of Rose Dugdale's June 1974 courtroom speech come from "Dr. Dugdale Gets Nine Years."

41. Warner, "The Revolution of Rose Dugdale," p. 10.

42. Robert Fisk, "Rose Dugdale, Jailed for Nine Years on Art Charge, Calls Britain 'A Filthy Enemy,'" *The Times* (UK), June 26, 1974, p. 2.

43. Kevin Moore, "RTE Storm as She Gets Nine Years," *Irish Independent*, June 26, 1974, p. 1.

44. "R.T.E. Row," *Sligo Champion*, June 28, 1974, p. 9.

45. "The Right to Know," *Irish Press*, June 26, 1974, p. 8.

46. "A Silent Dugdale Appears in Court," *Evening Herald*, October 21, 1974, p. 4.

47. "Dugdale and 2 Men on Hijacking Charge," *Irish Press*, November 26, 1974, p. 7.

48. "Palm Print," *Irish Press*, November 27, 1974, p. 7.

49. "Evidence of Explosives Man at Dugdale Trial," *Evening Herald*, November 26, 1974, p. 5.

50. "Dugdale and 2 Men on Hijacking Charge," *Irish Press*, November 26, 1974, p. 7.

51. "Hijack Case—Dugdale Found Guilty," *Irish Press*, November 27, 1974, p. 7.

52. "Dugdale Gets Nine Years in 'Copter Case," *Irish Press*, November 28, 1974, p. 7.

53. Ibid.

## chapter fourteen

1. Former IRA member, interview with the author, October 29, 2019.

2. Dunne, "A Rough Deal," pp. 6–9.

3. "Richard Behal and Acquaintance of Gallagher," *Munster Express*, October 17, 1975, p. 19.

4. "Big Manhunt for 19 Jailbreakers," *Irish Examiner*, August 19, 1974, p. 1.

5. "Top Tyrone IRA Man in Big Jail-Break," *Strabane Chronicle*, August 24, 1974, p. 1.

6. Kieran Patton, "Jail Escape 'Planned Two Months Ago,'" *Irish Press*, August 19, 1974, p. 1.

7. "Statement by Government," *Irish Press*, August 19, 1974, p. 4.

8. "Portlaoise: Big Dragnet for the 19 Goes On," *Irish Independent*, August 20, 1974, p. 16.

9. "Nineteen Provos Blast Out," *Irish Independent*, August 19, 1974, p. 18.

10. "Time Table of the Break-Out," *Irish Independent*, August 19, 1974, p. 18.

11. "Road Security Slack after Prison Escape," *Limerick Leader*, August 19, 1974, p. 1.

12. "Jail Escape 'Planned Two Months Ago,'" *Irish Press*, August 19, 1974, p. 1.

13. "Most Dramatic Escape So Far," *Irish Press*, August 19, 1974, p. 4.

14. "Top Tyrone IRA man in Big Jail-Break."

15. "Portlaoise: Big Dragnet for the 19 Goes On."

16. "Top Tyrone IRA Man in Big Jail-Break."

17. "Girl Freed of Garda Murder Attempt Charge," *Irish Independent*, October 24, 1974, p. 3.

18. "Manhunt for Jailbreakers," *Irish Examiner*, August 19, 1974, p. 14.

19. McCann, "Herrema's Kidnapper Explains His Motive."

20. Mangold, "The Case of Dr. Rose Dugdale," p. 27.

21. Mancini, "Playing Robin Hood for the IRA?"

22. Lansing, "Weird Orchid among Daisies."

23. Rose Dugdale, interview by John Murray, *The John Murray Show*.

24. Philip Bray with Anthony Galvin, *Inside Man: Life as an Irish Prison Guard* (Dublin: Gill & Macmillan, 2008), p. 57.

25. Anne McHardy, "Dr. Dugdale Has a Baby—and a Husband," *The Guardian*, December 14, 1974, p. 1.

26. Rose Dugdale, interview by John Murray, *The John Murray Show*.

27. Tony Purcell, "Mysterious Bouquets for Rose Dugdale," *The Cork Examiner*, December 14, 1974, back page.

28. Cabinet minutes of the Roinn an Taoisigh, December 12, 1974, number S.19337, "Limerick Women's Prison: Birth of Baby to Rose Dugdale."

29. Cabinet minutes of the Roinn an Taoisigh, "Limerick Women's Prison: Birth of Baby to Rose Dugdale."

30. "Why Dugdale Birth Was in Prison," *Irish Independent*, December 17, 1974, p. 1.

31. Rose Dugdale, interview by John Murray, *The John Murray Show*.

32. Irigoien, "Renunci a una vida de lujo la lucha armada antiimperialista en Irlanda."

33. "Why Dugdale Birth Was in Prison."

34. Bernard Levin, "Wild Imaginings That See a Baby as a Guerilla," *The Times* (UK), December 18, 1974, p. 14.

35. Purcell, "Mysterious Bouquets for Rose Dugdale."

36. "Why Dugdale Birth Was in Prison."

37. Brazil, "Cold, Committed and Naïve: The Rose Dugdale I Knew."

38. Rose Dugdale, interview by John Murray, *The John Murray Show*.

39. Bray with Galvin, *Inside Man*, p. 57.

40. Rose Dugdale interview, *Mná an IRA*.

41. Rose Dugdale, interview by John Murray, *The John Murray Show*.

42. "Luxury Home for Dugdale Baby," *Irish Press*, March 1, 1977, p. 1.

43. Rose Dugdale interview, *Mná an IRA*.

44. Henry McDonald, "IRA Victim's Brother Says Martin McGuiness Has Blood on His Hands," *The Guardian*, October 12, 2011, retrieved October 17, 2019, https://www .theguardian.com/politics/2011/oct/12/ira-relative-martin-mcguinness-blood.

45. Dunne, "A Rough Deal," pp. 6–9.

46. Rose Dugdale interview, *Mná an IRA*.

47. Ibid.

48. Warner, "The Revolution of Rose Dugdale," p. 18.
49. Letter from Iris Murdoch to the Department of Justice, July 2, 1977.
50. Justice Department official response to Iris Murdoch, September 1977.
51. "A Request from Dugdale," *The Irish Press*, January 6, 1975, p. 1.
52. Ibid.
53. Tony Purcell, "Dugdale to Be Deported?," *Irish Examiner*, January 3, 1975, p. 1.
54. "Dugdale Ends Fast," *The Irish Press*, May 30, 1975, p. 1.
55. "Dugdale in Fourth Week of Fast," *The Irish Times*, My 19, 1975, p. 3.
56. "Portlaoise Fast to Back Dugdale," *Irish Press*, May 15, 1975, p. 1.
57. "Jail Protest by Women," *Irish Press*, May 22, 1975, p. 5.
58. "Dugdale Ends Fast."
59. "Dugdale, Coyle in Prison Fighting," *The Irish Times*, November 27, 1975, p. 1.
60. "Dugdale Hacksaw Find Inquiry," *The Irish Times*, February 10, 1975, p. 1.
61. "Dugdale Escape Bid: No Staff Involved," *Sunday Independent*, February 16, 1975, p. 13.
62. "Dugdale Hacksaw Find Inquiry."
63. "Dugdale—Daughter in Revolt," *The Irish Times*, October 4, 1975, p. 9.
64. "Limerick Bombs Link with Dr. Dugdale?," *Irish Independent*, May 8, 1975, p. 11.

## chapter fifteen

1. Conor O'Clery, "IRA Ceasefire This Evening," *The Irish Times*, February 10, 1975, p. 1.
2. Christopher Owens, Review of *Gerry Adams: An Unauthorised Life*, The Pensive Quill blog, September 20, 2017, retrieved October 27, 2019, https://www.thepensivequill.com/2017/09/gerry-adams-unauthorised-life.html.
3. Interview of John Kelly, *Frontline*, retrieved October 27, 2019, https://www.pbs.org/wgbh/pages/frontline/shows/ira/inside/kelly2.html.
4. Dunne, "A Rough Deal," pp. 6–9.
5. UPI, "IRA Leader Arrested in Dublin," *The Orlando Sentinel*, January 9, 1975, p. 14.
6. McCann, "Herrema's Kidnapper Explains His Motive."
7. Ibid.
8. "Survey Shows Job Opportunities Best in Limerick," *The Irish Times*, December 14, 1973, p. 16.
9. "Redundancy in Ferenka to Stay at 160," *The Irish Times*, April 5, 1975, p. 8.
10. Kathy Sheridan, "Tiede Herrema: 'The Kidnappers Were Nervous. So Was I,'" *The Irish Times*, October 24, 2015, p. 41.
11. Much of Tiede Herrema's recollection of his ordeal comes from interviews he gave in 2005 based on the diary entries he wrote immediately upon his release while on a vacation. He provided details from the diaries in RTÉ Radio 1 documentary *Kidnapped—The Herrema Diaries*; Sheridan, "Tiede Herrema: 'The Kidnappers Were Nervous. So Was I'"; Damien Corliss, "This Day Forty Years Ago Nation Held Its Breath as Abduction by Rogue Republicans Played Out," *Independent*, October 3, 2015, retrieved November 17, 2019, https://www.independent.ie/irish-news/this-day-forty-years-ago-nation-held-its-breath-as-abduction-by-rogue-republicans-played-out-31578566.html.
12. Derek Brown, "Herrema Siege—IRA the Real Losers," *The Guardian*, November 10, 1975, p. 18.
13. "Branch Man Shot—Secret Kidnap Letter," *Irish Press*, November 1, 1975, p. 1.

14. "Kidnappers Stay Silent," *Irish Press*, October 6, 1975, p. 4.

15. Kevin O'Connor, "Exclusive: Dr. Herrema Safe," *Sunday Independent*, October 12, 1975, p. 20.

16. "Government Confronts Kidnappers," *The Irish Times*, October 4, 1975, p. 4.

17. "Provisionals Claim to Be Looking for Kidnappers," *The Irish Times*, October 7, 1975, p. 2.

18. Dunne, "A Rough Deal," pp. 6–9.

19. Noel Smith, "Kidnap: Provos Hunt £200,000 Suspect," *Irish Independent*, October 8, 1975, p. 1.

20. *Kidnapped—The Herrema Diaries*.

21. Ibid.

22. Paul Murray, "Herrema Dispels Myths," *The Irish Times*, November 10, 1975, p. 5.

23. Gordon Kerr and Phil Clarke, *Hostages: Dramatic Accounts of Real-Life Events* (Canary Press ebooks, 2011).

24. Andrew Blake, "'There's a Squad Coming . . . They're Going to Kill You,'" *The Washington Post*, September 6, 1979, retrieved November 9, 2019, https://www.washingtonpost.com/archive/politics/1979/09/06/theres-a-squad-coming-theyre-going-to-kill-you/367096d5-99cd-4eb6-999e-49c0eea0a0db.

25. Conor Brady, *The Guarding of Ireland—The Garda Síochána and the Irish State 1960–2014* (Dublin: Gill & Macmillan, 2014), p. 13.

26. *Irish Times* reporters, "Government Confronts Kidnappers," *The Irish Times*, October 4, 1975, p. 4.

27. Robert William White, *Ruairí O Bradaigh: The Life and Politics of an Irish Revolutionary* (Bloomington: Indiana University Press, 2006), p. 243.

28. McCann, "Herrema's Kidnapper Explains His Motive."

29. "Garda Chiefs Summoned to Herrema Trial," *Irish Examiner*, March 6, 1976, p. 9.

30. "Dugdale Child Seen by Gallagher," *Irish Independent*, October 22, 1975, p. 1.

31. Peter Hetherington, "Kidnap Man's Son in TV Plea for Mercy," *The Guardian*, October 6, 1975, p. 26.

32. "Parents in Vain Plea to Dugdale," *The Irish Press*, October 6, 1975, p. 4.

33. Rose Dugdale, interview by John Murray, *The John Murray Show*.

34. "How Herrema Survived Ordeal," *Sunday Independent*, November 9, 1975, p. 8.

35. "Irish Kidnappers Get Prison Terms," *Democrat and Chronicle* (Rochester, NY), March 12, 1976, p. 7.

36 "Luxury Home for Dugdale Baby."

37. "Prisoners Sue Minister," *Sunday Independent*, June 12, 1977, p. 10.

38. "Gallagher, Dugdale to Wed," *Irish Examiner*, August 20, 1977, p. 1.

39. "IRA Terrorists Wed at Prison Ceremony," *Democrat and Chronicle* (Rochester, NY), January 25, 1978, p. 15.

40. "IRA Terrorists Wed at Prison Ceremony."

41. "Gallagher Weds Wild Rose," *Evening Herald*, January 24, 1978, p. 1.

42. "His IRA Pa and IRA Ma Marry in Jail," *Detroit Free Press*, January 25, 1978, p. 17.

43. "Gallagher and Dugdale Wed in Prison," *Donegal Democrat*, January 27, 1978, p. 5.

44. "His IRA Pa and IRA Ma Marry in Jail."

### chapter sixteen

1. UPI, "English IRA Heiress Freed," *The Daily Herald*, October 12, 1980, p. 5.

2. "Dugdale Back in the Fold," *Evening Herald*, December 21, 1978, p. 1.

3. Joe Joyce, "Rose Dugdale on the Run from Press after Release from Gaol," *The Guardian*, October 13, p. 4.

4. Joyce, "Rose Dugdale on the Run from Press after Release from Gaol."

5. Rose Dugdale, interview by John Murray, *The John Murray Show*.

6. "Dr. Dugdale Brought Out the Crowd," *Tuam Herald*, November 29, 1980, p. 1.

7. Noel Smith and Tom Shiel, "Liberty!," *Irish Independent*, August 1, 1980, p. 1.

8. Beresford, "The Prison Graduate."

9. Irigoien, "Renunci a una vida de lujo la lucha armada antiimperialista en Irlanda."

10. Diane Chanteau, "Rose Dugdale—Publican," *Irish Press*, January 16, 1978, p 1.

11. "Dugdale to Join Staff of *An Phoblacht*," *Irish Press*, November 6, 1980, p. 3.

12. "Rose Dugdale Addresses Carrick H-Block March," *Leitrim Observer*, November 15, 1980, p. 1.

13. "Dr. Dugdale Brought Out the Crowd," *Tuam Herald*, November 29, 1980, p. 1.

14. "Dugdale Speech Seen as Set-Back to H-Block Campaign," *Donegal News*, April 4, 1981, p. 1.

15. Rose Dugdale, interview by John Murray, *The John Murray Show*.

16. Ibid.

17. Rose Dugdale interview, *Mná an IRA*.

18. Ibid.

19. Rose Dugdale, interview by John Murray, *The John Murray Show*.

20. Richard Jackson, Lee Jarvis, Jeroed Gunning, and Marie Breen-Smyth, *Terrorism: A Critical Introduction* (London: Red Globe Press, 2011), p. 87.

21. Harvey, "Celtic Fan Was IRA Terrorist."

## *epilogue*

1. Luke Jennings, "Every Picture Tells a Story . . . ," *Evening Standard*, December 3, 1999, pp. 16–19.

2. Mark Moloney, "Guinness's—'Steadfast in Their Loyalty to the British Crown,'" *An Phoblacht*, September 25, 2013, retrieved September 1, 2019, https://www.anphoblacht.com/contents/23408.

3. Barker, "Call Threat to Destroy the Vermeer."

# ACKNOWLEDGMENTS

The story of Rose Dugdale has lingered in my consciousness ever since I first encountered it back in 2005 while embarking on my journey into art theft research. Back then, I read Matthew Hart's excellent book *The Irish Game*, in which he included a beautifully written chapter about the heist at Russborough House. As the years passed, I collected a massive pile of research on Dugdale and, finally, I told my literary manager, Sharlene Martin of Martin Literary Management, about this incredible woman. I'm grateful to Sharlene for believing that Dugdale's was a story that should be told. Similarly, I'm indebted to the work and faith of my editor, Katie McGuire at Pegasus Books, for seeing the potential of the book. Katie's edits were vital to this manuscript and she raised many pertinent questions about it. I'm also grateful for the cover art of Chris Gilbert at Studio Gearbox.

Luke Jennings stunned me with his kindness and generosity in digging up a copy of his fascinating examination of the theft of *The Guitar Player* (and even sent me a great photo of Kenwood House). Legendary Scotland Yard art detective Charley Hill was instrumental in putting me in touch with fellow officer Arnie Cooke, who provided perspective on the investigation into the heist at Kenwood House.

I am deeply grateful to Walter Heaton for agreeing to answer my questions. Wally's memory is unusually sharp, and he was able to recall details about forty-five-year-old photographs that I showed him. He and his wife, Liz, were kind and very helpful, and I was fortunate to learn more about his time and shocking experiences as a guardsman—an important part of his life that for years was neglected when his background was mentioned.

Anthony McIntyre and Carrie Twomey provided me with quick, critical answers to my incessant questions, clearing up key facts with patience and warmth. Kevin Cullen gave me his time and perspectives on the Troubles that were useful in my understanding of the time period.

Dr. Steven Moysey helped direct me to some key resources, and his book *The Road to Balcombe Street* was an essential read. Dr. Victoria S. Reed provided valuable input on the manuscript, and Janet Moore was kind in her efforts to help me locate archival materials. Elizabeth Reluga provided useful guidance on copyright issues. Deborah Richards, Samantha Snodgrass, and Micha Broadnax at Mount Holyoke College Archives were indispensable to this project.

My most faithful reader, the incomparable Natalie Wolcott Williams, sped through the manuscript and encouraged me along the way. Kelly Horan lent me her expertise in framing a complicated story and answered countless questions about composition.

The kind assistance of Sharon O Suillibhan of Dublin, who helps publish the *1169 and Counting* blog, which keeps alive valuable articles from the era, was generous with her time and thoughts, keeping me laughing and informed. Kate Herlihy supplied great perspectives on the Price Sisters. Kristin Badgio helped with the organization of the project. Martin Foley also gave me thoughts on the matter and an interesting perspective on Rose Dugdale in his own inimitable style. My sister Lori Giorgi provided me with her usual inspiration and encouragement.

I'd be remiss if I didn't give special mention to what I consider to be the best website dedicated to an individual artist, Jonathan Janson's EssentialVermeer .com. The amount of information that it holds is staggering.

Documentarian and radio producer Alan Torney of RTÉ helped this project immeasurably, digging up a years-old radio interview with Rose Dugdale conducted by John Murray and by having recorded an important interview with Tiede Herrema.

Sarah D. Doherty was an exceptional resource in the production of this book, providing archival documents, translation, and ideas throughout its composition. I'm very thankful for her outstanding work and friendship. She's an immensely talented researcher.

Finally, I'm grateful for the many baristas who served me the countless cups of coffee necessary to complete this book, especially those at A&J King in Salem, Massachusetts, where, on a cold Sunday morning, their delicious brew inspired me to consult an all-knowing Oracle and run this book concept by them. When they said it sounded like a great idea, I knew I had to do it.